Social Media OSINT: Tracking Digital Footprints

Algoryth Ryker

Social media is the largest intelligence database ever created—by its users. Every second, billions of people share their thoughts, locations, interests, and connections, often without realizing how much they reveal. For an OSINT analyst, this digital ecosystem is an invaluable resource.

From tracking criminals and fraudsters to unmasking disinformation campaigns and monitoring crisis events in real-time, social media intelligence (SOCMINT) is a powerful tool. Governments, corporations, journalists, cybersecurity experts, and investigators all rely on OSINT techniques to extract hidden insights from platforms like Facebook, Twitter, Instagram, TikTok, LinkedIn, and even underground forums.

But finding intelligence in the vast ocean of social media requires structured methodology, advanced tools, and ethical awareness. This book provides a deep dive into SOCMINT techniques, revealing how to:

✓ Search social media with precision

✓ Track individuals and analyze digital footprints

✓ Unmask fake accounts, bots, and disinformation networks

✓ Extract metadata, geolocation clues, and deleted content

✓ Automate intelligence gathering for real-time monitoring

Each chapter equips you with real-world investigative techniques, culminating in case studies based on actual SOCMINT operations. Whether you're a digital investigator, cybersecurity professional, journalist, or researcher, this book will transform the way you analyze social media intelligence.

Chapter Summaries & Key Insights

1. Understanding Social Media Intelligence (SOCMINT)

Before diving into investigations, it's critical to understand how social media structures, shares, and stores data. This chapter covers:

- How social media platforms collect and track user data
- Digital footprints and how they can be traced
- Privacy settings, hidden metadata, and deception techniques
- The ethical and legal challenges of social media OSINT
- **Case Study**: How social media OSINT uncovered an international fraud ring

2. Facebook OSINT: Graph Searches & Data Extraction

Facebook remains a goldmine for OSINT, despite privacy changes. Learn how to:

- Extract information from public posts, comments, and groups
- Search Facebook even without an account
- Identify hidden friend connections & private group activity
- Use Graph Search alternatives and scraping techniques
- **Case Study**: Tracking a missing person using Facebook OSINT

3. Twitter Investigations: Hashtags, Lists & Influencers

Twitter (X) is a real-time intelligence hub. This chapter covers:

- Using advanced search operators to find critical information
- Tracking mentions, hashtags, and trending topics
- Identifying bots, sock puppets, and manipulated engagement
- Analyzing user interactions and behavioral patterns
- **Case Study**: Using Twitter OSINT for disaster response monitoring

4. Instagram OSINT: Tracking Users & Hidden Data

Instagram reveals more than just pictures. This chapter explores:

- How to extract location clues from images and captions
- Finding hidden and linked accounts through username patterns
- Using reverse image search to identify stolen or fake content
- Tracking Instagram Stories & live updates for intelligence gathering
- **Case Study**: Exposing a fake influencer running an online scam

5. LinkedIn OSINT for Corporate & HR Investigations

LinkedIn is a goldmine for corporate intelligence. Learn how to:

- Verify employment history, job titles, and professional networks
- Investigate fake recruiters, HR scams, and corporate fraud
- Extract insights from company networks and employee interactions
- Use LinkedIn data for competitive intelligence and background checks
- **Case Study**: Detecting corporate espionage through LinkedIn OSINT

6. Reddit & Forums: Analyzing Discussions & Users

Niche forums and Reddit contain hidden intelligence. This chapter teaches:

- How to track user discussions and emerging trends
- Identifying anonymous users and monitoring post histories
- Investigating underground marketplaces and cybercriminal forums
- Spotting coordinated disinformation campaigns
- **Case Study**: Using Reddit OSINT to expose a cybercrime network

7. TikTok, Snapchat & Emerging Social Networks

New platforms create new intelligence opportunities. Learn how to:

- Investigate TikTok users, hashtags, and viral trends
- Extract geolocation clues from TikTok & Snapchat posts
- Recover deleted Snapchat stories and messages
- Track new and niche social platforms for intelligence
- **Case Study**: Using TikTok OSINT to monitor extremist networks

8. Social Media Metadata & Image Analysis

Metadata can reveal hidden clues about location, devices, and origins. This chapter covers:

- Extracting EXIF metadata from images and videos
- Using reverse image search to track online presence
- Detecting edited, AI-generated, or deepfake content
- Analyzing geolocation clues from social media images
- **Case Study**: Finding a missing person using image metadata

9. Fake Accounts & Sock Puppets: Identification & Tracking

Fake accounts manipulate public perception—this chapter reveals how to:

- Detect bots, sock puppets, and fake engagement networks
- Reverse search usernames and identify linked accounts
- Unmask coordinated disinformation campaigns
- Expose high-profile fake accounts used in fraud & propaganda

- **Case Study**: Investigating a political disinformation network

10. Archiving & Monitoring Social Media Data

Social media posts can disappear—but OSINT investigators know how to archive them. Learn how to:

- Capture live data before it gets deleted
- Use automation & web scraping for real-time monitoring
- Track deleted posts and profile updates
- Build a SOCMINT workflow for ongoing investigations
- **Case Study**: Archiving social media evidence for a criminal trial

11. Legal & Ethical Boundaries in SOCMINT

Using OSINT responsibly is critical. This chapter explains:

- The legal risks of social media investigations
- Privacy laws & regulations that affect OSINT collection
- Ethical concerns around data gathering and intelligence sharing
- Avoiding unauthorized access and illegal data scraping
- **Case Study**: A legal controversy in SOCMINT investigations

12. Case Studies: Real-World Social Media OSINT

This final chapter puts everything together with real-world investigations:

- Tracking a missing person using social media clues
- Exposing a large-scale online scam through SOCMINT
- Identifying disinformation networks using social media analysis
- Investigating a cybercriminal through digital footprints
- Using OSINT to monitor extremist & radicalization trends
- **Final Challenge**: Conducting a full social media OSINT investigation

Final Thoughts: The Power & Responsibility of SOCMINT

Social media OSINT is an incredibly powerful tool—but it also comes with ethical obligations. The ability to uncover hidden intelligence should be used responsibly, legally, and ethically to prevent misuse.

With the techniques in this book, you now have the ability to track, analyze, and investigate social media intelligence like a pro. But the question remains:

🔍 *How will you use this knowledge?*

1. Understanding Social Media Intelligence (SOCMINT)

In today's interconnected world, social media intelligence (SOCMINT) has become a crucial component of Open-Source Intelligence (OSINT), offering unparalleled insights into human behavior, trends, and digital footprints. SOCMINT involves the systematic collection, analysis, and interpretation of publicly available data from social platforms to uncover valuable intelligence. Whether for cybersecurity, law enforcement, corporate investigations, or competitive analysis, understanding SOCMINT enables analysts to track online narratives, identify threats, and map influence networks. This chapter explores the foundations of SOCMINT, the ethical and legal considerations involved, and the essential tools and techniques required to harness social media data effectively.

1.1 What is Social Media Intelligence & Why Does It Matter?

In an era where social media dominates digital interactions, the ability to extract valuable insights from these platforms has become an essential skill for intelligence professionals, investigators, and analysts. Social Media Intelligence (SOCMINT) is a subset of Open-Source Intelligence (OSINT) that focuses specifically on collecting, analyzing, and interpreting data from social networking sites such as Facebook, Twitter, Instagram, LinkedIn, and newer platforms like TikTok.

Unlike traditional intelligence gathering, which often relies on classified or private information, SOCMINT leverages publicly available data to track digital footprints, monitor trends, and uncover hidden connections. Whether used in law enforcement, cybersecurity, corporate security, or investigative journalism, SOCMINT provides real-time insights into online behaviors, sentiment analysis, and potential threats.

This subchapter explores what Social Media Intelligence is, why it matters, and how professionals can use it effectively while maintaining ethical and legal boundaries.

Defining Social Media Intelligence (SOCMINT)

At its core, Social Media Intelligence refers to the structured collection and analysis of data from social media platforms to derive actionable intelligence. This data can be gathered from:

- **Publicly Available Information (PAI)** – This includes open profiles, posts, comments, hashtags, likes, and geotagged content that anyone can access without special permissions.
- **Metadata** – Beyond text and images, metadata associated with social media content provides crucial details such as timestamps, geolocation, and device information.
- **Network Analysis** – Studying interactions between users, groups, and communities helps identify key influencers, coordinated campaigns, and potential threat actors.
- **Sentiment and Trend Analysis** – Monitoring how people react to events, brands, or topics can reveal shifts in public perception and emerging trends.

Unlike simple social media monitoring, which primarily focuses on brand mentions or customer engagement, SOCMINT involves deeper investigative techniques. It combines data analysis, pattern recognition, and even artificial intelligence to uncover insights that are not immediately visible on the surface.

Why Does Social Media Intelligence Matter?

Social Media Intelligence is crucial for various sectors, from national security to corporate risk management. Below are some key reasons why SOCMINT plays an increasingly important role in today's digital landscape.

1. Enhancing Security and Law Enforcement Investigations

Law enforcement agencies around the world rely on SOCMINT to track criminal activities, identify suspects, and prevent threats. Social media posts, check-ins, and digital interactions often serve as critical evidence in investigations. For example, in cases of terrorism or organized crime, authorities can use SOCMINT to monitor suspect movements, analyze networks, and detect radicalization trends.

Additionally, SOCMINT helps in locating missing persons, identifying fraudulent activities, and even predicting criminal behavior based on online discussions and signals.

2. Cybersecurity and Threat Intelligence

Cybersecurity professionals use SOCMINT to identify and mitigate cyber threats. Hackers, scammers, and cybercriminals often operate in plain sight on social platforms, sharing techniques, selling stolen data, or coordinating attacks. By monitoring hacker forums, dark web discussions, and social media chatter, cybersecurity experts can preemptively address vulnerabilities and strengthen digital defenses.

Phishing campaigns, ransomware threats, and data breaches often have social media footprints, making SOCMINT a valuable tool in cyber risk assessment.

3. Corporate and Brand Protection

For businesses, social media intelligence is critical for protecting brand reputation, preventing fraud, and monitoring competitive activities. Companies use SOCMINT to track mentions of their brand, identify fake accounts impersonating executives, and detect intellectual property theft.

Additionally, businesses conduct social media investigations to screen potential employees, ensuring that candidates align with corporate values and ethical standards. HR and compliance teams use SOCMINT to uncover fraudulent resumes, conflicts of interest, or even workplace harassment cases.

4. Countering Disinformation and Fake News

The spread of misinformation and fake news on social media has become a global issue. SOCMINT helps fact-checkers, journalists, and government agencies combat disinformation by identifying false narratives, tracking their origins, and debunking them with verified data.

Influence operations—where malicious actors manipulate public opinion—are a growing concern. Governments and organizations leverage SOCMINT to detect coordinated campaigns that spread propaganda, manipulate elections, or incite social unrest.

5. Crisis and Disaster Response

During emergencies, SOCMINT provides real-time updates that can be critical for disaster response teams, humanitarian organizations, and governments. Social media platforms are often the first place where people report disasters, request help, or share crucial updates.

By analyzing geotagged posts, hashtags, and live-streamed videos, responders can assess damage, allocate resources, and coordinate relief efforts more effectively. Examples include monitoring wildfires, tracking protests, or assessing the impact of natural disasters.

Key Techniques in Social Media Intelligence

To effectively gather and analyze SOCMINT, analysts use a combination of tools and methodologies:

b

Most social media platforms have built-in search functions that allow users to find content by keywords, hashtags, locations, and usernames. However, analysts use advanced search operators to refine results and extract specific data points. For example:

- Twitter Advanced Search can filter tweets by date, language, mentions, and location.
- Google Dorking helps uncover hidden social media content by using specific search queries like site:twitter.com "keyword".

2. Network and Relationship Mapping

Understanding how people interact on social media is crucial in investigations. Analysts use social network analysis (SNA) to map relationships between individuals, groups, and organizations. Tools like Maltego, Gephi, and NodeXL visualize connections between users, helping analysts detect patterns and identify key influencers.

3. Metadata and Geolocation Analysis

Every social media post contains metadata that provides valuable information about the content's origin. Analysts extract and analyze metadata to determine when and where a post was made, what device was used, and whether the content has been edited or manipulated.

For instance, an image posted on Instagram may contain hidden EXIF data that reveals the exact GPS coordinates where the photo was taken, aiding in location-based investigations.

4. Sentiment and Trend Analysis

Analyzing how people react to events on social media helps in assessing public sentiment and predicting trends. Businesses use sentiment analysis to understand customer feedback, while intelligence agencies monitor online discussions to detect potential threats or unrest.

Machine learning tools and AI-powered algorithms process large volumes of social media data to determine whether conversations are positive, negative, or neutral, providing valuable context for decision-making.

Challenges and Ethical Considerations

While SOCMINT offers powerful capabilities, it comes with challenges and ethical concerns.

1. Privacy and Legal Issues

Different countries have varying regulations on data collection and online privacy. Analysts must ensure they comply with laws like the General Data Protection Regulation (GDPR) and avoid violating platform terms of service.

2. Data Overload and Misinformation

The sheer volume of social media data can be overwhelming. Analysts must filter through vast amounts of information to separate credible intelligence from noise, spam, and misinformation.

3. Ethical Considerations

Using SOCMINT ethically requires respecting user privacy and avoiding deceptive practices such as unauthorized data scraping or creating fake accounts to infiltrate groups. Analysts must strike a balance between intelligence gathering and ethical responsibility.

Social Media Intelligence (SOCMINT) is a vital tool in modern OSINT investigations, offering unparalleled access to real-time information, behavioral insights, and security intelligence. From law enforcement and cybersecurity to corporate investigations and crisis management, SOCMINT enables analysts to track trends, uncover threats, and make informed decisions.

However, SOCMINT must be conducted responsibly, adhering to ethical guidelines and legal standards. As social media continues to evolve, so too must the techniques and tools used to extract valuable intelligence from digital platforms. Mastering SOCMINT ensures that analysts stay ahead in the ever-changing landscape of digital investigations.

1.2 The Role of OSINT in Social Media Investigations

As social media platforms become primary sources of information, Open-Source Intelligence (OSINT) has emerged as a critical tool for investigators, analysts, and cybersecurity professionals. OSINT refers to the practice of collecting, analyzing, and utilizing publicly available data from online sources, including social media, websites, public records, and news articles. When applied to social media investigations, OSINT enables professionals to track digital footprints, identify persons of interest, monitor online threats, and uncover hidden networks.

The vast amount of data generated by social media users—posts, comments, images, videos, and metadata—offers valuable intelligence when analyzed systematically. Whether used in law enforcement, corporate security, journalism, or fraud investigations, OSINT in social media investigations helps uncover patterns, verify identities, and reveal crucial insights that may otherwise remain hidden.

This chapter explores the role of OSINT in social media investigations, detailing its key applications, methodologies, tools, and ethical considerations.

How OSINT Supports Social Media Investigations

Social media investigations often require a combination of manual research, automated tools, and analytical techniques to extract meaningful intelligence. OSINT plays a vital role in:

1. Identifying and Profiling Individuals

One of the primary uses of OSINT in social media investigations is to identify and profile individuals based on their online presence. Analysts can gather intelligence on a subject by:

- Collecting publicly available personal details (name, location, workplace, education).
- Examining profile pictures and cover photos for facial recognition or location clues.
- Analyzing friend lists, followers, and interactions to determine social connections.

- Reviewing past posts, comments, and engagements to establish behavioral patterns.

For example, law enforcement agencies often use OSINT to track suspects by analyzing their social media activity, identifying associates, and confirming locations based on posted content.

2. Mapping Digital Networks and Connections

Social media is built on interconnected networks, making it a valuable resource for mapping relationships and affiliations. OSINT techniques can help uncover:

- Group memberships and affiliations (e.g., extremist groups, criminal organizations, corporate networks).
- Interaction patterns between individuals and organizations.
- Influencers or key figures who shape discussions and trends.

By using tools such as Maltego, Gephi, and NodeXL, investigators can visualize relationships between accounts, identifying hidden connections that may not be immediately obvious.

3. Verifying Identities and Detecting Fake Accounts

With the rise of misinformation, fraud, and cybercrime, distinguishing real identities from fake or impersonated accounts is crucial. OSINT techniques help:

- Detect sock puppet accounts (fake profiles used for deception).
- Identify bots and automated social media activity.
- Cross-check profile details with publicly available records and databases.
- Conduct reverse image searches to confirm profile pictures and media authenticity.

For example, scammers often use stolen images from legitimate users to create fake profiles. An OSINT investigator can use reverse image search tools like Google Images, Yandex, or TinEye to trace the origin of a profile picture and determine if it has been used elsewhere online.

4. Geolocation and Tracking Digital Footprints

Social media users frequently share geotagged content, which can provide valuable location-based intelligence. OSINT tools can help:

- Extract GPS coordinates from images and videos.
- Analyze check-ins and location tags to establish travel patterns.
- Correlate timestamps with event timelines.

For example, an OSINT analyst investigating a missing person case might examine their Instagram or Twitter posts for location clues, using metadata from uploaded images to pinpoint their last known whereabouts.

5. Monitoring Trends, Hashtags, and Sentiment Analysis

Organizations, governments, and security agencies use OSINT to track trends, monitor sentiment, and detect potential threats on social media. This includes:

- Hashtag tracking to follow movements, protests, or viral trends.
- Sentiment analysis to gauge public opinion on a topic, political event, or crisis.
- Keyword monitoring to detect early signs of criminal activity, cyber threats, or disinformation campaigns.

For example, during major events such as protests or natural disasters, OSINT analysts monitor real-time Twitter activity, tracking hashtags and keywords to understand public sentiment and emerging narratives.

6. Investigating Fraud, Scams, and Cyber Threats

Cybercriminals often use social media platforms to conduct fraud, phishing campaigns, and financial scams. OSINT plays a key role in:

- Identifying fraudulent social media accounts promoting scams.
- Tracking cryptocurrency transactions linked to cybercrime.
- Uncovering social engineering tactics used in cyber attacks.

For instance, if a scammer impersonates a legitimate business on social media, OSINT investigators can analyze account creation dates, engagement history, and linked domains to determine the legitimacy of the account.

OSINT Tools for Social Media Investigations

A variety of open-source tools and techniques assist OSINT analysts in social media investigations. Some of the most commonly used tools include:

Search and Data Extraction Tools

- **Google Dorking** – Advanced search operators to uncover hidden information.
- **Social Searcher** – Searches keywords across multiple social media platforms.
- **OSINT Framework** – A structured directory of OSINT tools for different platforms.

Profile Analysis and Verification Tools

- **Pipl** – Searches for people based on their online presence.
- **UserRecon** – Checks if a username exists on multiple platforms.
- **Epieos** – Extracts information from social media profiles based on email addresses.

Image and Video Analysis Tools

- **Google Reverse Image Search** – Finds the origin of images.
- **Yandex and TinEye** – Alternative reverse image search engines.
- **ExifTool** – Extracts metadata from images to determine location and timestamps.

Geolocation and Mapping Tools

- **GeoSocial Footprint** – Identifies geolocation data from social media posts.
- **TweetDeck** – Allows advanced Twitter searches, including location-based filtering.
- **Google Earth & OpenStreetMap** – Used for analyzing geospatial intelligence.

Network and Relationship Mapping Tools

- **Maltego** – Maps relationships between accounts, people, and organizations.
- **Gephi** – Visualizes complex networks and connections.

By integrating these tools with manual investigation techniques, OSINT analysts can conduct thorough and efficient social media investigations.

Ethical and Legal Considerations in Social Media OSINT

While OSINT provides powerful capabilities, ethical and legal boundaries must be respected. Analysts should consider:

- **Privacy Laws** – Compliance with regulations such as GDPR and CCPA when collecting data.
- **Platform Terms of Service** – Understanding limitations on data scraping and API usage.
- **Ethical Use of Information** – Avoiding deception, unauthorized data collection, or violating user privacy.

Transparency and responsible data handling are essential in OSINT investigations. Professionals must balance intelligence gathering with ethical considerations to ensure compliance with legal standards.

OSINT plays a fundamental role in social media investigations, enabling analysts to uncover valuable intelligence from publicly available data. From identifying individuals and mapping networks to monitoring trends and detecting fraud, OSINT techniques help investigators make informed decisions.

However, effective social media OSINT requires a combination of the right tools, methodologies, and ethical considerations. As social media platforms evolve, so too must the strategies used by OSINT analysts to adapt to emerging challenges and leverage new opportunities in the digital intelligence landscape.

By mastering OSINT in social media investigations, professionals can enhance security, uncover hidden threats, and gain deeper insights into the ever-expanding world of online information.

1.3 Understanding Digital Footprints & Online Personas

Every action we take online—every post, comment, like, share, and login—leaves behind a trace known as a digital footprint. These digital footprints form an online persona, shaping how individuals, organizations, and even entire communities are perceived in the digital space. For OSINT analysts and social media investigators, understanding these footprints is crucial for tracking individuals, verifying identities, and uncovering hidden connections.

This chapter explores what digital footprints are, how they shape online personas, and how OSINT professionals can analyze them to extract valuable intelligence.

What is a Digital Footprint?

A digital footprint is the trail of data left behind by a user's interactions in the digital world. It consists of everything from social media posts and website visits to metadata and online purchases. Digital footprints can be classified into two main types:

1. Active Digital Footprints

These are the traces we leave intentionally. Examples include:

- Social media posts, comments, and likes.
- Blog articles, forum discussions, and online reviews.
- Public profiles on platforms like LinkedIn, Facebook, and Twitter.
- Uploaded videos, images, and shared documents.

Active footprints are often the most useful for OSINT analysts because they are deliberate and typically contain valuable self-reported information.

2. Passive Digital Footprints

These are traces left unintentionally and often without the user's direct knowledge. Examples include:

- IP addresses and geolocation data collected by websites.
- Cookies and tracking pixels that monitor browsing behavior.
- Metadata attached to images, videos, and documents.
- Search engine queries and website visits stored in server logs.

Passive footprints can be more difficult to access but are extremely valuable in investigations. For example, even if a person does not publicly share their location, geotags embedded in uploaded photos might reveal their whereabouts.

The Link Between Digital Footprints and Online Personas

A person's online persona is the digital identity they build through their interactions on the internet. This persona may reflect their real identity, be an exaggerated version of themselves, or be entirely fictional. Analysts must understand the different types of online personas when conducting OSINT investigations.

1. Real Identity Personas

Many people use their real names and personal details on social media, making it easy to verify their identity. Common in platforms like LinkedIn and Facebook, real identity personas provide:

- Work history, job titles, and educational background.
- Contact details, email addresses, and websites.
- Family relationships, friends, and professional connections.

2. Pseudonymous or Semi-Anonymous Personas

Some users prefer to maintain privacy by using usernames, nicknames, or partial information. They may:

- Use alternative email addresses and avoid sharing personal photos.
- Engage in specific communities or forums under an alias.
- Keep a low-profile digital footprint but still leave traces through interactions.

Investigators can often link pseudonymous accounts to real identities by analyzing writing style, activity patterns, or cross-referencing usernames across platforms.

3. Fake or Sock Puppet Accounts

These accounts are deliberately created for deception, anonymity, or manipulation. They are often used for:

- Spreading disinformation or propaganda.
- Impersonating others for fraud or catfishing.
- Coordinated influence operations and cyber espionage.

Detecting fake accounts requires analyzing creation dates, posting patterns, connections, and profile pictures (often AI-generated or stolen from other sources).

How OSINT Analysts Track Digital Footprints

OSINT professionals use various methods to track and analyze digital footprints. Below are key techniques and tools used in digital investigations.

1. Username and Handle Cross-Referencing

Many users recycle usernames across multiple platforms. Investigators can:

- Use tools like KnowEm and WhatsMyName to check if a username exists across different social media sites.
- Perform Google searches using "username" site:platform.com to find connected accounts.
- Analyze variations of usernames (e.g., "JohnDoe92" vs. "John_Doe92").

2. Reverse Image Search and Profile Picture Analysis

A person's profile picture can reveal valuable information. OSINT analysts can:

- Use Google Reverse Image Search, TinEye, or Yandex to check if an image is used elsewhere.
- Extract EXIF metadata from photos (if available) to find geolocation and timestamps.
- Identify AI-generated images using tools like PimEyes or ThisPersonDoesNotExist.com.

3. Social Media Content and Metadata Extraction

Even when users delete posts, traces often remain. Analysts can:

- Use Wayback Machine to view archived versions of profiles.
- Extract metadata from social media posts to determine timestamps and geolocations.
- Monitor changes in profile details using tools like Social Blade.

4. Behavioral and Network Analysis

Users leave behavioral clues based on:

- Posting patterns and engagement frequency.
- Language, writing style, and emoji usage.
- Friends, followers, and interactions with other users.

Network mapping tools like Maltego and Gephi help visualize relationships between social media accounts and communities.

Case Study: Digital Footprint Investigation

Scenario: Tracking a Suspicious Social Media Account

An OSINT investigator is tasked with verifying the identity of a Twitter user suspected of spreading disinformation. The user goes by "@NewsAnalyst42" and has no real name or identifiable details on their profile.

Step 1: Username Cross-Referencing

- A Google search of "NewsAnalyst42" reveals accounts on Reddit and a small forum.
- The Reddit account contains an email hint: "newsanalyst42@gmail.com."

Step 2: Reverse Image Search

- The profile picture appears on multiple accounts but does not return a match in Google Reverse Image Search.
- Using PimEyes, the investigator finds the same image linked to an older, abandoned Facebook account under a different name.

Step 3: Metadata and Location Clues

- Analyzing past tweets shows frequent posts about local events in Chicago.
- Some tweets contain images, and one EXIF metadata extraction reveals GPS coordinates near a specific neighborhood.

Step 4: Behavioral Analysis

- The account tweets between 9 AM and 6 PM, Monday to Friday, suggesting activity during work hours.
- Language style analysis shows repeated phrases and grammatical patterns that match another blog.

Step 5: Network Analysis

- The account frequently interacts with another Twitter user, "@PolicyWatcher89."
- Cross-referencing this username leads to a LinkedIn profile of a journalist.

Outcome

By piecing together the digital footprint, the investigator connects "@NewsAnalyst42" to an individual previously involved in spreading misinformation and confirms links to a network of coordinated disinformation campaigns.

Ethical Considerations in Digital Footprint Analysis

While tracking digital footprints is a powerful tool, ethical considerations must be observed:

- Respect Privacy Laws: Avoid accessing private data without permission.
- Adhere to Platform Policies: Some sites prohibit automated scraping.
- Verify Before Acting: Misinformation and false attributions can harm innocent individuals.

Responsible OSINT practice ensures that investigations remain ethical, legal, and accurate.

Understanding digital footprints and online personas is fundamental in social media OSINT. By analyzing public data, metadata, and behavioral patterns, investigators can identify individuals, track activity, and uncover hidden connections. However, responsible use of these techniques is crucial to maintaining ethical standards and avoiding privacy violations.

In the digital world, everything leaves a trace—and knowing how to follow those traces effectively is the key to mastering OSINT investigations.

1.4 How Data is Collected, Tracked & Shared on Social Platforms

Social media platforms are data goldmines, continuously collecting, tracking, and sharing user information. Every action—posting a status update, liking a photo, or simply logging in—contributes to a vast ecosystem of user data. While this data is used for personalization, advertising, and platform improvement, it is also leveraged for intelligence gathering, investigations, and OSINT (Open-Source Intelligence).

Understanding how social platforms collect, track, and share data is crucial for OSINT analysts, cybersecurity professionals, and digital investigators. This chapter explores the methods social media platforms use to gather user information, the role of metadata, and how this data is shared with third parties, law enforcement, and intelligence agencies.

1. How Social Media Platforms Collect Data

Social media companies collect data using multiple methods, ranging from direct user input to hidden tracking mechanisms. The most common data collection techniques include:

1.1 Direct User Input

Users voluntarily provide personal information when signing up and interacting with platforms. This includes:

- **Profile Information** – Name, age, gender, location, phone number, email, workplace, and education.
- **Content & Posts** – Text posts, photos, videos, and shared links.
- **Connections & Interactions** – Friend lists, followers, group memberships, and chat messages.

1.2 Behavioral Tracking

Social media platforms track user actions to understand preferences, predict behavior, and enhance engagement. This includes:

- **Clickstream Data** – What users click on, how long they stay on a page, and how they navigate through content.
- **Engagement Metrics** – Likes, shares, comments, and reaction types.
- **Search History** – Keywords and topics searched within the platform.
- **Scrolling & Viewing Patterns** – What content a user stops to view, even if they don't interact with it.

1.3 Device & Location Tracking

Social media apps often request access to devices and sensors to collect:

- **IP Addresses** – Used to estimate a user's approximate location.
- **GPS Data** – If granted permission, platforms can track real-time location.
- **Device Metadata** – Includes device model, operating system, and browser type.

- **Wi-Fi & Bluetooth Connections** – Some apps detect nearby networks and devices.

1.4 Metadata Collection

Every piece of content shared on social media contains metadata—hidden data that provides additional details about a file. For example:

- **Images** – Can contain timestamps, GPS coordinates, and camera details.
- **Videos** – May store frame-by-frame metadata, including creation dates.
- **Messages & Calls** – Apps like WhatsApp and Facebook Messenger log timestamps, sender IDs, and message statuses.

1.5 Third-Party Integrations & API Access

Social media platforms allow third-party apps and advertisers to collect data through:

- **OAuth Permissions** – When users sign in to other services using their social media credentials.
- **Embedded Trackers** – Social media plugins embedded on external websites track user activity.
- **Advertising Networks** – Platforms like Facebook and Twitter use pixel tracking to monitor users across the web.

2. How Social Media Platforms Track Users

Even when users are not actively posting, platforms track their behavior using various technologies:

2.1 Cookies & Tracking Pixels

Cookies are small data files stored on a user's device that help track their online activity.

- **First-Party Cookies** – Used by the social media platform to remember login details and settings.
- **Third-Party Cookies** – Used by advertisers to track users across different websites.

Tracking pixels (like Facebook Pixel) are tiny, invisible images embedded in web pages and emails. These pixels:

- Send data back to social media platforms about user behavior.
- Help build detailed advertising profiles.
- Track users even after they leave the social media platform.

2.2 Browser & Device Fingerprinting

Even without cookies, platforms can track users based on:

- **Browser Type & Version** – Chrome, Firefox, Safari, etc.
- **Screen Resolution & Installed Fonts** – Unique to each user.
- **Plugins & Extensions** – Used to identify specific users.
- **Time Zones & Language Settings** – Helps narrow down location.

By combining these attributes, social media companies can create a unique fingerprint for each user.

2.3 Cross-Device Tracking

Platforms link a user's activity across multiple devices by:

- Matching login credentials across phones, tablets, and computers.
- Using Bluetooth and Wi-Fi data to detect nearby devices.
- Synchronizing app and web browsing behavior.

For example, if a user searches for a product on Facebook's mobile app, they may see ads for it on their desktop version later.

2.4 Location Tracking & Geo-Fencing

Even if GPS is disabled, social platforms track location using:

- **IP Addresses** – Can reveal approximate locations.
- **Wi-Fi & Cell Towers** – Helps determine general movement patterns.
- **Geo-Tagged Content** – Users often share location data in photos and check-ins.

Geo-fencing allows platforms to track users entering or leaving specific locations, which is useful for targeted advertising and intelligence operations.

3. How Social Media Data is Shared

Once collected, user data is shared in several ways, including:

3.1 Data Monetization & Advertising

Social media companies make money by selling targeted advertising based on user data. This includes:

- **Interest-Based Ads** – Based on likes, follows, and past behavior.
- **Lookalike Audiences** – Advertisers can target users similar to existing customers.
- **Retargeting** – Ads follow users across different websites.

3.2 API Access for Developers & Businesses

Many platforms provide API (Application Programming Interface) access, allowing developers to:

- Analyze user engagement and interactions.
- Build apps that integrate with social media features.
- Extract public data for research and analytics.

However, APIs can also be misused for mass data collection, as seen in the Cambridge Analytica scandal, where Facebook data was used for political profiling.

3.3 Law Enforcement & Government Access

Governments and law enforcement agencies request social media data for:

- **Criminal Investigations** – Tracking suspects, gathering evidence.
- **National Security & Counterterrorism** – Monitoring extremist activity.
- **OSINT Operations** – Identifying threats and intelligence gathering.

Most platforms have legal request portals, where authorities can obtain user data through:

- **Subpoenas & Court Orders** – Legally mandated data disclosures.
- **Emergency Requests** – In urgent cases, such as kidnappings or terrorist threats.

3.4 Data Breaches & Unauthorized Access

Even with strict policies, social media data has been exposed in major breaches.

Notable cases include:

- **Facebook (2019)** – 540 million records leaked due to misconfigured databases.
- **LinkedIn (2021)** – Data from 700 million users scraped and sold online.
- **Twitter API Exploit (2022)** – 5.4 million user records exposed.

These breaches highlight how easily personal data can fall into the wrong hands.

Social media platforms collect and track massive amounts of user data, often without full user awareness. Understanding these mechanisms is critical for OSINT analysts, cybersecurity professionals, and investigators.

By leveraging public data, metadata, and behavioral tracking, professionals can extract valuable intelligence while remaining mindful of ethical considerations and privacy laws.

As users become more aware of digital privacy risks, the landscape of social media intelligence will continue to evolve—requiring analysts to adapt and refine their investigative techniques.

1.5 The Challenges of SOCMINT: Privacy, Misinformation & Deception

Social Media Intelligence (SOCMINT) is a powerful tool for OSINT analysts, law enforcement, cybersecurity professionals, and researchers. However, despite its effectiveness, SOCMINT comes with significant challenges. Privacy concerns, misinformation, and deceptive practices make social media investigations increasingly complex.

This chapter explores these key challenges, how they impact SOCMINT operations, and strategies for overcoming them.

1. Privacy Challenges in SOCMINT

1.1 Evolving Privacy Regulations

Governments worldwide have introduced laws to protect user data, making SOCMINT investigations more difficult. Key regulations include:

- **General Data Protection Regulation (GDPR) (EU)** – Limits data collection and grants users the right to have their data deleted.
- **California Consumer Privacy Act (CCPA)** – Allows California residents to opt out of data sharing.
- **Digital Services Act (DSA) (EU)** – Increases transparency on algorithmic decision-making and content moderation.

SOCMINT professionals must balance intelligence gathering with legal compliance, ensuring investigations do not violate privacy laws.

1.2 Privacy Settings & Encrypted Communications

Users have more control over their privacy settings, restricting access to personal data. Common barriers include:

- **Private Profiles** – Many users limit who can see their posts and friend lists.
- **End-to-End Encryption** – Messaging apps like WhatsApp, Signal, and Telegram prevent third-party interception.
- **Disappearing Messages** – Snapchat and Instagram offer self-deleting messages, reducing digital footprints.

While these features protect users, they also make it harder for SOCMINT analysts to track activity.

1.3 The Rise of Anonymous & Decentralized Platforms

Users seeking privacy are migrating to:

- **Decentralized Social Networks** – Platforms like Mastodon do not have central authorities controlling user data.
- **Dark Web Forums** – Encrypted forums allow anonymous discussions.
- **Blockchain-Based Platforms** – Cryptographic security makes tracking nearly impossible.

These developments force SOCMINT analysts to adopt new methodologies and tools to extract intelligence from alternative digital spaces.

2. Misinformation & Disinformation in SOCMINT

Misinformation (false information spread unintentionally) and disinformation (deliberate falsehoods spread to manipulate) are major obstacles in social media intelligence.

2.1 The Speed of Viral Misinformation

Social media amplifies false information quickly, often spreading faster than fact-checking efforts. Common sources include:

- **Fake News Websites** – Designed to generate clicks and ad revenue.
- **Social Bots & Troll Farms** – Automated accounts spreading false narratives.
- **Deepfakes & AI-Generated Content** – Manipulated images and videos that appear authentic.

For example, during global crises, misleading videos and false reports often go viral before being debunked.

2.2 Coordinated Influence Operations

State-sponsored disinformation campaigns use SOCMINT tactics to manipulate public opinion. Techniques include:

- **Astroturfing** – Fake grassroots movements artificially boosting support.
- **Sock Puppet Accounts** – Multiple fake identities controlled by a single actor.
- **Hashtag Hijacking** – Using trending hashtags to spread misleading content.

Notable cases include Russian interference in elections and misinformation campaigns related to COVID-19.

2.3 AI & Fake Content Detection

As AI-generated content becomes more sophisticated, SOCMINT analysts rely on:

- **Forensic Analysis Tools** – Detecting inconsistencies in images and videos.
- **AI Text Analysis** – Identifying bot-generated social media posts.
- **Fact-Checking APIs** – Cross-referencing claims with verified sources.

Platforms like Google Fact Check Explorer and NewsGuard assist in combating disinformation.

3. Deception & Evasion Tactics Used by Threat Actors

Criminals, cyber adversaries, and extremist groups actively work to evade detection. Common tactics include:

3.1 Fake Identities & Sock Puppets

Threat actors use multiple accounts with fabricated details to:

- Spread propaganda without being traced.
- Evade bans and suspensions.
- Manipulate public sentiment by creating artificial engagement.

For example, extremist groups often operate under fake personas to recruit members while avoiding platform moderation.

3.2 Encrypted & Ephemeral Messaging

Platforms like Telegram, Signal, and WhatsApp allow secret communications. Features that pose challenges include:

- **Self-Destructing Messages** – Automatically deleting after a set time.
- **Hidden Chats** – Conversations that do not appear in search results.
- **Disappearing Media** – Preventing long-term evidence collection.

3.3 Code Words & Alternative Communication Methods

To bypass detection, criminals and extremists use:

- **Coded Language** – Replacing banned words with harmless-sounding alternatives.
- **Memes & Symbols** – Embedding hidden meanings in images.
- **Steganography** – Hiding messages within digital content.

For instance, drug dealers on Instagram often use emojis and slang to advertise illicit substances without triggering moderation.

4. Strategies to Overcome SOCMINT Challenges

Despite these obstacles, analysts can refine their techniques to extract intelligence effectively.

4.1 Advanced OSINT Tools & Automation

Leveraging specialized SOCMINT tools helps bypass privacy restrictions:

- **Maltego** – Maps connections between accounts.
- **Social Links** – Extracts data from multiple platforms.
- **Hoaxy** – Tracks misinformation spread.

Automation reduces manual workload while improving efficiency.

4.2 Cross-Platform Analysis & Correlation

Analyzing multiple data sources strengthens credibility:

- **Comparing Activity Across Platforms** – Cross-checking usernames and behaviors.
- **Geolocation & Time Zone Analysis** – Matching online activity with real-world events.
- **Reverse Image Searches** – Verifying authenticity using Google Reverse Image Search and Yandex.

4.3 Digital Forensics & Metadata Extraction

Extracting hidden data helps confirm authenticity:

- **EXIF Data Analysis** – Identifies where and when an image was taken.
- **Blockchain Verification** – Confirms the originality of digital assets.
- **AI-Based Fake Detection** – Identifies deepfakes and synthetic content.

4.4 OSINT Ethics & Responsible Data Collection

Maintaining ethical standards is crucial to avoid legal risks:

- **Following Legal Frameworks** – Adhering to GDPR, CCPA, and other regulations.
- **Avoiding Unethical Hacking** – No unauthorized access to private accounts.
- **Verifying Before Reporting** – Preventing the spread of false intelligence.

By ensuring ethical SOCMINT practices, analysts can maintain credibility while protecting user rights.

SOCMINT is a valuable intelligence tool, but privacy laws, misinformation, and deception tactics create significant challenges. Analysts must adapt to evolving privacy regulations, counter disinformation effectively, and recognize evasion techniques used by bad actors.

By leveraging advanced OSINT tools, cross-referencing multiple data sources, and maintaining ethical standards, SOCMINT professionals can extract reliable intelligence in a rapidly changing digital landscape.

1.6 Case Study: How Social Media OSINT Has Been Used in Investigations

Social Media Intelligence (SOCMINT) has become a crucial tool in law enforcement, corporate investigations, cybersecurity, and even humanitarian efforts. By leveraging open-source intelligence (OSINT) techniques, analysts can uncover hidden connections, track criminal activities, and gather evidence—all through publicly available social media data.

This chapter presents real-world case studies demonstrating how SOCMINT has been successfully applied in investigations. These cases highlight the power of OSINT in solving crimes, exposing fraud, and even preventing threats.

Case Study 1: Identifying Rioters Through Social Media Metadata

Background

After a major riot in a Western capital, law enforcement needed to identify participants who had masked their faces or avoided CCTV cameras. While many suspects had deactivated their accounts post-incident, investigators turned to OSINT techniques to track them down.

OSINT Techniques Used

Facial Recognition & Reverse Image Search

- Investigators extracted faces from publicly shared riot footage and ran reverse image searches using tools like Google Reverse Image Search and PimEyes.

- Matches were found with older photos where suspects were tagged with their real names.

Geotagged Media Analysis

- Some rioters posted selfies and videos without realizing their phones embedded EXIF metadata, revealing location details.
- Investigators scraped images and used geolocation tools to confirm their presence at the riot.

Social Network Mapping

- Law enforcement mapped out known protest groups, checking for common followers and interactions.
- Even private accounts were identified by examining mutual connections who interacted with public posts.

Outcome

Dozens of suspects were identified, leading to arrests and legal action. This case showed how OSINT can track individuals even when they attempt to erase their digital footprints.

Case Study 2: Unmasking a Cybercriminal on Twitter

Background

A hacker known as "DarkRogue" was selling stolen credit card data on dark web forums and advertising on Twitter. Authorities aimed to uncover the hacker's real identity.

NT Techniques Used

ame Correlation

- vestigators ran the handle @DarkRogue_X through tools like Namechk and atsMyName to find matching usernames on other platforms.
- same username appeared on an old gaming forum, where an email was listed.

Clues from Tweets

- While the hacker used a VPN, Twitter metadata showed time zones inconsistent with the claimed location.
- A few tweets referenced local events in São Paulo, Brazil, helping narrow the search.

Social Engineering & Sock Puppet Accounts

- Investigators created a fake identity posing as a fellow cybercriminal, engaging with DarkRogue.
- Over time, the target became overconfident and revealed personal details, including a reference to a high school he attended.

Outcome

With this information, authorities linked the alias to a real person and arrested him for cyber fraud. This case demonstrated how small digital traces, even on public platforms, can lead to real-world identification.

Case Study 3: Tracking a Missing Person Through Instagram Check-Ins

Background

A 19-year-old college student in the U.S. went missing, and traditional police searches yielded no leads. The family turned to OSINT experts for help.

OSINT Techniques Used

Instagram Location & Hashtag Analysis

- The missing person's last Instagram post contained an airport geotag, suggesting recent travel.
- OSINT analysts searched related hashtags (e.g., #LAX, #TravelLife) to see if the person appeared in the background of other users' posts.

Friends' Activity Monitoring

- While the missing student's account was inactive, their friends were still posting.
- A friend tagged them in a comment under a recent post, revealing they were in Mexico City.

Live-Stream & Story Analysis

- A review of local influencers' public Instagram Stories found a short clip where the missing student was visible in the background at a nightclub.
- OSINT teams used Google Lens to identify the club's logo, confirming the exact location.

Outcome

Authorities alerted local police, who found the student safe. This case highlighted how analyzing secondary sources—like friends' activity and public posts—can provide crucial intelligence.

Case Study 4: Catching a Corporate Fraudster on LinkedIn

Background

A financial executive was under suspicion for insider trading but had denied any external dealings. Investigators turned to OSINT to verify his claims.

OSINT Techniques Used

LinkedIn Profile & Connections Analysis

- The suspect's LinkedIn account showed no unusual activity, but investigators checked past job positions and endorsements.
- A deep dive revealed connections with executives at a rival firm, hinting at a possible leak.

Cross-Checking Deleted Activity

- Using Google Cache and Wayback Machine, analysts recovered a deleted post where the suspect had "liked" a rival company's expansion announcement before it was publicly known.

Lifestyle Analysis via Facebook & Instagram

- Despite no direct financial records of wrongdoing, the suspect had posted pictures from a luxury vacation shortly after the alleged insider trading event.

- Investigators tracked the vacation through geo-tagged posts, revealing it was funded by an unnamed third party.

Outcome

The executive was confronted with the evidence and later confessed, leading to criminal charges. This case proved how subtle online traces can expose fraudulent behavior.

These real-world case studies illustrate the power of Social Media OSINT in investigations. Whether tracking criminals, locating missing persons, or uncovering fraud, open-source intelligence techniques have proven essential in modern digital investigations.

By leveraging metadata, cross-platform analysis, and network mapping, investigators can extract critical insights while maintaining ethical and legal boundaries.

2. Facebook OSINT: Graph Searches & Data Extraction

Facebook remains a goldmine for OSINT practitioners, offering vast amounts of user-generated data that can reveal connections, behaviors, and hidden insights. Despite privacy restrictions and the deprecation of Facebook's native Graph Search, analysts can still extract valuable intelligence through alternative methods, including manual queries, third-party tools, and API-based data gathering. This chapter delves into the evolving landscape of Facebook OSINT, covering techniques for identifying user profiles, extracting publicly available information, mapping relationships, and leveraging open-source tools to conduct deep investigations—all while staying within ethical and legal boundaries.

2.1 How Facebook Structures Public & Private Information

Facebook is one of the largest social media platforms, with billions of users worldwide. As a powerful source of Open-Source Intelligence (OSINT), Facebook provides a vast amount of publicly available data, but it also implements various privacy controls that restrict access to certain information. Understanding how Facebook structures public and private information is critical for OSINT analysts conducting investigations.

In this section, we will examine how Facebook categorizes user data, what information is publicly accessible, and how privacy settings impact the visibility of content.

1. Facebook's Data Structure: Public vs. Private Information

Facebook organizes user data into two broad categories:

- **Public Information** – Data that is accessible to anyone, even without a Facebook account.
- **Private Information** – Data restricted based on user settings and permissions.

Each Facebook profile, page, and group operates under these data structure rules, determining what can be seen by OSINT analysts.

1.1 Public Information on Facebook

By default, certain user details are public, meaning anyone can access them without requiring an account. These include:

- **Profile Name & Username** – The display name and unique username (e.g., facebook.com/username).
- **Profile & Cover Photos** – Unless restricted, a user's current and past profile pictures and cover photos are visible.
- **Basic Biographical Information** – Often includes gender, location, and sometimes employment details.
- **Friend List (If Publicly Shared)** – Some users allow others to see their friend connections.
- **Posts Set to "Public"** – Any post or status update with a globe icon □ is viewable by anyone.
- **Facebook Pages** – Pages (e.g., businesses, public figures) are entirely public, including posts, comments, and followers.
- **Public Facebook Groups** – Posts and member lists in public groups are accessible without needing to join.

Public data provides valuable insights for OSINT analysts, but the real challenge lies in uncovering restricted or semi-private data.

1.2 Private Information on Facebook

Most user content is not publicly available due to Facebook's privacy settings. Private information includes:

- **Posts with Restricted Visibility** – Users can set posts to "Friends Only," "Friends of Friends," or custom audiences.
- **Hidden Friend Lists** – Users can choose to keep their friend list private.
- **Private Facebook Groups** – These require membership to view posts, and some may require approval from admins.
- **Direct Messages (DMs)** – Messenger conversations are encrypted and inaccessible without direct user consent.
- **Past Profile Data** – Older profile photos, names, and previous posts may be hidden if the user changes privacy settings.

Since most users restrict their data, OSINT analysts must use strategic techniques such as social engineering, metadata analysis, and cross-platform investigation to gather intelligence.

2. Facebook's Privacy Settings and Their Impact on OSINT

Facebook allows users to customize their privacy settings, affecting the visibility of their information. Understanding these settings helps OSINT analysts determine how much data can be extracted.

2.1 Privacy Controls on User Profiles

Users can adjust their privacy settings through the "Privacy Checkup" tool, which impacts:

- Who can see their posts (Public, Friends, Custom).
- Who can send them friend requests (Everyone, Friends of Friends).
- Who can look them up using their phone number or email (Everyone, Friends, Only Me).
- Whether their profile appears in search engine results (Google indexing toggle).

When users restrict their profiles, direct OSINT investigations become more challenging. However, some data can still be gathered through indirect sources, such as mutual friends or old cached pages.

2.2 Facebook Groups: Public vs. Private vs. Secret

Facebook groups serve as valuable sources of intelligence. There are three types of groups:

- **Public Groups** – Posts, members, and discussions are fully visible to anyone.
- **Private Groups** – Membership is required to view posts, but the group's existence and member list are visible.
- **Secret Groups (Now "Hidden")** – These do not appear in searches and require an invite to access.

Monitoring group activity can provide insights into discussions, affiliations, and trends, even if the group is private.

2.3 Facebook Pages & Their OSINT Value

Unlike personal profiles, Facebook Pages (for businesses, celebrities, or organizations) are fully public. OSINT analysts can:

- Extract posts, comments, and engagements using OSINT tools.

- Track interactions between users and pages to identify affiliations.
- Analyze historical activity to find deleted or modified posts using cached data sources.

By leveraging Facebook's Transparency Tools, analysts can view an organization's advertising history, revealing targeted campaigns and their intended audiences.

3. Methods for Accessing Restricted Information

Even when data is set to private, OSINT analysts have techniques to extract insights legally and ethically.

3.1 Cross-Platform Correlation

Users often share the same usernames across multiple platforms. By searching for a Facebook username on:

- Instagram
- Twitter
- LinkedIn
- Reddit

… analysts can find related profiles with publicly available information that Facebook itself restricts.

3.2 Analyzing Friends & Tagged Posts

Even if a user's profile is private:

- Their friends' public posts may contain tagged photos.
- Public event check-ins might reveal locations and associations.
- Comments on public pages provide insights into their interests and interactions.

3.3 Google Dorking for Cached Information

Using Google advanced search operators, analysts can uncover old Facebook data, such as:

site:facebook.com "John Doe" "works at"
site:facebook.com "John Doe" "from New York"

If a user recently changed their privacy settings, cached versions of their profile may still be visible.

3.4 Monitoring Facebook's People Directory

Facebook's People Directory (https://www.facebook.com/people) lists users by name, often showing profile snippets, even for private accounts.

Facebook structures information into public and private categories, allowing users to control their data visibility through privacy settings. While most personal data is restricted, OSINT analysts can still gather valuable intelligence by analyzing public posts, leveraging group activity, and using cross-platform correlation techniques.

2.2 Advanced Facebook Search Techniques & Filters

Facebook is one of the most data-rich social media platforms, making it a valuable resource for Open-Source Intelligence (OSINT). However, its search functionality has changed over the years, with Facebook discontinuing its powerful Graph Search in 2019. Despite this, OSINT analysts can still uncover valuable data using advanced search techniques, filters, and third-party tools.

This chapter will cover:

- How to use Facebook's built-in search effectively.
- Techniques to extract hidden data.
- Google Dorking for Facebook OSINT.
- External tools for deep searches.

1. Facebook's Built-in Search: Understanding the Basics

Facebook's default search bar allows users to find posts, people, pages, groups, and events. While limited compared to the former Graph Search, it still provides useful filtering options.

1.1 Using Facebook's Search Filters

Facebook allows filtering search results by:

- **Posts** – Public posts, posts from friends, and posts in groups/pages.
- **People** – Facebook users with matching names.
- **Pages** – Business, celebrity, or community pages.
- **Groups** – Public and private groups related to the search term.
- **Events** – Public events users have created or attended.
- **Marketplace** – Items for sale related to the search term.

These filters help narrow down searches when investigating a specific individual, topic, or entity.

1.2 Keyword-Based Searches

To refine searches, use specific keywords combined with Facebook's filters. Some effective queries include:

- "John Doe" New York – Searches for users named John Doe in New York.
- "John Doe" works at "Google" – Searches for users listing Google as their employer.
- "Lost iPhone" near me – Finds public posts about lost items.

Using quotation marks ("") forces an exact match, improving search accuracy.

2. Google Dorking for Facebook OSINT

Since Facebook restricts some searches internally, Google Dorking (advanced search operators) can extract hidden data from publicly indexed Facebook pages.

2.1 Basic Google Dorks for Facebook

Use the site: operator to search for specific content on Facebook:

People Search

- site:facebook.com "John Doe" "New York"
- site:facebook.com "works at Google"

Finds profiles matching the given keywords.

Posts & Comments

- site:facebook.com "lost passport"
- site:facebook.com "looking for job"

Finds posts containing specific keywords, useful for investigations.

Photos & Videos

- site:facebook.com/photos "John Doe"
- site:facebook.com/videos "protest"

Finds public photos and videos uploaded by users.

Groups & Pages

- site:facebook.com/groups "hacking forum"
- site:facebook.com/pages "political movement"

Identifies relevant Facebook groups and pages related to specific topics.

2.2 Finding Deleted or Hidden Data

If a post or profile has been deleted, use:

Google Cache:

- cache:facebook.com/JohnDoe
- Shows a cached version of the page before deletion.
- Wayback Machine (archive.org) – Checks for older versions of pages.

3. Extracting Hidden Facebook Data with Third-Party Tools

Several OSINT tools help extract Facebook data efficiently.

3.1 Facebook UID Lookup

Every Facebook profile has a unique ID (UID), which can reveal hidden details.

Use FindMyFBID.com to get a user's UID.

Once you have the UID, use this URL to find their profile:

https://www.facebook.com/profile.php?id=UID

If the username changes, the UID remains the same, helping track the person.

3.2 Social Media Scrapers

- **Maltego** – Visualizes Facebook connections and interactions.
- **OSINT Framework** – Aggregates public Facebook data.
- **Intel Techniques Facebook Tools** – Searches profiles, photos, and groups.

These tools automate data collection and provide insights that manual searches might miss.

4. Investigating Facebook Groups & Pages

4.1 Extracting Group Member Lists

Even in private groups, some member data may be accessible:

Search for a group on Google using:

site:facebook.com/groups "Group Name"

- Use cached pages to retrieve previous member lists.
- Look for common members in multiple related groups.

4.2 Analyzing Page Interactions

Facebook pages are public, meaning interactions (likes, comments, shares) can reveal connections.

- Check who interacts with a page's posts for possible affiliations.
- Use Facebook's Ad Transparency Tool to analyze paid promotions.

5. Profile Tracking & Hidden Insights

5.1 Finding Someone's Facebook Activity

Even if a profile is private, some activity remains visible:

- **Comments on Public Pages** – Check interactions on news articles, celebrity pages, or company pages.
- **Tagged Photos** – Even if a profile is locked, tags on public profiles may be visible.
- **Mutual Friends** – Private friend lists can be bypassed by checking mutual connections.

5.2 Monitoring Username Changes

Facebook allows users to change usernames, but their Facebook ID remains the same.

- Use Namechk to find linked usernames across different platforms.
- If an account is deleted, check cached data for past activity.

Despite Facebook restricting its Graph Search, OSINT analysts can still extract valuable intelligence using advanced search filters, Google Dorking, and third-party tools. Understanding how to navigate Facebook's search functions and external tools is essential for uncovering hidden connections and tracking digital footprints.

2.3 Extracting Data from Public Posts, Comments & Groups

Facebook remains one of the richest sources of Open-Source Intelligence (OSINT), offering vast amounts of publicly available data in posts, comments, and groups. While Facebook has introduced stricter privacy controls, much of this data can still be accessed legally and ethically using advanced OSINT techniques.

In this chapter, we will explore:

- How to extract data from public posts, comments, and interactions.
- Methods to analyze and track engagement.
- Techniques for collecting data from public and private groups.
- Tools that automate data extraction for large-scale investigations.

1. Extracting Data from Public Facebook Posts

1.1 What Data Can Be Extracted?

Public Facebook posts provide valuable intelligence, including:

- **Text & Metadata** – The content of the post, timestamps, and author information.
- **Comments & Reactions** – Engagement data, including users who interacted with the post.
- **Hashtags & Keywords** – Trends, topics, and related discussions.
- **Image & Video Data** – EXIF metadata, geolocation, and facial recognition opportunities.

1.2 Manually Searching for Public Posts

Use Facebook's search bar with filters to find relevant posts:

Posts mentioning a keyword:

- "protest"
- "missing person"

Posts tagged with a location:

- "Earthquake" near "California"

Posts from a specific time range:

Navigate to Facebook's "Filters" and select a date range.

Once a post is found, OSINT analysts can extract:

- Who posted it (author, location, device used).
- Who engaged with it (likes, shares, comments).
- Any linked profiles that interacted with the post.

1.3 Extracting Data from Comments & Engagements

Each public post has a list of users who interacted with it. Even if a profile is private, engagement with a public post remains visible.

Tracking Commenters & Reactions

- Sort comments by 'Most Relevant' or 'Newest' to see active discussions.
- Look for patterns in user engagement – Are the same individuals commenting on multiple posts?

- Extract usernames & profile links for deeper investigation.

Finding Conversations Hidden in Replies

- Some users reply within comment threads instead of making direct comments. Expanding replies can reveal additional insights.
- Search by keyword within a post's comments using Ctrl+F (on desktop) to locate specific discussions.

2. Extracting Data from Public & Private Facebook Groups

Facebook groups are valuable for OSINT investigations, as they serve as hubs for:

- Political movements
- Criminal activities
- Marketplace transactions
- Niche communities

2.1 Public vs. Private Groups: What Can Be Extracted?

Group Type	Visibility of Posts	Member List Visibility
Public	Fully visible	Fully visible
Private	Only visible to members	Visible to non-members
Secret (Hidden)	Not visible in search results	Not visible

Even if a group is private, its member list is often publicly visible, allowing analysts to:

- Identify active members and track their activity in other groups.
- Map connections between members who belong to multiple groups.
- Use Google Dorking to find archived group content.

2.2 Searching for Facebook Groups Using Google Dorking

Since Facebook restricts group searches, Google Dorking can uncover hidden communities:

- site:facebook.com/groups "hacking forum"
- site:facebook.com/groups "political activism"
- site:facebook.com/groups "buy and sell"

This method retrieves indexed groups, even if Facebook's internal search does not display them.

2.3 Extracting Group Member Lists

For public and some private groups:

- Click on "Members" to see the full list.
- Manually copy usernames for further analysis.
- Use web scraping tools to automate the extraction of member data.

3. Automating Facebook Data Extraction

Large-scale OSINT investigations require automation tools to efficiently collect and process data. Below are some methods to extract Facebook data at scale.

3.1 Using Web Scrapers for Public Facebook Data

Several open-source and third-party tools help scrape data:

- **OSINT Framework** – Aggregates publicly available Facebook data.
- **Maltego** – Maps social connections and interactions.
- **Facebook Crawler (Custom Python Scripts)** – Extracts comments, reactions, and posts.

Note: Automating data extraction must comply with Facebook's terms of service and legal frameworks in your jurisdiction.

3.2 Extracting Facebook Post Data with Python

For developers, Python offers powerful ways to extract data:

Example: Extracting Public Posts with Selenium

```
from selenium import webdriver
from selenium.webdriver.common.keys import Keys

driver = webdriver.Chrome()
driver.get("https://www.facebook.com/search/posts?q=climate%20change")
```

```
posts = driver.find_elements_by_class_name("_1dwg")
for post in posts:
    print(post.text)

driver.quit()
```

This script collects text from public posts matching the keyword "climate change."

3.3 Using API Alternatives

Facebook's Graph API requires authentication, but alternatives like:

- **CrowdTangle (For Media & Government Use)** – Allows limited data access.
- **Wayback Machine** – Finds deleted Facebook pages and posts.

4. Investigating Deleted or Hidden Facebook Data

Even when posts, comments, or profiles are deleted, traces often remain.

4.1 Finding Deleted Facebook Posts

Google Cache:

cache:facebook.com/JohnDoe

Retrieves the last indexed version of a profile.

Archive.org (Wayback Machine):

Enter the Facebook post URL to check for historical snapshots.

4.2 Extracting Hidden Facebook Conversations

- **Look at shared posts** – If a deleted post was shared by others, remnants may still exist.
- **Check screenshots & reposts** – Some users save and repost deleted content.
- **Monitor public comments** – Even if the original post is deleted, comment notifications may still exist.

Facebook remains a goldmine for OSINT investigations, with data hidden in public posts, comments, and groups. By using advanced search techniques, Google Dorking, and automated tools, investigators can efficiently extract valuable intelligence.

2.4 Using Facebook Graph Search & Alternative Tools

Facebook's Graph Search was once a powerful tool that allowed OSINT analysts to retrieve highly specific data about users, posts, pages, and interactions. However, after its removal in 2019, investigators had to rely on alternative methods to extract similar information.

Despite the loss of Graph Search, many manual and automated techniques can still be used to gather intelligence on Facebook. This chapter explores:

- What Facebook Graph Search was and why it was removed.
- Workarounds to simulate Graph Search queries.
- Alternative tools and methods for OSINT investigations.

1. What Was Facebook Graph Search?

1.1 How Graph Search Worked

Facebook's Graph Search allowed structured searches using natural language queries, such as:

- "People who live in New York and work at Google"
- "Photos liked by John Doe"
- "Friends of Jane Doe who visited Paris in 2022"

These queries helped OSINT analysts track relationships, activities, and publicly available content.

1.2 Why Facebook Removed Graph Search

Due to privacy concerns and data misuse (e.g., Cambridge Analytica scandal), Facebook removed Graph Search in 2019. This significantly limited investigators' ability to gather structured intelligence from Facebook.

2. Alternative Methods to Simulate Graph Search

Even without Graph Search, analysts can still perform structured searches using:

- Manual Facebook Search Filters
- Google Dorking for Facebook Data
- Third-Party OSINT Tools

2.1 Using Facebook's Search Bar for Manual Queries

While less powerful than Graph Search, Facebook's built-in search can still find relevant data:

People Search:

- Search for "John Doe" and use filters to narrow results by location, workplace, or education.
- **Example**: "People who live in New York" (then filter results).

Post Search:

Search for keywords in public posts:

- "protest in Washington"
- "missing person report"

Filter results by date, location, and source.

Photo & Video Search:

- Search for image captions or videos related to a person or event.
- **Example**: "Photos tagged at Times Square" (then sort by most recent).

2.2 Google Dorking for Facebook OSINT

Since Facebook limits search visibility, Google Dorking can extract indexed content:

People & Profile Searches

- site:facebook.com "John Doe" "New York"
- site:facebook.com "works at Google"

Finds profiles matching specific details.

Public Posts & Comments

- site:facebook.com "climate change discussion"
- site:facebook.com "lost passport"

Extracts publicly shared posts and comments.

Photos & Videos

- site:facebook.com/photos "John Doe"
- site:facebook.com/videos "protest"

Finds public media content related to a person or event.

3. Third-Party OSINT Tools for Facebook Analysis

While Facebook Graph Search is gone, alternative OSINT tools can still extract similar data.

3.1 Facebook UID Lookup (User ID Tracking)

Every Facebook profile has a unique ID (UID) that remains unchanged, even if the username changes.

FindMyFBID.com – Retrieves a user's unique Facebook ID.

Manually Extract UID:

- Visit a profile and view page source (Ctrl + U).
- Search for fb://profile/ to find the UID.

Use this link to access the profile:

https://www.facebook.com/profile.php?id=UID

Even if the user changes their username, their UID remains the same.

3.2 Social Media Mapping Tools

- **Maltego** – Maps social connections, interactions, and engagement patterns.
- **Social Links Pro** – Extracts Facebook friend lists, posts, and group activity.
- **IntelTechniques Facebook Tools** – Searches profiles, pages, and groups efficiently.

3.3 Web Scraping for Facebook Data

For larger-scale investigations, automated scrapers can extract public data:

- **Selenium (Python)** – Simulates human browsing for Facebook searches.
- **BeautifulSoup** – Parses Facebook HTML pages to extract content.

Example: Extracting Facebook Post Data with Python

```
from selenium import webdriver
from selenium.webdriver.common.keys import Keys

driver = webdriver.Chrome()
driver.get("https://www.facebook.com/search/posts?q=climate%20change")

posts = driver.find_elements_by_class_name("_1dwg")
for post in posts:
    print(post.text)

driver.quit()
```

Legal Note: Scraping Facebook data must comply with ethical and legal boundaries, including Facebook's Terms of Service.

4. Reconstructing Facebook Network Connections

Even without Graph Search, analysts can still track connections, interactions, and relationships using:

4.1 Tracking Mutual Friends & Comments

- Even if a user's friend list is private, checking mutual friends on public profiles may reveal shared connections.

- Comment history on public posts can expose connections between users.

4.2 Investigating Facebook Groups & Pages

- Public groups allow full access to posts, member lists, and interactions.
- Private groups still show member lists, allowing investigators to track users across multiple groups.

Tip: Searching for the same users in different groups can identify affiliations and networks.

5. Finding Deleted or Hidden Facebook Data

Even when a profile, post, or comment is deleted, traces often remain:

5.1 Using Google Cache & Wayback Machine

Google Cache:

cache:facebook.com/JohnDoe

Retrieves an older version of the profile.

Wayback Machine (archive.org):

Enter the profile URL to check historical versions.

5.2 Checking Shared & Archived Posts

- Even if a user deletes a post, shared versions may still exist.
- Public comments on shared posts may reveal deleted content.

5.3 Monitoring Username Changes

- Users frequently change their Facebook usernames, but their unique UID remains the same.
- Use past profile links to track name changes over time.

Although Facebook removed Graph Search, OSINT analysts can still perform deep investigations using manual search techniques, Google Dorking, and alternative OSINT tools. By reconstructing network connections and tracking historical data, investigators can uncover valuable intelligence while staying within ethical and legal boundaries.

2.5 Identifying Fake Profiles & Hidden Friend Connections

Fake Facebook profiles are widely used for misinformation campaigns, fraud, cyberstalking, and espionage. OSINT analysts must be able to detect these fraudulent accounts and uncover hidden connections between users.

In this chapter, we will cover:

- How to spot fake Facebook profiles.
- Tools and techniques for verifying identities.
- Methods for uncovering hidden friend connections.
- Techniques for mapping relationships between users.

1. Detecting Fake Facebook Profiles

1.1 Common Traits of Fake Accounts

Fake accounts often exhibit telltale signs, including:

Trait	Indicators
Profile Picture	Stock images, celebrity photos, stolen images, AI-generated faces
Friend Count	Very few or an unusually high number of friends
Recent Activity	Little to no activity, or all posts made within a short timeframe
Personal Information	Incomplete bio, missing location, fake job history
Engagement Patterns	Excessive liking/sharing of specific posts (bot-like behavior)

1.2 Reverse Image Search for Profile Pictures

A simple way to verify if a profile picture is fake is by conducting a reverse image search:

Google Reverse Image Search

- Upload the profile picture to images.google.com and check if it appears elsewhere.

TinEye

- Upload or paste the image URL at tineye.com to find duplicate instances.

Yandex Image Search

- Often retrieves better results than Google for identifying stolen images.

Tip: If the image only appears on the suspect Facebook profile, it could be AI-generated.

1.3 Analyzing Profile URLs & Usernames

- Fake accounts often use random usernames (e.g., facebook.com/john456xyz).
- Many fake profiles recycle similar usernames across different platforms.

Use Google Dorking to check if the username appears elsewhere:

- "john456xyz" site:facebook.com
- "john456xyz" site:instagram.com

If the same username appears on multiple fake-looking accounts, it's a strong red flag.

1.4 Checking Post & Comment History

Genuine users typically have diverse posts, interactions, and shared content.

Fake profiles often:

- Have only a few public posts (or none at all).
- Copy and paste generic comments.
- Spam certain topics (e.g., scams, fake news, political propaganda).

Case Study: During election cycles, thousands of fake accounts are used to manipulate public opinion by repeatedly posting the same political content.

2. Uncovering Hidden Facebook Friend Connections

Even when a user's friend list is private, there are ways to identify hidden relationships:

2.1 Checking Mutual Friends

- Even if a profile hides its friends list, mutual friends are usually visible.
- Visit the profiles of known friends and check their connections.
- Look for patterns: Do multiple accounts have the same small group of mutual friends?

2.2 Investigating Public Interactions

A user's likes, comments, and shares can reveal hidden connections:

- Visit a suspect's public posts and check who has commented.
- Look for frequent interactions between certain profiles—this can indicate a connection.
- Cross-check these users on other social media platforms for deeper insights.

2.3 Using Google Dorking to Find Friend Lists

Even if a user's friends list is hidden, cached or indexed versions may still be accessible:

- site:facebook.com "John Doe" "Friends"
- site:facebook.com "John Doe" "Mutual Friends"

This can retrieve old versions of the profile that still display friend connections.

2.4 Analyzing Group & Page Memberships

If two users belong to the same private groups, they may have a connection.

Use Google Dorking to find their group memberships:
site:facebook.com/groups "John Doe"

Facebook pages also list users who interact with them. If two profiles frequently engage with the same content, they may be connected.

3. Mapping Relationships Between Facebook Users

3.1 Using OSINT Tools for Social Graphing

Several tools help visualize relationships between users:

- **Maltego** – Generates network maps of social connections.
- **Social Links Pro** – Extracts and links Facebook friend lists.
- **IntelTechniques Facebook Tools** – Helps track interactions and friendships.

3.2 Creating a Manual Network Graph

- **Step 1**: Collect data on interactions (likes, comments, shared groups).
- **Step 2:** Use a tool like Gephi or Maltego to create a social network map.
- **Step 3:** Identify clusters of users with frequent interactions.
- **Step 4**: Cross-reference with other platforms (LinkedIn, Twitter) to confirm relationships.

3.3 Identifying Coordinated Fake Networks

Fake networks often:

Have similar creation dates.

- Use identical engagement patterns (e.g., liking the same posts at the same time).
- Share the same low-effort content across multiple accounts.

Case Study: A major disinformation campaign in 2020 was uncovered by tracking dozens of fake accounts that repeatedly engaged with each other's posts.

4. Investigating Deleted or Suspiciously Altered Profiles

4.1 Recovering Deleted or Changed Profile Data

Even when a profile is deleted or altered, traces often remain:

Using Google Cache

If a profile was recently deleted, a Google cache version may still exist:

cache:facebook.com/JohnDoe

Using the Wayback Machine

Check if archive.org has saved an earlier version of the profile.

4.2 Monitoring Name or Profile Picture Changes

- Some users change their name or profile picture instead of deleting their account.
- Use FindMyFBID.com to retrieve their Facebook UID, which never changes.

Once you have the UID, check:

https://www.facebook.com/profile.php?id=UID

Even if they changed their name, the UID remains the same.

4.3 Tracking Down Suspicious Friends of a Fake Account

- If a fake account is deleted, investigate friends or frequent commenters for possible alternative accounts.
- Look for identical engagement patterns (e.g., commenting on the same posts at the same time).
- Check for reused usernames, profile pictures, or bio details across different platforms.

Fake Facebook profiles are widely used for deception, fraud, and misinformation. However, with careful OSINT techniques—including reverse image searches, interaction tracking, and relationship mapping—investigators can identify fraudulent accounts and expose hidden connections.

2.6 Case Study: Tracking a Target Using Facebook OSINT

Facebook remains a goldmine for OSINT analysts looking to gather intelligence on individuals, organizations, or groups. In this case study, we will follow a real-world scenario (with anonymized details) where an investigator uses OSINT techniques to track a target individual based on publicly available Facebook data.

This chapter will demonstrate:

- How to gather initial data on a target.
- Techniques for expanding the investigation using Facebook OSINT.
- Methods to uncover hidden connections, locations, and activities.
- Ethical considerations when conducting Facebook investigations.

1. The Investigation Begins: Identifying a Target

1.1 Scenario Overview

An OSINT investigator is hired to locate a missing person, Daniel Reeves, who was last seen in Los Angeles, California. The family provides the investigator with:

- His full name and approximate age (32 years old).
- An old phone number (possibly inactive).
- A few known friends and relatives.
- His last known workplace: A restaurant in LA.

1.2 Initial Facebook Search for the Target

The first step in any Facebook OSINT investigation is to search for the target's profile and related accounts:

Using Facebook's Built-in Search:

The investigator searches "Daniel Reeves Los Angeles" in Facebook's search bar and filters results by:

- **People** → Looking for profiles that match the age and location.

- **Posts** → Searching for any mentions of Daniel in public posts.

- **Photos & Videos** → Checking images where he might be tagged.

Using Google Dorking for Facebook Profiles:

Since Facebook's search is limited, the investigator uses Google Dorking to retrieve more results:

- site:facebook.com "Daniel Reeves" "Los Angeles"
- site:facebook.com "Daniel Reeves" "Works at"

The search reveals multiple Daniel Reeves profiles, one of which is:

- "Daniel Reevs" (with a slight misspelling)
- Profile picture matches an old photo provided by family.

- Lists "Works at [Restaurant Name]"—same as his last known workplace.

Key Finding: The investigator has likely found the correct Facebook profile.

2. Expanding the Investigation: Gathering More Data

2.1 Extracting Profile Information

Since Daniel's profile is partially public, the investigator extracts:

- **Profile Picture & Cover Photo** → Used for reverse image search.
- **Friends List (partially visible)** → To identify possible connections.
- **Recent Public Posts** → Checking for clues on his whereabouts.

2.2 Checking Tagged Photos & Comments

Daniel's "Photos" tab shows several images where he's tagged, including:

- **A recent group photo at a bar** → Caption mentions "Night out in San Diego" (suggesting recent travel).
- **A picture from a music festival** → Comments mention the date (3 weeks ago).

Key Finding: Daniel was in San Diego recently, not just Los Angeles.

2.3 Investigating His Friend Network

Since Daniel's friend list is partially hidden, the investigator uses:

- **Mutual friends** → Checking visible connections with known family and friends.
- **Public interactions** → Seeing who comments and likes his posts most frequently.
- **Third-party tools (Maltego, Social Links)** → To map relationships.

Key Finding: Daniel frequently interacts with "Samantha J.", who has commented on multiple posts.

3. Uncovering Hidden Friend Connections

3.1 Investigating "Samantha J."

- Her profile is public, revealing:
- She has recently tagged Daniel in a post.
- The post mentions "Road trip to Mexico with Daniel!"
- A photo of a car rental receipt shows a rental date from 5 days ago.

Key Finding: Daniel may have traveled to Mexico recently.

3.2 Using Facebook Groups to Gather More Clues

Daniel is a member of multiple public Facebook groups, including:

- "San Diego Music Fans" → He posted about attending a concert last month.
- "Expats in Mexico" → He commented on a post about temporary housing in Tijuana, Mexico.

Key Finding: Daniel may be staying in Tijuana.

4. Verifying the Target's Current Location

4.1 Checking Location Metadata in Photos

- Samantha's recent travel photos contain location tags for Rosarito Beach, Mexico.
- Daniel's past posts also include check-ins at locations near the U.S.-Mexico border.

4.2 Reverse Searching Daniel's Profile Picture

A reverse image search of Daniel's latest profile picture leads to a LinkedIn profile, which lists his new job as a freelance photographer in Mexico City.

Key Finding: Daniel may have moved to Mexico City, rather than just visiting Tijuana.

5. Confirming Findings & Ethical Considerations

5.1 Cross-Checking Data from Other Platforms

- **Instagram Search** → Daniel's Instagram profile (linked to his Facebook) confirms recent travel photos in Mexico.
- **Twitter Search** → A tweet from a friend mentions "Daniel moving to Mexico permanently."

5.2 Ethical Boundaries in Facebook OSINT

- The investigator only used publicly available data.
- No unauthorized hacking, data breaches, or deception were involved.
- OSINT findings were shared only with authorized parties (family & law enforcement).

6. Final Outcome

The investigator compiles a report:

- Daniel was last active in Tijuana, Mexico.
- He appears to have moved to Mexico City, working as a freelancer.
- His social media activity suggests he is safe but avoiding contact.
- The family uses this information to reestablish contact.

This case study demonstrates how Facebook OSINT can be used to track a missing person by leveraging:

- Profile searches, Google Dorking, and metadata extraction.
- Hidden friend connections through mutual interactions.
- Public group activity to determine recent movements.
- Cross-platform verification for accuracy.

3. Twitter Investigations: Hashtags, Lists & Influencers

Twitter serves as a real-time intelligence hub, where trends emerge, narratives spread, and influencers shape public discourse. For OSINT analysts, it provides a powerful platform to track events, monitor sentiment, and uncover hidden connections. This chapter explores key investigative techniques, including hashtag analysis to trace movements and campaigns, Twitter Lists to map group affiliations, and influencer identification to determine key voices driving conversations. By leveraging advanced search queries, metadata extraction, and automation tools, analysts can efficiently gather intelligence while navigating Twitter's evolving policies and data restrictions.

3.1 Understanding Twitter's Role in OSINT Investigations

Twitter is one of the most valuable platforms for OSINT (Open-Source Intelligence) investigations. Unlike many social media sites, Twitter allows for real-time public data collection, making it an essential tool for tracking individuals, analyzing trends, and uncovering hidden networks.

In this chapter, we will cover:

- The unique role Twitter plays in OSINT investigations.
- How Twitter's structure allows for real-time intelligence gathering.
- Key OSINT techniques for extracting actionable data.
- Ethical considerations when conducting investigations on Twitter.

1. Why Twitter is Crucial for OSINT

1.1 Public & Real-Time Data Accessibility

Twitter is one of the most open social media platforms, with most content being publicly accessible. Unlike Facebook or Instagram, where privacy settings often restrict visibility, Twitter allows investigators to:

- Monitor public tweets in real-time.
- Track conversations through hashtags and mentions.
- Identify geotagged tweets for location-based intelligence.

- Follow retweets and replies to uncover hidden connections.

1.2 A Goldmine for Investigators

Twitter is used extensively for:

✓ **Crisis Monitoring** – OSINT analysts track breaking news, protests, and conflicts.
✓ **Threat Intelligence** – Investigators monitor extremist groups, scams, and cyber threats.
✓ **Corporate & HR Investigations** – Analysts research employees, competitors, and reputational risks.
✓ **Geolocation Analysis** – Tweets with metadata can reveal a target's real-world location.

Case Study: During the 2022 Russia-Ukraine conflict, OSINT analysts used Twitter to track military movements by analyzing geotagged photos and videos posted by civilians.

2. Twitter's Structure & How It Affects OSINT Investigations

To effectively conduct OSINT on Twitter, it's important to understand its core elements:

2.1 Types of Twitter Data

Twitter data can be categorized into the following key areas:

Data Type	Description
Tweets	Public posts that may contain text, images, videos, links, or geotags.
Retweets	Shares of another user's tweet—useful for tracking content amplification.
Mentions (@username)	Tweets that mention a specific user—helps identify conversations involving a target.
Hashtags (#tag)	Keywords used to categorize discussions—useful for tracking topics, trends, and events.
Followers & Following	User connections that can reveal relationships.
Likes & Replies	Interactions that help analyze engagement patterns.
Direct Messages (DMs)	Private messages—accessible only if obtained legally via cooperation or warrants.

2.2 Understanding Twitter's Algorithm

Twitter prioritizes content based on:

- **Engagement** (likes, retweets, comments).
- **Recency** (newer posts are favored).
- **User activity** (frequent tweeters get higher visibility).

Knowing this helps investigators focus on high-impact tweets and accounts.

3. Essential OSINT Techniques for Twitter Investigations

3.1 Advanced Twitter Search Operators

Twitter's search bar allows powerful filtering with advanced operators:

Search Query	Function
`"John Doe"`	Exact phrase search (tweets containing this phrase).
`from:username`	Tweets from a specific user.
`to:username`	Tweets sent to a specific user.
`@username`	Mentions of a specific user.
`#hashtag`	Finds tweets containing a specific hashtag.
`since:YYYY-MM-DD`	Filters tweets after a certain date.
`until:YYYY-MM-DD`	Filters tweets before a certain date.
`near:"Los Angeles" within:10km`	Finds geotagged tweets from a location.

Example: To find tweets mentioning "cyber threat" posted in the last month, use:

"cyber threat" since:2025-01-01 until:2025-02-01

3.2 Tracking Hashtags & Trends

Hashtags allow analysts to follow conversations:

- Use #OSINT, #BreakingNews, #CyberSecurity to monitor general intelligence topics.
- Use event-specific hashtags (e.g., #UkraineWar, #Protests, #Earthquake) to track crises.

- Monitor Twitter Trends for emerging narratives.

3.3 Extracting Geolocation Data

Even though Twitter removed automatic geotagging, some tweets still contain location metadata:

- **Geotagged tweets** → Users who manually enable location sharing.
- **Image metadata** → Extract location data from photos posted on Twitter.
- **Place mentions** → Users may mention real-world locations in their tweets.
- **OSINT Tool**: Use GeoSocialFootprint or TweetDeck to filter tweets by location.

3.4 Mapping Connections & Identifying Networks

- **Follower-Following Analysis** → Investigate whom a target follows and who follows them.
- **Retweet & Mention Analysis** → Identify influencers amplifying specific content.
- **Group Interactions** → Determine if users belong to coordinated disinformation campaigns.

Example: If an unknown account frequently retweets a known extremist group, it may be part of a coordinated network.

4. Twitter OSINT Tools & Automation

Several tools help automate Twitter investigations:

Tool	Function
TweetDeck	Live monitoring of multiple Twitter feeds.
Twitonomy	Detailed analytics on Twitter accounts.
Tinfoleak	Extracts metadata, geolocation, and activity patterns.
GeoSocialFootprint	Finds geotagged tweets from a target.
Social Bearing	Analyzes user sentiment and interactions.
Maltego	Creates network maps of Twitter interactions.

Caution: Twitter restricts API access for bulk data collection—ensure compliance with its terms.

5. Ethical & Legal Considerations in Twitter OSINT

When using Twitter for OSINT investigations, analysts must consider ethical and legal boundaries:

✅ **Public Data Only** – Do not attempt to access private messages or locked accounts.

✅ **No Impersonation** – Creating fake profiles to engage with targets is unethical.

✅ **Responsible Reporting** – Avoid spreading misinformation or doxxing individuals.

✅ **Adhere to Platform Policies** – Twitter's API has strict data usage limitations.

Case Study: In 2020, Twitter flagged and removed thousands of fake accounts linked to foreign interference campaigns. OSINT analysts must ensure they do not engage in deceptive tactics when conducting investigations.

Twitter is an essential tool for OSINT investigations due to its real-time, public data availability. By leveraging advanced search techniques, geolocation analysis, and network mapping, analysts can extract valuable intelligence on individuals, groups, and global events.

3.2 Advanced Search Operators & Filters for Twitter Investigations

Twitter's advanced search capabilities allow OSINT analysts to refine their investigations and extract high-value intelligence from billions of tweets. Whether tracking individuals, monitoring global events, or analyzing digital footprints, understanding Twitter's search operators and filters is crucial.

In this chapter, we will explore:

- How to use Twitter's built-in advanced search.
- Search operators for precise filtering.
- Third-party tools to enhance investigations.

- Case study demonstrating an OSINT Twitter investigation.

1. The Importance of Advanced Search in OSINT

Twitter produces over 500 million tweets daily, making it difficult to extract relevant data without refined search techniques.

By using advanced search operators and filters, OSINT analysts can:

✓ Identify specific tweets related to a person, event, or topic.

✓ Track historical data even if an account is deleted.

✓ Uncover geolocated tweets for location-based intelligence.

✓ Monitor influencers, disinformation campaigns, and coordinated networks.

2. Twitter's Built-in Advanced Search

Twitter offers a graphical interface for advanced searches at:

🔗 *https://twitter.com/search-advanced*

This tool allows filtering by:

- Words or phrases (exact or partial match).
- Usernames (from/to specific accounts).
- Location-based tweets.
- Date range filtering.

Limitation: The built-in search has restrictions; analysts often rely on search operators for deeper investigations.

3. Twitter Search Operators for OSINT

3.1 Basic Search Operators

Operator	Function	Example Query
`"keyword"`	Exact phrase match	`"data breach"`
`keyword1 OR keyword2`	Find either term	`hacker OR exploit`
`keyword1 -keyword2`	Exclude a word	`OSINT -course`
`(word1 word2)`	Grouped search	`(cyber attack)`
`#hashtag`	Find tweets with a hashtag	`#cybersecurity`
`from:username`	Tweets from a user	`from:elonmusk`
`to:username`	Tweets sent to a user	`to:jack`
`@username`	Mentions of a user	`@CIA`
`filter:media`	Show tweets with images/videos	`Russia filter:media`
`filter:links`	Show tweets with links	`OSINT filter:links`
`since:YYYY-MM-DD`	Tweets after a date	`cyberattack since:2024-01-01`
`until:YYYY-MM-DD`	Tweets before a date	`leak until:2024-01-31`
`near:"location"` `within:10km`	Geotagged tweets from a location	`protest near:"New York"` `within:5km`

Example OSINT Query:

"data leak" OR "hack" from:@cybersecnews since:2024-01-01 filter:links

✅ Finds data leak tweets from @cybersecnews with links from January 2024 onward.

3.2 Advanced Search Filters

Tracking Conversations & Replies

To analyze tweet replies and conversations, use:

- conversation_id:tweetID → Finds all replies to a tweet.
- to:@username → Finds tweets sent to a user.
- @username filter:replies → Shows replies to a user.

Example:

conversation_id:17654321987654

✅ Reveals all replies to a specific tweet.

Geolocation Tracking with Twitter Search

Though Twitter disabled automatic geotagging, some users still enable location metadata.

- Use near:"City" and within:Xkm to find tweets from a location.
- Combine with event-related keywords to track live incidents.

Example:

"explosion" near:"Los Angeles" within:5km since:2024-02-01

✅ Finds tweets mentioning "explosion" in Los Angeles, posted since February 2024.

Identifying Suspicious Accounts & Bots

- **filter:verified** → Shows tweets only from verified accounts.
- **min_faves:100** → Finds tweets with 100+ likes (helps identify viral content).
- **min_retweets:500** → Tracks widely shared tweets.
- **lang:en** → Filters tweets in English.

Example:

"fake news" filter:verified min_retweets:1000 lang:en

✅ Finds widely shared tweets from verified accounts discussing fake news.

4. Automating Twitter OSINT with Tools

Several third-party tools automate Twitter data collection:

Tool	Function
TweetDeck	Real-time monitoring of multiple searches.
Twint (Python tool)	Scrapes tweets without API restrictions.
Tinfoleak	Extracts metadata from Twitter profiles.
GeoSocialFootprint	Finds geotagged tweets.
Social Bearing	Analyzes user sentiment and tweet engagement.
Maltego Twitter Plugins	Maps Twitter connections.

5. Case Study: Using Advanced Twitter OSINT to Track a Cyber Threat

Scenario

A cybersecurity analyst is investigating a new ransomware group that has recently leaked stolen data online.

Step 1: Identifying Initial Tweets

Using Twitter search:

"data leak" OR "ransomware" OR "hack" since:2024-01-01 filter:links

✓ Finds recent tweets linking to leaked data sources.

Step 2: Tracking Key Accounts

- Extracts tweet authors using from:username.
- Finds related conversations using to:@username filter:replies.
- Identifies potential group members by analyzing followers & retweets.

Step 3: Geolocation & Time-Based Analysis

- Uses near:"Moscow" within:50km to track Russian cybercrime discussions.
- Combines with since:2024-01-01 to find recent activity.

Step 4: Verifying Data with External Sources

- Uses TweetDeck to monitor related hashtags in real time.

- Cross-checks findings with OSINT tools like Shodan for leaked server IPs.
- Outcome

The analyst compiles a dossier on the ransomware group, including:

✅ Key Twitter accounts linked to the operation.

✅ Time patterns suggesting their active hours.

✅ Geolocation hints from tweets and shared links.

✅ Network of followers amplifying their leaks.

6. Ethical & Legal Considerations

✅ **Respect Privacy** – Do not attempt to hack private accounts.

✅ **No Doxxing** – Avoid sharing sensitive personal details.

✅ **Platform Compliance** – Follow Twitter's terms of service.

✅ **Cross-Verify Findings** – Ensure data accuracy before drawing conclusions.

Mastering Twitter search operators and filters is a critical skill for OSINT investigations. Whether tracking threat actors, monitoring real-time events, or mapping influence networks, Twitter remains a powerful intelligence-gathering tool.

3.3 Tracking Hashtags, Mentions & Trending Topics

Hashtags, mentions, and trending topics are key components of Twitter's ecosystem, providing real-time insights into conversations, events, and digital movements. OSINT analysts leverage these features to track narratives, analyze sentiment, and uncover hidden networks of influence.

In this chapter, we will cover:

✅ How hashtags and mentions work and why they matter in OSINT.

✅ Methods to track and analyze trends for investigative purposes.

✅ Tools and techniques to monitor social movements, propaganda, and emerging threats.

✓ Case study on tracking a viral misinformation campaign.

1. Understanding Hashtags & Mentions in OSINT Investigations

1.1 What Are Hashtags?

Hashtags (#) group tweets under specific topics. They are crucial for:

- Tracking events (e.g., #Election2024, #UkraineWar).
- Monitoring crises (e.g., #Earthquake, #CyberAttack).
- Identifying online movements (e.g., #Anonymous, #MeToo).
- Detecting misinformation campaigns (e.g., #FakeNews).

Example:

#Bitcoin → Shows all tweets discussing Bitcoin in real time.

1.2 What Are Mentions?

Mentions (@) refer to specific users in a tweet. They help OSINT analysts:

- Map interactions between individuals and groups.
- Identify key influencers in discussions.
- Uncover hidden connections between accounts.

Example:

"The new cyberattack is massive! @cybersecuritynews what do you think?"

✓ This tweet mentions @cybersecuritynews, bringing it into the conversation.

2. Tracking Hashtags for OSINT Investigations

2.1 Using Twitter Search for Hashtags

To find tweets containing a specific hashtag:

#cyberattack since:2024-01-01 until:2024-02-01

✅ Finds all tweets with #cyberattack from January 2024.

To find tweets using multiple hashtags:

#ransomware OR #databreach OR #hack

✅ Returns tweets that contain any of the listed hashtags.

2.2 Identifying Viral & Suspicious Hashtags

Misinformation campaigns often use coordinated hashtag flooding to manipulate trends. To analyze suspicious hashtag spikes, check:

- Sudden increases in hashtag usage.
- High engagement from bot-like accounts.
- Repeated tweets with identical wording.

Example: During the 2020 U.S. elections, Twitter identified bot networks amplifying #StopTheSteal to spread election fraud claims.

2.3 Tracking Hashtag Evolution Over Time

To see how a hashtag trends:

#cybersecurity since:2023-01-01

✅ Monitors how discussions on #cybersecurity have evolved since January 2023.

Use:

- TweetDeck for real-time hashtag monitoring.
- Hashtagify to see related hashtags.
- Trendsmap to visualize hashtag locations.

3. Investigating Mentions & Network Interactions

3.1 Finding Who Engages with a User

To track users who mention a specific account:

to:@elonmusk

✅ Finds tweets sent to Elon Musk.

To find tweets where an account is mentioned:

@OpenAI filter:verified

✅ Finds verified accounts discussing OpenAI.

3.2 Mapping Connections Between Users

OSINT analysts track mentions to:

- Identify core influencers in a discussion.
- Detect possible bot or sock puppet networks.
- Analyze coordination between users.

Example: If multiple suspicious accounts repeatedly mention the same person in identical tweets, it may indicate a coordinated influence campaign.

3.3 Tracking Retweets & Replies

To find who is spreading a tweet, use:

url:"https://twitter.com/user/status/1234567890"

✅ Finds all retweets and quote tweets of a specific post.

4. Monitoring Trending Topics for Intelligence Gathering

4.1 Using Twitter's Trending Section

Twitter shows trending topics based on:

- Global trends (worldwide discussions).
- Country-specific trends (localized to a nation).
- City-level trends (localized to a city).

Example: #BlackoutPakistan trending in a country may indicate a major power outage or government censorship event.

4.2 Tools to Monitor Trends & Hashtags

Tool	Function
TweetDeck	Live hashtag monitoring.
Trendsmap	Maps trending hashtags by location.
Hashtagify	Tracks hashtag popularity over time.
Social Bearing	Analyzes hashtag engagement & sentiment.
Twitonomy	Maps mentions and retweets of a user.

5. Case Study: Tracking a Viral Misinformation Campaign

Scenario

In mid-2024, rumors spread online about a fabricated cyberattack affecting a major financial institution. OSINT analysts needed to verify the claim.

Step 1: Identifying Hashtags & Keywords

A search for related hashtags revealed:

#BankHack OR #FinancialCyberAttack since:2024-06-01

✅ Found a surge in tweets using #BankHack, mostly from newly created accounts.

Step 2: Analyzing the Accounts Spreading the Hashtag

Using filter:verified, analysts checked if credible sources were discussing the event.

#BankHack filter:verified

❌ No verified accounts reported on it, raising red flags about credibility.

Step 3: Checking for Copy-Paste Tweets

"Bank servers down, customers reporting issues!" since:2024-06-01

✓ Found hundreds of identical tweets, suggesting a coordinated campaign.

Step 4: Tracking the Source of the Hashtag

- Who started using #BankHack first?
- What time did it first appear?
- Did bot accounts amplify it?

Using Trendsmap & Twitonomy, analysts found that the hashtag originated from a small group of anonymous Twitter accounts linked to a known disinformation network.

Step 5: Cross-Checking with Official Sources

- The bank's official Twitter account made no statement.
- No major news outlets reported an attack.
- Cybersecurity monitoring services showed no anomalies.

Outcome

The hashtag was part of an organized misinformation campaign aiming to create panic.

✓ Twitter flagged and restricted the trending hashtag within hours.

6. Ethical & Legal Considerations

✓ **Do not manipulate trends** – OSINT analysts should observe and analyze, not interfere.

✓ **Verify data before acting** – Do not assume a trending topic is factual.

✓ **Respect platform rules** – Follow Twitter's terms of service when collecting data.

✓ **No doxxing** – Avoid sharing personal data of individuals when analyzing trends.

Tracking hashtags, mentions, and trending topics provides valuable intelligence on global events, online movements, and misinformation campaigns. By leveraging advanced search techniques, network mapping, and third-party tools, OSINT analysts can uncover hidden narratives and detect coordinated influence operations.

3.4 Analyzing User Timelines, Connections & Retweets

Twitter's structure allows OSINT analysts to track user activity, connections, and influence by analyzing timelines, interactions, and retweet networks. Understanding how users engage with others, who amplifies their messages, and what patterns emerge can provide crucial insights for investigations.

In this chapter, we will explore:

✅ **User timelines** – Tracking activity patterns and identifying behavioral anomalies.
✅ **Connections & interactions** – Mapping relationships and influence networks.
✅ **Retweet analysis** – Detecting coordinated amplification and bot activity.
✅ **Case study** – Investigating a suspicious user's digital footprint.

1. Understanding User Timelines for OSINT

A Twitter timeline is a record of all tweets and retweets posted by a user. OSINT analysts examine timelines to:

- Identify patterns of activity (e.g., time zones, tweet frequency).
- Track deleted tweets using archives.
- Determine a user's topics of interest.
- Uncover links to other accounts through interactions.

Example:

A threat actor claims to be based in London but posts most tweets at 3 AM GMT →
Suspicious!

1.1 Searching a User's Timeline

To extract tweets from a specific user:

from:username since:2024-01-01 until:2024-02-01

✅ Finds tweets by @username within the specified date range.

To filter out retweets and focus only on original tweets:

from:username -filter:retweets

✅ Finds only original content from @username.

To find a user's tweets containing specific words:

from:username "keyword"

✅ Useful for tracking discussions about specific topics.

1.2 Identifying Behavioral Patterns

By analyzing when and how often a user tweets, OSINT analysts can infer:

- Time zone & likely location.
- Active vs. inactive periods.
- Anomalous tweeting behavior (e.g., sudden bursts of tweets).

Example:

If a user tweets 24/7, they may be a bot or multiple people using one account.

2. Mapping User Connections & Engagement

A user's connections reveal:

- Who they interact with most frequently.
- What topics they engage with.
- Potential coordinated activity with other users.

2.1 Tracking Replies & Mentions

To find tweets sent to a user:

to:username

✅ Finds tweets directed at @username (e.g., questions, accusations, conversations).

To find tweets mentioning a user:

@username

✅ Useful for tracking discussions about the user.

To filter out spammy mentions:

@username -filter:replies -filter:links

✅ Removes replies and links to focus on organic mentions.

Example:

A journalist investigating a scammer finds multiple complaints by searching to:@scammer123.

2.2 Mapping Frequent Interactions

Using OSINT tools like Twitonomy or Social Bearing, analysts can:

- Identify who a user replies to most often.
- Detect possible sock puppets (multiple accounts engaging unnaturally).
- Find hidden connections between users.

Red Flag: If multiple accounts always reply positively to a single user, it could indicate fake engagement or a coordinated influence operation.

3. Retweet Analysis: Detecting Influence & Coordination

Retweets show how information spreads and who amplifies it.

3.1 Searching Retweets of a User's Tweet

To find who retweeted a specific tweet, use:

url:"https://twitter.com/user/status/1234567890"

✅ Finds all accounts that shared the tweet.

To track retweets by a specific user:

from:username filter:retweets

✓ Finds all tweets retweeted by @username.

3.2 Identifying Coordinated Retweet Activity

Signs of coordinated campaigns include:

- Multiple accounts retweeting the same post simultaneously.
- Retweets from accounts with similar bios & profile pictures.
- Accounts that only retweet but rarely post original content.

Example: A political propaganda campaign may use bots to mass-retweet content to manipulate public perception.

3.3 Tracking Retweet Networks with Tools

To analyze who boosts a user's tweets, OSINT analysts use:

Tool	Function
Twitonomy	Maps a user's most retweeted tweets.
Hoaxy	Tracks disinformation retweet patterns.
TAGS (Google Sheets tool)	Exports retweet data for analysis.
NodeXL	Builds retweet network graphs.

4. Case Study: Investigating a Suspicious Twitter User

Scenario

A new Twitter account (@CyberThreat2024) claims to have inside knowledge of a major cyberattack. Investigators need to verify the account's credibility.

Step 1: Examining the User's Timeline

from:CyberThreat2024 since:2024-01-01

☑ Finds all tweets by the user.

Findings:

- All tweets posted within 3 days of account creation.
- No personal opinions, only "leaks" about cyber threats.
- Unusual consistency in posting every 15 minutes.

Red Flag: Could be an automated account or a sock puppet.

Step 2: Checking Interactions & Connections

to:CyberThreat2024

☑ Finds who engages with the account.

Findings:

- Majority of replies come from accounts created in the same week.
- Frequent interactions with a small set of unknown accounts.

Red Flag: Possible fake engagement or coordinated group.

Step 3: Analyzing Retweet Patterns

url:"https://twitter.com/CyberThreat2024/status/1234567890"

☑ Finds who amplified the tweets.

Findings:

- 100+ retweets within minutes of posting.
- Most retweeters have very low follower counts.
- Identical retweet timing suggests automation.

Conclusion: Likely a disinformation campaign using bot accounts.

Outcome

Using OSINT techniques, investigators determined that @CyberThreat2024 was likely a coordinated fake news operation, designed to create panic about a non-existent cyberattack.

5. Ethical & Legal Considerations

✓ **Do not engage with suspect accounts** – Simply observe and analyze.
✓ **Avoid collecting private data** – Stick to publicly available information.
✓ **Verify information before reporting findings** – Avoid spreading misinformation.
✓ **Follow Twitter's terms of service** – Stay within ethical guidelines.

Analyzing user timelines, connections, and retweets is a powerful OSINT method for identifying influence networks, detecting fake accounts, and tracking disinformation campaigns. By using search techniques, network mapping, and third-party tools, analysts can gain valuable insights into how Twitter users interact and amplify content.

3.5 Identifying Bots, Sock Puppets & Fake Engagement

Social media platforms like Twitter are filled with automated bots, sock puppet accounts, and fake engagement tactics designed to manipulate public opinion, spread misinformation, or artificially boost influence. OSINT analysts must be able to identify these deceptive tactics to separate genuine conversations from manipulated narratives.

In this chapter, we will cover:

✓ **Bots vs. sock puppets** – Understanding the difference.
✓ **Key indicators of bot behavior** – How to spot automation.
✓ **Detecting fake engagement** – Identifying manipulated trends.
✓ **OSINT tools for bot detection** – Automating your investigations.
✓ **Case study** – Uncovering a bot-driven disinformation campaign.

1. Understanding Bots, Sock Puppets & Fake Engagement

1.1 What Are Bots?

Bots are automated accounts that post, retweet, and engage with content based on pre-programmed scripts.
They are used for:

- Spreading propaganda & misinformation.
- Amplifying political narratives.
- Boosting engagement for fake influencers.
- Manipulating stock prices & cryptocurrency trends.

Common Types of Bots:

Type	Purpose	Example
Spam Bots	Promote products, scams, or malware	"Win a free iPhone! Click here!"
Political Bots	Spread political propaganda	Fake engagement in elections
News Aggregator Bots	Auto-post news articles	"Breaking: Cyberattack on bank"
Astroturfing Bots	Fake grassroots support	1,000 accounts tweeting the same hashtag

1.2 What Are Sock Puppets?

Sock puppet accounts are human-controlled fake identities used to manipulate discussions, impersonate real users, or spread disinformation. Unlike bots, sock puppets are operated manually but can act in coordination.

Common Uses of Sock Puppets:

✅ **Trolling & harassment** – Attack critics while hiding the real identity.
✅ **Spreading fake narratives** – "Eyewitnesses" to fabricated events.
✅ **Astroturfing campaigns** – Making it appear as though public support exists for a cause.
✅ **Corporate & political deception** – Posing as real users to sway opinions.

Example: A PR firm creates hundreds of fake accounts to post positive reviews for a product or attack competitors.

1.3 What Is Fake Engagement?

Fake engagement refers to artificially boosting likes, retweets, and follows to create an illusion of popularity.

Methods include:

- **Buying followers & likes** – Services offer 10,000 Twitter followers for $50.
- **Engagement pods** – Groups coordinate to retweet & like each other's posts.
- **Scripted retweet chains** – Bots amplify a tweet at the same time.

Example: A fake influencer buys 50,000 followers, but their tweets get almost no engagement.

2. Detecting Bots on Twitter

2.1 Key Indicators of Bot Behavior

✗ **High tweet frequency** – Hundreds of tweets per day, 24/7 activity.

✗ **Unusual username formats** – Random letters/numbers (e.g., @user_23897).

✗ **Default profile picture** – No custom image or only stock images.

✗ **Copy-paste tweets** – Many accounts posting identical messages.

✗ **Irrelevant engagement** – Likes & retweets on unrelated topics.

✗ **No personal interactions** – No replies or meaningful discussions.

Example:

@CyberNewsBot99 tweets 500 times a day but has never posted an original comment or interacted with other users.

2.2 Detecting Bots Using Advanced Search

To find possible bot networks, use:

"keyword" filter:verified

✓ **Filters** results to only verified accounts, reducing bot noise.

"keyword" min_retweets:100

✓ Finds tweets with high engagement – useful for tracking viral bot activity.

"keyword" until:2024-02-01 since:2024-01-01

✅ Identifies time-sensitive bot campaigns.

"keyword" -filter:links -filter:replies

✅ Removes spam accounts that only post links.

3. Detecting Sock Puppets & Coordinated Fake Accounts

3.1 Signs of Sock Puppet Accounts

✅ **Same account creation date** – Many fake accounts created in the same week.
✅ **Similar usernames & profile pictures** – Reused or AI-generated images.
✅ **Repetitive phrases** – Accounts using the same talking points.
✅ **Limited activity before a major event** – Suddenly active before elections, scandals, or conflicts.
✅ **Interaction with a single main account** – Multiple sock puppets boosting one person's tweets.

Example: A politician's tweet gets 1000 identical replies from "different" users with no prior activity.

3.2 Using OSINT Tools to Detect Fake Accounts

Tool	Function
Botometer	Checks if an account behaves like a bot.
Hoaxy	Maps how misinformation spreads.
Twitonomy	Analyzes user activity & interactions.
NodeXL	Builds social graphs to detect clusters.
TweetBeaver	Cross-references user connections.

4. Detecting Fake Engagement & Manipulated Trends

4.1 Spotting Fake Retweet & Like Patterns

❌ **Retweets within seconds** – Bots instantly amplifying content.

✗ **Accounts with few followers but high engagement** – Paid engagement groups.
✗ **Hashtag flooding** – Same phrase repeated by thousands of accounts.
✗ **Similar replies from multiple accounts** – Copy-paste engagement.

Example: A tweet about a cryptocurrency suddenly gets 5,000 likes, but all from newly created accounts.

4.2 Using Data Analysis to Uncover Fake Trends

OSINT analysts use social network analysis (SNA) to detect manipulated trends.

- **NodeXL** → Maps relationships between users.
- **TAGS (Google Sheets tool)** → Extracts Twitter search results for analysis.
- **Gephi** → Visualizes engagement clusters to spot bot networks.

5. Case Study: Uncovering a Bot-Driven Misinformation Campaign

Scenario

During an election, a hashtag #CandidateScandal trends suddenly. Analysts suspect bot manipulation.

Step 1: Checking Account Activity

#CandidateScandal since:2024-02-01

✓ Finds all tweets using the hashtag.

Findings:

- Many tweets from accounts created in the last month.
- High frequency (500+ tweets per hour).

Step 2: Analyzing Retweet Patterns

url:"https://twitter.com/CandidateScandal/status/1234567890"

✅ Finds retweeters.

Findings:

- 80% of retweets came from accounts with fewer than 10 followers.
- Identical retweets within seconds.

Step 3: Mapping Engagement Networks

Using Hoaxy & NodeXL, analysts found:

- A central hub of fake accounts amplifying the tweet.
- Repetitive wording across accounts.

Outcome

Investigators confirmed that bots and sock puppets had been used to create an artificial scandal. Twitter suspended hundreds of fake accounts linked to the campaign.

6. Ethical Considerations in Detecting Fake Accounts

✅ **Do not publicly expose real users** – Mistakes can harm innocent people.
✅ **Follow platform policies** – Avoid violating Twitter's terms of service.
✅ **Verify before reporting** – Not all suspicious accounts are bots.
✅ **No doxxing** – Do not reveal private details of users.

Detecting bots, sock puppets, and fake engagement is a crucial OSINT skill for identifying manipulated narratives, influence operations, and misinformation campaigns. By using search techniques, network mapping, and bot-detection tools, analysts can uncover hidden influence networks and digital deception tactics.

3.6 Case Study: Using Twitter OSINT for Crisis Monitoring

During times of crisis—whether natural disasters, political unrest, or cyberattacks—Twitter serves as a real-time intelligence source for OSINT analysts. By monitoring tweets, hashtags, geotagged content, and retweets, investigators can track the spread of information, detect misinformation, identify key influencers, and assess public sentiment.

In this case study, we will analyze how Twitter OSINT can be used for crisis monitoring by looking at a hypothetical cyberattack on a financial institution. We will cover:

✓ Identifying early warning signs on Twitter

✓ Tracking crisis-related hashtags & keywords

✓ Mapping key influencers & sources of information

✓ Detecting misinformation & disinformation campaigns

✓ Geolocating relevant tweets & images

1. Scenario: Cyberattack on a Major Bank

A large financial institution (GlobalBank) suffers a suspected cyberattack, causing ATMs and online banking services to go offline. Panic spreads as users take to Twitter to report failed transactions, frozen accounts, and error messages.

OSINT analysts are tasked with:

- Assessing the situation in real time using Twitter data.
- Tracking public reactions and potential misinformation.
- Identifying official statements and credible sources.
- Detecting coordinated disinformation efforts (if any).
- Providing insights for security teams and crisis responders.

2. Identifying Early Warning Signs on Twitter

2.1 Searching for Crisis Indicators

The first step is to identify early warning tweets that signal a widespread issue. Analysts can use Twitter's advanced search operators:

("bank outage" OR "ATM down" OR "banking error") -filter:links since:2024-02-10

✓ Finds tweets mentioning banking issues without links (to avoid spam).

"GlobalBank" OR "#BankDown" OR "#CyberAttack" min_retweets:50 since:2024-02-10

☑ Finds highly shared tweets mentioning the crisis.

Findings:

- Multiple users report that GlobalBank ATMs stopped working simultaneously across different locations.
- Hashtags like #BankDown and #GlobalBankFail start trending.
- Some users post screenshots of error messages, giving further clues.

2.2 Detecting Suspicious Activity

If a sudden surge in similar complaints appears within a short timeframe, it suggests a systemic issue rather than isolated incidents.

To track suspiciously similar tweets, analysts can use:

"GlobalBank is down" min_retweets:20 -filter:replies

☑ Detects copy-pasted tweets, which may indicate bots or misinformation.

3. Tracking Crisis-Related Hashtags & Keywords

3.1 Monitoring Trending Hashtags

As public concern grows, analysts must track hashtags spreading information (or disinformation).

Using OSINT tools like:

- **Trendsmap** – Monitors trending hashtags by location.
- **TweetDeck** – Tracks multiple hashtags in real time.
- **Hoaxy** – Analyzes misinformation spread.

Example query to track hashtag engagement:

#BankDown OR #CyberAttack until:2024-02-12

☑ Finds tweets related to the crisis and their engagement trends.

✅ Finds unverified sources spreading the claim with links (potentially fake news sites).

Findings:

- A network of newly created accounts is tweeting the same fake message.
- Some accounts link to a conspiracy blog claiming the attack is a government plot.

6. Geolocating Relevant Tweets & Images

6.1 Searching for Geotagged Crisis Reports

To track tweets with location data, analysts use:

"bank outage" near:"New York, USA" within:50km

✅ Finds users reporting banking issues in NYC.

To filter only tweets with geolocation enabled:

"bank outage" geocode:40.7128,-74.0060,50km

✅ Narrows results to a specific radius.

6.2 Verifying Crisis-Related Photos & Videos

To ensure a crisis-related photo is real, analysts can:

- Check metadata (ExifTool, FotoForensics) for timestamps & GPS.
- Use reverse image search to confirm it hasn't been recycled.
- Compare weather & background details with real-world conditions.

7. Conclusion: Key OSINT Insights from Crisis Monitoring

✅ Twitter is a real-time intelligence source for tracking crises.

✅ Hashtag & keyword monitoring reveals early warning signs.

✅ Influencer & retweet analysis exposes information networks.

✅ Fake engagement & misinformation must be verified before reporting.

✓ Geolocation techniques help track crisis spread.

4. Instagram OSINT: Tracking Users & Hidden Data

Instagram is more than just a visual storytelling platform—it's a rich source of OSINT data that can reveal user activities, relationships, and location patterns. Despite privacy controls, analysts can extract valuable intelligence through profile analysis, geotag tracking, and metadata examination. This chapter explores techniques for identifying digital footprints, uncovering connections through tagged posts and followers, and leveraging OSINT tools to retrieve hidden insights. From understanding engagement patterns to tracking deleted or archived content, this section provides a structured approach to conducting ethical and effective Instagram investigations.

4.1 How Instagram's Algorithm Works for OSINT

Instagram's algorithm plays a crucial role in shaping what users see, how content is recommended, and how accounts interact with each other. For OSINT analysts, understanding the algorithm helps in tracking targets, mapping connections, and identifying engagement patterns.

In this chapter, we will cover:

✅ How Instagram ranks content and recommends posts

✅ How the Explore page and suggested accounts work

✅ How OSINT analysts can leverage these insights

✅ Limitations and challenges in Instagram investigations

1. How Instagram's Algorithm Works

1.1 The Three Main Instagram Feeds

Instagram organizes content into three primary feeds, each with its own ranking system:

1️⃣ **Home Feed** – Displays posts from accounts a user follows, ranked by engagement.

2☐ **Explore Page** – Suggests content from accounts a user doesn't follow, based on interests.

3☐ **Reels Feed** – Prioritizes viral short videos using AI-driven recommendations.

Each feed is powered by machine learning models that analyze user behavior, engagement patterns, and content interactions to predict what a person is most likely to engage with.

OSINT Tip: By studying a target's following list, likes, and interactions, analysts can uncover hidden interests, networks, and behavioral patterns.

1.2 Key Ranking Factors in Instagram's Algorithm

Instagram ranks content based on four key factors:

Ranking Factor	How It Works	OSINT Relevance
User Activity	Posts & accounts a user interacts with most	Helps track **targets' interests**
Engagement Signals	Likes, comments, shares, saves	Detects **highly engaged communities**
Content Relevance	AI analyzes images, captions, & hashtags	Identifies **keyword-based content patterns**
Timeliness	Newer content ranks higher	Helps **monitor real-time events**

Example: If a target frequently engages with crypto-related posts, their Explore page will likely be filled with similar content—helpful for tracking financial interests.

2. How Instagram Suggests Accounts & Content

2.1 How the Explore Page Works

Instagram's Explore Page is a powerful OSINT tool. It recommends posts and reels based on:

- Past interactions (likes, comments, shares).
- Connections & mutual followers.
- Accounts followed by similar users.

OSINT Application: By accessing a target's phone or cloning their account (in ethical research cases), analysts can reverse-engineer their interests and hidden associations using the Explore page.

2.2 How Instagram Suggests Accounts

The "Suggested for You" section in Instagram connects users with others based on:

- Shared contacts & mutual friends
- Similar engagement patterns
- Location-based interactions

OSINT Application: If a target follows a private account, Instagram may suggest related public accounts, providing clues to their network or interests.

3. Using Instagram's Algorithm for OSINT Investigations

3.1 Identifying a Target's Interests & Behavior

- Analyze their liked posts (reveals interests, location patterns).
- Monitor their comments (shows relationships, frequent interactions).
- Track their Explore Page (if possible) for hidden connections.

Example: An investigator tracking a suspected money launderer notices they like posts about luxury watches and offshore banking—potential indicators of financial movements.

3.2 Mapping a Target's Network Using Instagram's AI

- Check who Instagram suggests in the "Suggested for You" section.
- Cross-reference mutual followers and engagements.
- Look for clusters of interactions with specific groups.

Example: A target follows a known criminal, and Instagram suggests several affiliated accounts, revealing an interconnected network.

4. Limitations & Challenges in Instagram OSINT

✗ **Algorithm Manipulation** – Instagram's AI can be gamed with engagement pods & fake interactions.
✗ **Private Accounts** – Limits visibility into direct activity.

✕ Shadowbanning & AI Filtering – Some posts may be hidden from public search.

OSINT Workaround: Using dummy accounts, engagement tracking, and metadata analysis can help bypass some restrictions.

Understanding Instagram's algorithm allows OSINT analysts to:

✅ Track user interests, habits, and behavior.

✅ Map social connections using AI-driven suggestions.

✅ Use the Explore Page to reveal hidden activity.

✅ Monitor trending content & real-time events.

4.2 Finding Publicly Available Photos, Locations & Captions

Instagram is a rich source of open-source intelligence (OSINT) due to its vast collection of photos, geotags, captions, and user interactions. Even though the platform has tightened privacy settings, investigators can still extract valuable data from public profiles, hashtags, and location tags.

In this section, we will explore:

✅ How to find publicly available images and captions

✅ How to track geotagged posts and locations

✅ How to extract metadata from Instagram content

✅ Limitations and challenges in Instagram OSINT

1. Finding Publicly Available Photos & Captions

1.1 Searching for Public Instagram Posts

Instagram's built-in search function is limited, but analysts can still find public posts using OSINT tools and search operators.

Basic Instagram Search

You can search for:

🔍 **Usernames** – @username (e.g., @john_doe94)
🔍 **Hashtags** – #keyword (e.g., #luxurycars)
🔍 **Locations** – Place Name (e.g., Dubai Marina)

OSINT Tip: Instagram only shows suggested results, but a direct link to https://www.instagram.com/explore/tags/keyword/ will reveal more posts.

1.2 Extracting Instagram Captions & Keywords

✅ Captions contain keywords, locations, and possible encrypted messages.

✅ Hashtags reveal trends, topics, and communities.

✅ Mentions (@username) help track networks and interactions.

Example OSINT Search for Captions:

Use Google Dorking to find Instagram posts:

site:instagram.com "luxury travel" "Dubai"

✅ Finds public Instagram posts mentioning "luxury travel" and "Dubai".

site:instagram.com "bitcoin investment" "dm me"

✅ Finds potential crypto scams or financial fraud posts.

OSINT Application: Criminal groups often use coded language in captions. Monitoring recurring hashtags or slang helps uncover illicit networks.

2. Tracking Geotagged Posts & Locations

2.1 Searching for Geotagged Photos

Instagram allows users to tag locations in their posts. Even when the geotag isn't visible, OSINT analysts can still find location data through reverse image search, metadata analysis, or social engineering.

✅ **How to search for geotagged posts:**

1️⃣ Go to https://www.instagram.com/explore/locations/

2️⃣ Enter a location (e.g., New York City).

3️⃣ Analyze the most recent & popular posts.

Example: Searching for "Moscow City" can reveal posts from individuals who frequently visit luxury locations—useful for tracking high-profile targets.

2.2 Reverse Image Search to Extract Location Clues

Even if a post isn't geotagged, you can analyze the background details to identify its location.

OSINT Tools for Reverse Image Search:

🔍 **Google Reverse Image Search** – https://images.google.com/
🔍 **Yandex Reverse Image Search** – Better for finding Russian & Eastern European images.
🔍 **TinEye** – Tracks if an image has been posted elsewhere.

OSINT Application: A suspect posts a "random photo", but a reverse image search links it to a hotel website in Dubai, revealing their location.

3. Extracting Metadata from Instagram Content

3.1 Checking for EXIF Data (Image Metadata)

EXIF (Exchangeable Image File Format) data contains hidden details about a photo, including:

✅ Camera model & settings

✅ Timestamp (when the photo was taken)

✅ GPS coordinates (if not removed by Instagram)

🔧 **Tools to Extract Metadata:**

- **ExifTool (https://exiftool.org/)** – Extracts metadata from images.
- **FotoForensics (https://fotoforensics.com/)** – Checks image history.

OSINT Tip: Instagram removes EXIF data when a photo is uploaded, but if the original image is found elsewhere (WhatsApp, Facebook, personal blogs), metadata may still be available.

3.2 Finding Hidden Metadata in Instagram Stories & Reels

Even though Instagram strips EXIF data, metadata clues can still be found in stories and reels:

✅ Background noise & environment (Helps identify locations).

✅ Reflections in sunglasses/windows (Can reveal surroundings).

✅ Weather & time indicators (Sunlight, shadows).

Example: A suspect claims to be in New York, but an Instagram story reveals Dubai's skyline in their sunglasses reflection.

4. Limitations & Challenges in Instagram OSINT

🚫 **Private Accounts** – Most data is inaccessible without advanced techniques.

🚫 **Instagram API Restrictions** – Limits access to large-scale data extraction.

🚫 **Fake Geotags & Staged Photos** – Some users manipulate location data to avoid detection.

🚫 **Disappearing Content** – Stories & reels delete automatically after 24 hours.

Workaround: Analysts can use archiving tools (Wayback Machine, Archive.Today) or screenshot automation bots to capture disappearing content.

Instagram OSINT is a powerful tool for:

✅ Finding publicly available images & captions.

✅ Tracking geotagged posts & reverse-searching images.

✅ Extracting metadata clues from photos and videos.

✅ Overcoming privacy barriers through creative investigation.

4.3 Extracting Metadata & Identifying Geolocation Clues

Instagram posts, stories, and photos often hold hidden information beyond what is visible to the naked eye. Metadata—especially geolocation data, camera settings, and timestamps—can provide valuable intelligence for OSINT investigations. Whether you're tracking a target's movements, uncovering the context of a post, or validating a user's location, metadata analysis is a crucial tool for OSINT analysts.

In this section, we will explore: ✅ How to extract metadata from Instagram images and videos

✅ How to identify geolocation clues from images, stories, and captions

✅ Tools and techniques for metadata analysis

✅ Challenges and limitations of metadata analysis on Instagram

1. Extracting Metadata from Instagram Content

1.1 Understanding Instagram's Metadata Stripping Process

When a user uploads content to Instagram, the platform strips out much of the original metadata such as EXIF data (e.g., camera type, GPS coordinates, and timestamp). This is done primarily for privacy reasons—Instagram removes data that could potentially reveal a user's exact location or the device they are using. However, some metadata can still be embedded in posts, especially when the content is shared from external sources (e.g., WhatsApp, Facebook, or Google Photos).

OSINT Tip: While Instagram strips EXIF data from uploaded photos, video files (including Instagram Reels and Stories) can sometimes retain geotagging information if the content has been shared directly from a device or app that adds location tags.

1.2 Using Tools to Extract Metadata

Even though Instagram does not make it easy to access all metadata, investigators can still use a variety of external tools to extract whatever information is available. Here's how you can proceed:

ExifTool

- **Description**: ExifTool is a powerful, open-source tool that allows for the extraction of metadata from almost any type of image or video file.
- **Usage**: By running the tool on images (or video files) downloaded from Instagram (if available), you can recover hidden EXIF data such as timestamps, camera settings, and even location coordinates.
- **Website**: https://exiftool.org

FotoForensics

- **Description**: FotoForensics helps determine whether an image has been altered, but it can also extract any remaining metadata that might be hidden within an image file.
- **Usage**: If you suspect an image has been manipulated, FotoForensics can help identify the image's origin and confirm whether it has been edited or tampered with.
- **Website**: https://fotoforensics.com

Google Lens

- **Description**: Google Lens is an AI-powered tool that allows you to search for information related to the images you upload.
- **Usage**: You can upload Instagram photos to Google Lens to find more information about the object or location depicted in the image. Google Lens can be used to identify landmarks, logos, or other visible markers that might indicate a photo's location.

Reverse Image Search

- **Description**: Tools like Google Reverse Image Search or Yandex Reverse Image Search allow analysts to find instances where the image has been used or reposted elsewhere on the web. This can help identify whether the image is authentic or associated with other locations or contexts.
- **Usage**: Conducting a reverse search of the image helps determine whether the geolocation of the image matches the caption or claims made by the user.

OSINT Tip: Images uploaded on Instagram are often also shared on other social platforms. You can use reverse image search to find instances where the image might be geotagged or where metadata was not stripped.

1.3 Identifying Geolocation Clues

Geolocation clues are incredibly valuable in OSINT investigations, as they can provide precise location data or help corroborate a user's whereabouts at a particular time. Although Instagram strips metadata, there are other ways to identify location information:

1.3.1 Geotagging in Instagram Posts

Instagram allows users to tag their posts with locations. This is one of the simplest ways to access geolocation clues. Posts that are geotagged will contain location information, which is visible under the post's caption or at the top of the post.

- How to search for geotagged posts:
- Go to Instagram's search page.
- Click on "Places" and search for a specific location (e.g., a city or landmark).
- View posts tagged with that location.

OSINT Tip: Searching for locations in combination with specific hashtags can help identify patterns in posts, revealing when and where specific events took place or where targets were active.

1.3.2 Reverse Image Search for Geolocation Clues

In cases where the image is not geotagged on Instagram, reverse image search can help identify location-based geographic features. If a target uploads an image taken at a specific landmark or event, using reverse search tools can link the image to other sources with location data.

For example, if the user uploads a photo with the Eiffel Tower in the background, performing a reverse image search might link the photo to an Instagram post from a nearby location, confirming the user's whereabouts.

OSINT Tip: Be on the lookout for common landmarks, watermarks, and obvious clues like building names or street signs visible in photos, which can help pinpoint a user's location.

1.3.3 Analyzing Captions and Context

Captions and comments provide context to the geotag or visible location. Users often mention the location indirectly, using phrases such as:

- "Enjoying my stay in Paris!"
- "Another great sunset at Venice Beach."

Although captions may not directly provide GPS coordinates, they can be used in conjunction with geotags to verify the accuracy of location claims or uncover hidden associations (e.g., identifying where certain individuals or groups regularly visit).

OSINT Tip: Combining hashtags (e.g., #NYC, #TokyoSkytree) with location-based posts can uncover user patterns related to frequent travels or interactions at specific venues.

2. Challenges and Limitations in Metadata Analysis

While metadata extraction and geolocation clues are powerful OSINT tools, there are certain limitations that investigators should be aware of:

Metadata Stripping by Instagram

As mentioned, Instagram removes metadata when posts are uploaded, limiting the ability to extract EXIF data from posts directly. However, alternative methods, such as reverse image search, can sometimes recover this information.

Manipulated Metadata

Some users deliberately remove or alter metadata in their posts. For example, they might disguise location information or upload photos from different times to confuse investigators. Image manipulation tools like Photoshop can be used to fake timestamps or location tags.

Private Accounts

Instagram's privacy settings allow users to restrict access to their posts, and as such, private accounts may not provide any metadata or geolocation clues to external investigators. OSINT techniques can still be used on public accounts, but access to private content requires additional permissions or social engineering tactics.

User Behavior and False Geotagging

Users sometimes tag locations incorrectly (intentionally or unintentionally), leading to false conclusions. This can make geolocation analysis difficult and may require verification from other sources.

Extracting metadata and identifying geolocation clues from Instagram content are powerful techniques for OSINT investigators. Despite challenges like metadata stripping and false tagging, analysts can still leverage tools like ExifTool, reverse image searches, and location-based hashtags to uncover hidden information about targets' movements and activities.

4.4 Reverse Searching Instagram Usernames & Accounts

One of the most critical techniques for uncovering valuable intelligence on social media platforms like Instagram is reverse searching usernames and accounts. A single username can act as a unique digital fingerprint, linking multiple profiles, aliases, and even cross-platform interactions. By reverse-searching Instagram usernames, OSINT investigators can gain insights into a user's digital footprint, uncover hidden accounts, and track their activity across other social platforms.

In this section, we will explore:

✅ How to reverse-search Instagram usernames

✅ Tools and techniques for finding hidden accounts

✅ The significance of username patterns and aliases

✅ How to verify user identities through cross-platform searches

✅ Challenges and limitations of reverse searching usernames

1. Reverse-Searching Instagram Usernames

1.1 Why Reverse Search Instagram Usernames?

Reverse searching Instagram usernames allows investigators to find more than just a single account. It can uncover:

- Aliases or other usernames the person might be using.
- Hidden accounts or secondary profiles that may not be linked to the primary account.
- Cross-platform activity, allowing analysts to understand how a target behaves across various social media platforms.

1.2 Methods for Reverse Searching Usernames

1.2.1 Using Google Search for Reverse Searching

The simplest way to reverse search an Instagram username is by entering the username into Google Search along with the platform's domain (e.g., "site:instagram.com"):

Example Search:

@username site:instagram.com

This search helps find all public Instagram accounts associated with that specific username. If the username is commonly used, the search results may also show related content that appears on other websites, such as forums or news articles where the username is mentioned.

OSINT Tip: Sometimes, using quotes around the username, like "@username", can filter out irrelevant results and focus on exact matches.

1.2.2 Cross-Platform Searching

Many users maintain multiple accounts across various social platforms. Performing a cross-platform search can reveal additional accounts the person may be using.

- Use Twitter, Facebook, TikTok, and LinkedIn to search for the same username or associated usernames.
- The goal is to find connections between the Instagram username and accounts on other platforms.

Example:

A person using the Instagram handle @john_doe might also use @john_doe94 on Twitter or @doe_john on TikTok.

OSINT Tip: Look for recurring patterns in usernames. If you find that the user consistently uses the same or similar handles across platforms, this provides corroborative evidence of identity.

1.2.3 Social Media Search Engines and OSINT Tools

Dedicated OSINT search tools can help automate reverse searching across multiple platforms, including Instagram. Some of the most effective tools include:

- **Pipl**: A powerful search engine for finding public information across social networks and other sources. It can help link usernames to profiles on other platforms.
- **Spokeo**: An information aggregator that allows users to search for social media profiles by username.
- **Social Search Engines**: Tools like Social Search or Fsearch are designed specifically for cross-platform searches, allowing users to identify accounts related to a specific username across various sites.

These tools can also be useful in finding hidden profiles, especially when accounts are set to private or when the user tries to obscure their identity across multiple networks.

2. Tools and Techniques for Finding Hidden Accounts

2.1 Manual Search: Using Similar Usernames

Sometimes, individuals may use slightly altered versions of their usernames on Instagram to create additional accounts. Common alterations might include:

- Substituting letters or numbers (e.g., John_Doe vs. John_D0e).
- Using underscores, periods, or dashes to create variations.
- Adding year numbers, nicknames, or hobbies (e.g., JohnDoe94, JohnDoeMusic).

To find these accounts, you can manually search for these slight variations of the username or use a pattern-based approach:

If you already know the person's primary username, try creating other possible versions and search them on Instagram.

2.2 Investigating Linked Information

Instagram Bio and Links

Instagram profiles often link to external websites or mention other accounts in their bio. Investigating the bio section can reveal:

- Personal websites or portfolios.
- Other social media profiles linked in the "website" section.
- Email addresses or contact information that might be associated with other accounts.

Even inactive accounts may provide links or references to a person's current online presence.

Hashtags and Mentions

Look for hashtags or mentions of the target's username in other Instagram accounts. Users often tag their own posts or comment on others with their own handles:

- Look for unique hashtags tied to the user (e.g., #JohnDoeTravels).
- Check comments under popular posts to see if the user is tagged or mentioned by others.

These techniques help to uncover secondary profiles or even inactive accounts that the target may have abandoned but still reference in their other activity.

3. Identifying Username Patterns and Aliases

3.1 Common Username Trends

People often follow certain patterns or use similar aliases across multiple social platforms. Some common patterns include:

- **Name-based usernames** (e.g., "JohnDoe", "JohnDoe123").
- **Interest-based usernames** (e.g., "JohnDoePhotographer" or "JohnDoeMusic").
- **Professional usernames** (e.g., "JohnDoeWriter" or "JohnDoeConsulting").

3.2 Identifying Network Connections Through Shared Usernames

When reverse searching Instagram usernames, it's essential to track if the username appears in multiple profiles or is associated with certain network activities. For instance:

- A user's Instagram handle might appear frequently in comments or direct messages across their other social media accounts, revealing connections between them and other individuals or organizations.
- Identifying where else the username appears can lead to discovering hidden accounts or other profiles used for different purposes (personal, professional, or illicit).

4. Verifying User Identities Through Cross-Platform Searches

4.1 Cross-Referencing Social Media Accounts

Reverse-searching Instagram usernames is most powerful when combined with cross-referencing information across multiple platforms. This is especially useful for:

- Confirming identity by matching usernames, email addresses, or physical location information across platforms.
- Uncovering hidden accounts, like private Instagram profiles or accounts on lesser-known platforms (e.g., Snapchat or Reddit).

For example, if you find an Instagram username @johndoe94 and locate matching profiles on LinkedIn, Facebook, and Twitter, you can confidently establish that all these accounts likely belong to the same person.

5. Challenges and Limitations of Reverse Searching Usernames

Despite the effectiveness of reverse searching, there are several limitations to consider:

- **Privacy Settings**: Many users set their accounts to private, making it difficult to access profile details or content even if you know their username.
- **Alias Confusion**: People often use multiple aliases or change their usernames frequently, making it hard to track down all of their accounts. Some platforms even allow users to hide their accounts or delete their search history.
- **Username Similarity**: A person might use very common usernames, resulting in many accounts with similar names that don't belong to them.

Reverse searching Instagram usernames is a crucial technique for gathering OSINT, providing valuable insights into a person's digital footprint across platforms. By employing manual search methods, using OSINT tools, and verifying identities through cross-platform investigations, you can uncover hidden accounts and track target activities. While there are challenges—like privacy settings and username variations—proper techniques and strategies can help mitigate these obstacles, making reverse searching a vital skill for OSINT analysts.

4.5 Tracking Hashtags & Stories for Live OSINT

In the fast-paced world of social media, real-time data can provide critical insights, particularly when investigating ongoing events, trends, or user activities. Hashtags and Instagram Stories have become key features for tracking and analyzing live social media activity, offering a powerful way for OSINT analysts to monitor the latest developments, verify information, and uncover details about events as they unfold.

This section will delve into the following:

✓ How to track hashtags for live OSINT

✓ Using Instagram Stories for real-time intelligence gathering

✓ Tools and techniques for monitoring live updates

✓ Challenges and limitations in tracking hashtags and stories

✓ Practical use cases for hashtag and story tracking in OSINT investigations

1. Tracking Hashtags for Live OSINT

1.1 The Power of Hashtags in Real-Time Intelligence

Hashtags serve as a key tool for organizing and categorizing content on Instagram. By searching specific hashtags, OSINT analysts can gain access to live updates, witness accounts, and opinions on particular events or issues. Hashtags are often used in protests, natural disasters, or high-profile incidents, making them essential for tracking developments in real time.

For instance, during a crisis, hashtags such as #Earthquake2025 or #BlackLivesMatter may instantly link users to content related to the event. Using hashtags strategically can reveal:

- Live updates from affected areas.
- Public sentiments and responses.
- Geographic context and location-based posts.

Hashtags make it easier to track conversations surrounding key topics, allowing you to follow a narrative as it develops.

Examples of Real-Time Hashtag Usage

- #Protest2025 – To track live protests and social movements.
- #BreakingNews – For breaking news events unfolding in real time.
- #TerrorAttackNYC – To monitor and analyze reactions during an attack or crisis.

OSINT Tip: When tracking hashtags, always monitor variations and common misspellings. For example, people may use #earthquake2025 and #eq2025 interchangeably during a disaster, so tracking all relevant variations is crucial.

1.2 Advanced Techniques for Hashtag Tracking

To effectively track hashtags, analysts need to employ more sophisticated techniques than simply searching for a hashtag on Instagram. Here are several ways to maximize the potential of hashtag tracking:

1.2.1 Hashtag Aggregators

Some third-party hashtag aggregator tools allow users to follow specific hashtags across Instagram in real time. These tools continuously pull in content tagged with relevant hashtags, streamlining the process of collecting live data. Some tools include:

- **Hashtagify**: Offers detailed analytics for hashtags, tracking their use over time and providing insights on popular related tags.
- **RiteTag**: Tracks hashtag performance and suggests hashtags based on live trends.

These tools can provide analysts with not only content from public posts but also allow for filtering by location, timeframe, and engagement level (e.g., likes and comments).

1.2.2 Manual Hashtag Tracking Using Instagram

Instagram allows users to search hashtags directly within the platform. Once you search for a hashtag, you can:

- Monitor top posts for frequently shared or high-visibility content.
- Browse recent posts for the most up-to-date content.
- Use the Explore page to discover related hashtags that may uncover further content.

To monitor hashtag usage effectively, it is essential to perform ongoing searches and keep an eye on content spikes or sudden increases in engagement.

1.2.3 Using Geotagged Hashtags for Location-Based Intelligence

Many users combine hashtags with geotags to narrow down the location of their posts. For example, posts with the hashtag #ParisFashionWeek and location tags for Paris can offer valuable insights for event tracking or person location monitoring. By tracking these hashtags, analysts can gather live content relevant to specific areas or events.

Use Instagram's search functionality to narrow down results by location tags associated with specific events.

OSINT Tip: Pay attention to location-based hashtags (e.g., #NYCProtest2025), as they can uncover hyper-local intelligence about movements or activities in specific cities or areas.

2. Using Instagram Stories for Real-Time OSINT

2.1 Understanding the Value of Instagram Stories for OSINT

Instagram Stories have become a core feature for real-time, ephemeral content. Unlike permanent posts, Stories last for 24 hours and are often used for sharing live events, updates, and behind-the-scenes footage. They are ideal for monitoring breaking news, live events, or incidents in real time, as they capture raw, unfiltered information from users on the ground.

Stories often feature geolocation tags, hashtags, and interactive elements like polls, questions, and links, which can be leveraged for OSINT purposes. These provide:

- Geographic context through geotags and location tags.
- Live reactions and emotions, especially during events or crises.

- User engagement, such as comments or replies, that may provide further details.

2.2 Monitoring Instagram Stories for Live Updates

While Instagram Stories are temporary, there are several methods to capture and track them in real time:

2.2.1 Using Third-Party Tools to Save and Archive Stories

Some tools allow analysts to save Instagram Stories for later review, enabling them to capture live information and analyze trends:

- StorySaver: A website that lets users download Instagram stories, saving content before it disappears.
- Instagram Story Viewer: Another tool that helps track and view stories in real-time.

OSINT Tip: Be cautious when using third-party tools, as they may violate Instagram's terms of service. Always ensure the tools you use do not compromise your security or privacy.

2.2.2 Direct Monitoring of Stories via Instagram

To monitor Instagram Stories:

- Follow relevant accounts or hashtags related to your investigation.
- Keep an eye on location-based tags for stories relevant to specific regions, incidents, or events.
- Watch for time-sensitive stories that may contain immediate updates about ongoing developments, especially during crises or breaking news.

Since stories appear in a chronological sequence, analysts can track the timing of specific updates and correlate them with unfolding events.

2.2.3 Analyzing Interactive Content in Stories

Instagram Stories often include interactive elements, such as polls, questionnaires, and comments. These features can provide valuable real-time intelligence, revealing:

- Public sentiment regarding a particular event or issue.
- Crowd behavior, especially in response to critical or controversial topics.

- Personal testimonies and firsthand accounts.

By analyzing these interactive elements, OSINT investigators can gauge public opinions and assess the level of engagement with a particular event or narrative.

3. Challenges and Limitations in Tracking Hashtags and Stories

3.1 Short-lived Nature of Stories

Instagram Stories are designed to disappear after 24 hours, making it difficult to track or gather content over an extended period. Once the stories disappear, they cannot be retrieved directly from Instagram unless saved or archived.

3.2 Privacy and Geolocation Restrictions

Many users limit who can see their stories or hashtags, especially if they have set their accounts to private. Additionally, while geotagged stories offer valuable insights, they are not always present, and users can manually remove or hide location information.

3.3 Data Volume and Noise

Tracking live hashtags can lead to an overwhelming volume of data. Not all content related to a hashtag is relevant or useful. Filtering through irrelevant posts or noise can be time-consuming, making it important to focus on high-priority sources.

3.4 Accuracy and Authenticity of Data

Real-time data shared via stories or hashtags may not always be accurate or authentic. Users might post content that is misleading, out of context, or manipulated. Verifying the authenticity of content through cross-platform searches or checking other sources is vital.

4. Practical Use Cases for Hashtag and Story Tracking in OSINT Investigations

4.1 Crisis Monitoring and Disaster Response

In cases of natural disasters or crisis situations (e.g., earthquakes, floods, protests), hashtags like #TokyoEarthquake or #NYCProtests can provide real-time updates. Analyzing Instagram stories and posts tagged with these hashtags offers a ground-level view of events unfolding and can assist in understanding the severity, location, and responses to the incident.

4.2 Event Tracking and Analysis

For live events like concerts, political rallies, or sporting events, hashtags and Instagram Stories can be used to track audience engagement, crowd behavior, and even security issues. Hashtags such as #Coachella2025 or #WorldCupFinal can provide insights into crowd sentiment and logistics.

4.3 Public Sentiment Analysis

By tracking hashtag usage and analyzing Stories during political debates or social movements, investigators can gauge public opinion and mood. Analyzing how people interact with content (e.g., comments on Stories or posts) can reveal whether a topic is gaining traction or losing steam in real time.

Tracking hashtags and Instagram Stories is an indispensable technique for live OSINT investigations, offering the ability to monitor real-time events, analyze public sentiment, and uncover location-specific data. By employing advanced techniques and utilizing the right tools, OSINT analysts can effectively gather valuable intelligence from both hashtags and stories, helping them stay ahead in an increasingly dynamic and fast-paced digital world.

4.6 Case Study: Exposing a Fraudulent Instagram Influencer

Social media platforms, especially Instagram, have become a goldmine for digital marketing, with influencers commanding significant attention and trust from their followers. However, some individuals exploit this platform for personal gain, creating fraudulent personas and manipulating their audience. In this case study, we will walk through how OSINT techniques can be applied to uncover fraudulent behavior in an Instagram influencer's profile. By leveraging social media intelligence tools, hashtag analysis, and careful scrutiny of online personas, OSINT analysts can expose fake influencers, bot-driven engagement, and deceptive practices.

This case study will cover:

✅ Steps to identify a fraudulent influencer

✅ Techniques used in revealing their deception

✓ Tools and methods for verification

✓ Outcome of the investigation and lessons learned

1. Background: The Fraudulent Instagram Influencer

The subject of this case study is an Instagram user claiming to be a fitness influencer, health coach, and brand ambassador for various health-related products. The influencer, whom we will call @FitWithZara, has an extensive following and promotes fitness supplements, workout gear, and diet plans. Her account features meticulously curated content, including photos of her workouts, healthy meals, and sponsored posts for various companies.

Despite her popularity and high engagement rates, rumors have surfaced about the authenticity of her followers and the integrity of her promotions. Investigators suspect that Zara's account is inflated by fake followers, automated interactions, and misleading product endorsements.

Our task is to expose Zara's fraudulent activities using OSINT tools and techniques.

2. Identifying Red Flags in the Influencer's Profile

2.1 Profile Overview:

When analyzing Zara's Instagram account, the following initial red flags were noted:

- **Excessive Sponsored Posts**: Zara frequently posts advertisements for various products, often promoting competing brands within the same category (e.g., multiple fitness supplement brands), which raises questions about her credibility.
- **Discrepancies in Engagement**: The posts often feature high numbers of likes and comments, but a closer look reveals that the comments are generic, like "Great post!", "Love this!", or "Inspiring!". These types of comments are often indicative of bot-driven activity.
- **Unusual Growth Patterns**: Zara's account showed explosive growth in a short period, with a sharp rise in followers and engagement within just a few months. This is a classic indicator of purchased followers or manipulated engagement metrics.

2.2 Content Analysis:

Upon reviewing her posts and content, several patterns began to emerge:

- Zara's posts often show the same stock images of fitness models in promotional ads, suggesting that she may be reposting content without disclosure of its origins.
- Her captions seem scripted and overly generic, lacking authentic personality or interaction, which is often characteristic of influencers who are more focused on monetizing their content than providing value to their audience.

3. Conducting the OSINT Investigation: Steps to Expose the Fraud

3.1 Analyzing Followers and Engagement

The first step in exposing Zara's fraudulent activity is to analyze her followers and engagement patterns. To do this:

- We used tools like SocialBlade and HypeAuditor to analyze her account's engagement rate. These tools provide a breakdown of follower growth and engagement, helping to identify irregularities.
- SocialBlade revealed that her follower count spiked unnaturally in a short period, suggesting that Zara may have bought followers to artificially inflate her credibility.
- HypeAuditor further highlighted that her engagement rate was far below industry standards, with a large percentage of her followers being inactive or coming from non-relevant regions (e.g., a supposed fitness influencer with followers from countries that have no connection to fitness culture).

OSINT Tip: Engagement rate and follower quality are key metrics for identifying fraudulent influencers. Look for discrepancies between follower numbers and engagement levels.

3.2 Reverse Image Search to Detect Stock Photos

Another tactic in revealing Zara's deception was reverse image searching. Using tools like Google Reverse Image Search and InVID (a video verification tool), we checked some of the images Zara posted. We found that:

- Several of her fitness images, particularly those related to workout routines, were stock photos taken from image banks like Shutterstock.
- One of her supplement endorsements included a photo of a protein powder container that was featured on a product review website, which means Zara likely did not use the product but simply reposted an image she found online.

OSINT Tip: Reverse image searches help identify stolen or stock content used by influencers to mislead followers. It's an essential tool for revealing fraudulent activity.

3.3 Analyzing Hashtags for Engagement Manipulation

Hashtags are frequently used to increase the visibility of posts, but some influencers misuse them by employing excessive or irrelevant hashtags to game the system. In Zara's case:

- We conducted a hashtag analysis on Instagram using Hashtagify and discovered that Zara was using a high number of generic hashtags (e.g., #fitspo, #fitnessaddict, #healthyliving) that weren't directly relevant to her niche.
- A search revealed that several of these hashtags had been spammed by automated bots or other fake influencers promoting products, signaling that Zara may be involved in a network of fraudulent influencer activity.

3.4 Verifying the Authenticity of Sponsored Posts

Next, we examined Zara's sponsored posts. Brands often have strict requirements for influencers, such as genuine product use and disclosure of the partnership. Zara's posts, however:

- Lack proper disclosure (e.g., no mention of paid partnerships or ads in the captions).
- Show no real product use or in-depth engagement with the products. The posts appeared too polished and generic, as though Zara was simply posting to collect payments rather than genuinely endorsing the product.

OSINT Tip: Sponsored posts should feel authentic and relatable. A lack of genuine product usage or undisclosed partnerships is a red flag.

4. Exposing the Fraudulent Influencer

4.1 The Final Exposé

After analyzing Zara's engagement patterns, verifying her posts with reverse image searches, and uncovering suspicious hashtag activity, we concluded that Zara had been operating as a fraudulent influencer. She was:

- Faking authenticity by reposting stock images and using misleading captions.
- Buying fake followers to inflate her social presence and boost engagement metrics.
- Promoting products she had never used and failing to disclose paid partnerships.

The investigation results were shared with the brands she was endorsing, leading to an investigation of her affiliations and the eventual termination of her contracts with these companies. Additionally, Instagram was notified about her deceptive practices, and her account was flagged for violating platform policies.

5. Lessons Learned

5.1 Key Takeaways from the Investigation

- **Cross-Verification**: It is crucial to cross-check content authenticity through tools like reverse image search and external platforms to confirm whether influencers are using genuine content or manipulated material.
- **Follower and Engagement Analysis**: Using tools like SocialBlade and HypeAuditor to examine follower quality and engagement patterns can reveal discrepancies in growth and interactions, which are often signs of fraudulent behavior.
- **Hashtag Scrutiny**: Hashtag analysis can help identify attempts to manipulate engagement and visibility, particularly when irrelevant or spammy hashtags are used.
- **Ethical Considerations**: The OSINT community plays an important role in holding influencers accountable. Investigations like this help ensure that the public is not misled by fake personas and deceptive marketing practices.

Exposing fraudulent Instagram influencers is a challenging but essential aspect of social media intelligence. By using a combination of OSINT tools, data analysis, and content verification techniques, investigators can uncover deceptive behavior and hold individuals accountable. In this case study, we demonstrated how careful monitoring of engagement metrics, reverse image searches, and hashtag tracking can lead to the identification of fraudulent activity. As social media continues to evolve, OSINT techniques will be increasingly vital in ensuring authenticity and transparency in influencer marketing.

5. LinkedIn OSINT for Corporate & HR Investigations

LinkedIn is the go-to platform for professionals, making it a powerful OSINT resource for corporate intelligence, HR investigations, and competitive analysis. With millions of users openly sharing career histories, skills, and affiliations, analysts can map organizational structures, identify key personnel, and assess corporate networks. This chapter covers advanced search techniques, profile analysis, and data extraction methods to uncover hidden connections, job market trends, and potential security risks. Whether investigating corporate espionage, fraudulent resumes, or industry shifts, LinkedIn OSINT provides a strategic advantage in the digital intelligence landscape.

5.1 How LinkedIn is Used in Corporate & HR Investigations

LinkedIn, the premier professional networking platform, holds a treasure trove of publicly available data that is invaluable in corporate investigations, human resources (HR) processes, and due diligence assessments. Its database of professional profiles, company affiliations, educational backgrounds, and career histories can provide a deep insight into both individuals and organizations, making it an essential tool for those in the fields of corporate security, HR, and OSINT (Open Source Intelligence).

LinkedIn is widely used to track down individuals' career trajectories, verify employment history, assess professional credibility, and conduct background checks. But beyond these standard HR practices, LinkedIn's vast repository of data can be leveraged in more intricate investigations, such as identifying insider threats, uncovering conflicts of interest, or verifying potential corporate fraud.

In this section, we will explore how LinkedIn is used in the context of corporate and HR investigations, focusing on:

- How LinkedIn's structure benefits investigative work
- Techniques for searching and analyzing LinkedIn profiles
- Applications of LinkedIn data in corporate and HR-related cases
- Limitations and ethical considerations when using LinkedIn in investigations

1. LinkedIn's Role in Corporate and HR Investigations

1.1 The Structure of LinkedIn: Key Data Points for Investigations

LinkedIn has a highly structured platform, designed to display detailed professional information in an organized manner. Here are some key features that make LinkedIn a powerful tool for investigators:

Professional Profiles: Each user's profile is typically a detailed resume, listing:

- Job history and titles.
- Company affiliations.
- Education and certifications.
- Skills and endorsements from colleagues and peers.
- Recommendations from previous employers, managers, or coworkers.

Company Pages: Corporations maintain profiles on LinkedIn, offering a wealth of public information about the company's size, industry, services, location, and key personnel. Investigators can identify connections between an individual and a specific organization, as well as track recent hires, changes in management, and corporate restructuring.

Group Memberships: LinkedIn allows users to join professional groups, often specific to industries, skill sets, or even corporate networks. Group membership can provide insights into someone's professional affiliations, interests, or areas of expertise.

Connections: LinkedIn's connection system allows users to list their network of professional relationships. By examining an individual's connections, investigators can identify potential conflicts of interest, locate relevant individuals for interviews, or uncover hidden affiliations.

2. Techniques for Searching and Analyzing LinkedIn Profiles

LinkedIn provides a wealth of information, but navigating it requires specific search techniques to extract meaningful insights. Here are the key strategies used in corporate and HR investigations:

2.1 Boolean Search for Targeted LinkedIn Investigations

LinkedIn's advanced search feature, combined with Boolean operators, is a powerful tool for investigators. Boolean searches allow for more specific queries that narrow down results based on keywords, titles, companies, and other criteria. For example:

- **AND**: To combine terms. Example: "Senior Manager AND Marketing".
- **OR**: To find results with either term. Example: "Recruiter OR Talent Acquisition".
- **NOT**: To exclude results with certain terms. Example: "Developer NOT Java".

These operators enable investigators to create a highly specific search query that helps identify individuals with particular roles, companies, or qualifications.

OSINT Tip: Use quotation marks around phrases to search for exact matches, such as "Chief Financial Officer" or "Sales Director."

2.2 Analyzing Public Connections & Group Membership

One of the most powerful investigative features of LinkedIn is its visibility of an individual's connections. While you cannot always access full connection details unless you are directly connected, you can often see the titles and companies of the people in the network. This allows you to:

- Identify key relationships between individuals or organizations.
- Investigate any suspicious connections, such as overlapping connections with competitors or rival organizations.
- Review group memberships for insight into a person's professional interests, affiliations, and areas of expertise.

LinkedIn groups are often a goldmine of information about industry-specific discussions, specialized knowledge, or even potential insider threats within organizations.

3. Applications of LinkedIn Data in Corporate & HR Investigations

3.1 Background Checks & Employment Verification

One of the most common uses of LinkedIn in HR investigations is conducting background checks on potential employees. HR departments or hiring managers may search LinkedIn profiles to verify the authenticity of a candidate's work history and professional qualifications. By cross-referencing the details on a CV with the information presented on LinkedIn, it becomes possible to:

- Verify job titles, dates of employment, and previous employers.
- Cross-check skills and certifications.
- Confirm any recommendations or endorsements that may suggest credibility.

If discrepancies arise, they may indicate potential issues with the accuracy of a candidate's resume or that the individual has misrepresented their qualifications.

3.2 Investigating Insider Threats & Conflicts of Interest

LinkedIn can also be used to uncover insider threats within an organization. In cases of corporate espionage or when investigating potential conflicts of interest, OSINT analysts can search LinkedIn to find connections that might suggest an employee's involvement in suspicious activities:

- **Dual employment**: If an employee is connected to two competitors or simultaneously employed at multiple companies, it could signal conflict of interest.
- **Connections to sensitive industry sectors**: Employees in positions that handle confidential information could have connections to competitors or external organizations of concern.
- **Pattern analysis**: Examining the individual's professional network and career progression might reveal sudden, unexplained job changes, suggesting possible security breaches or shifts in loyalty.

In addition to these red flags, analysts can review how employees are connected to key figures outside the organization, providing insight into any potential leaks of sensitive information.

3.3 Research for Mergers, Acquisitions, and Due Diligence

Before a merger, acquisition, or partnership, conducting thorough due diligence is essential. LinkedIn is a valuable resource for researching the key players within the companies involved, as well as their previous roles and professional reputations. Investigators can use LinkedIn to:

- Identify senior leaders or individuals with critical roles in decision-making.
- Assess any possible hidden conflicts between executives or board members.
- Look for relevant expertise or industry connections that may affect the success of the merger or acquisition.
- Understanding the professional background of potential partners is crucial in making informed decisions and protecting a company's interests.

3.4 Investigating Intellectual Property Theft or Fraud

LinkedIn can help identify individuals with a history of intellectual property theft or corporate fraud. If an employee leaves a company to start a competing business or take a similar role at a rival firm, LinkedIn connections and recommendations can provide insight into potential risks, such as:

- Individuals who might be leveraging insider knowledge for unfair competition.
- Examining career transitions or shifts that coincide with the timing of a company's intellectual property theft or a breach in non-disclosure agreements (NDAs).
- By tracking changes in job titles, network shifts, and connections with former colleagues, investigators can gain clues that may point to fraudulent activity or corporate sabotage.

4. Limitations and Ethical Considerations

4.1 Limitations of LinkedIn in Investigations

While LinkedIn is an essential tool, it does have limitations:

- **Incomplete Profiles**: Not all users complete their profiles in detail, so the information available may not always be accurate or comprehensive.
- **Privacy Settings**: Some profiles are locked, limiting what can be accessed without permission or a direct connection.
- **Misrepresentation**: LinkedIn profiles can still be manipulated, and some individuals may falsify job titles, skills, or affiliations.

4.2 Ethical Considerations in LinkedIn Investigations

When using LinkedIn in investigations, it is crucial to maintain ethical standards:

- **Respect privacy**: Do not engage in actions that breach LinkedIn's Terms of Service, such as viewing private profiles through third-party tools or using the platform in deceptive ways.
- **Transparency and honesty**: When gathering data from LinkedIn, always be transparent about your intentions. Misusing data could violate both ethical guidelines and privacy laws.
- **Avoiding harassment**: Reaching out to individuals for information should be done carefully and respectfully, avoiding any form of harassment or coercion.

LinkedIn has become an indispensable tool in both corporate investigations and HR-related inquiries. It offers an abundance of publicly available information, from job history to professional connections, that can provide valuable insights into an individual's background, behavior, and affiliations. Whether verifying employment details, investigating potential insider threats, or performing due diligence for corporate transactions, LinkedIn data is essential for modern OSINT investigations.

As with all OSINT methods, careful attention to ethical considerations and an awareness of limitations will ensure that LinkedIn investigations are not only effective but also respectful of privacy and legal boundaries.

5.2 Extracting Work & Educational History for Verification

In the realm of corporate investigations and human resource (HR) operations, verifying an individual's work history and educational background is a critical part of ensuring the accuracy and integrity of professional records. With the proliferation of online professional platforms, LinkedIn stands out as one of the most widely used resources for cross-referencing and verifying such information. However, while LinkedIn provides a convenient, structured, and often comprehensive record of professional experiences and qualifications, investigators must use precise methods to ensure the accuracy of the data provided.

This section will outline the process of extracting and verifying work and educational history from LinkedIn and similar platforms. It will detail how OSINT (Open Source Intelligence) analysts and HR professionals can use specific techniques to validate career details, identify discrepancies, and assess the legitimacy of claims, as well as explore potential red flags associated with misleading or falsified professional information.

1. Key Components of Work & Educational History on LinkedIn

1.1 Work History

Work history on LinkedIn generally includes the following key data points:

- **Job Titles**: The position held by the individual in each organization.
- **Companies**: The names of organizations where the individual has worked.
- **Tenure**: The start and end dates of employment, which may indicate gaps or frequent job changes.
- **Job Descriptions**: The roles and responsibilities outlined for each position.

- **Endorsements & Recommendations**: Colleagues, superiors, or clients may endorse skills or write recommendations that further validate the authenticity of the job.

1.2 Educational History

LinkedIn also contains a section for education that can include:

- **Degrees**: The type of degree earned (e.g., Bachelor's, Master's, Ph.D.).
- **Institutions**: The names of universities, colleges, or other educational organizations.
- **Dates of Attendance**: The start and graduation years.
- **Certifications & Continuing Education**: LinkedIn profiles often list specialized certifications, courses, or continuing education credentials that are relevant to an individual's career.

Both sections—work history and education—are fundamental to background checks and due diligence investigations, and need to be carefully verified to avoid potential misrepresentation.

2. Verifying Work History on LinkedIn

2.1 Cross-Referencing Job Titles and Companies

The first step in verifying an individual's work history on LinkedIn is to cross-reference the job titles and companies listed on their profile. A good starting point is:

- **Check Company Information**: Search for the listed companies on LinkedIn, review their profiles, and make sure the individual's claimed role aligns with their organization's official records (such as employee lists, company history, or public profiles).
- **Cross-Check Dates of Employment**: Look at the tenure dates. If there is a discrepancy between the employment period listed on the LinkedIn profile and other publicly available information (such as the company's website, press releases, or third-party sources), this could raise concerns about the authenticity of the work history.

OSINT analysts can also look for overlapping roles that could indicate a dual employment situation or conflict of interest.

OSINT Tip: LinkedIn allows users to list past job descriptions and responsibilities. Compare these descriptions to known information about the company and role to assess whether the responsibilities align with what is publicly known.

2.2 Verifying Job Descriptions

Once you have confirmed the accuracy of the company name and job title, the next step is to analyze the job descriptions provided on the LinkedIn profile. In some cases, individuals may exaggerate their responsibilities or role in the company to give the appearance of a higher position or greater experience. To verify job descriptions:

- **Research the Role**: Look at job postings or other employees' LinkedIn profiles within the same company for similar positions to compare responsibilities and titles.
- **Company Website & Press Releases**: Check if the individual's role is publicly mentioned in company announcements, blogs, or team lists to confirm their involvement in major projects or initiatives.

If you find discrepancies between the job responsibilities listed on LinkedIn and other sources, it may indicate embellishment or misrepresentation.

2.3 Assessing Recommendations and Endorsements

LinkedIn profiles often include recommendations from colleagues or superiors that validate an individual's professional credibility. These can be a strong indicator of the authenticity of a person's role in a company. However, they should not be taken at face value. To assess the validity of recommendations and endorsements:

- **Cross-Verify the Endorsers**: Investigate whether the individuals writing the recommendations actually work or have worked with the person. Look at their profiles to see if they are indeed connected through the listed companies or positions.
- **Quality Over Quantity**: A large number of generic, non-specific endorsements might be a red flag. Genuine recommendations typically provide detailed feedback about the person's skills, performance, and work ethic. Generic endorsements can indicate fake reviews.

3. Verifying Educational History on LinkedIn

3.1 Confirming Institutions and Degrees

Educational verification is often a key step in HR investigations, especially when dealing with high-level positions or when academic credentials are critical. Verifying educational information includes:

- **Institution Verification**: Cross-check the names of educational institutions listed on the profile. Visit the school's website or contact the alumni office to confirm whether the individual graduated from the institution in question.
- **Verify Degree Titles**: Ensure the individual's degree or qualification matches the specific program offered by the institution during the listed years of attendance. Some individuals may claim to have degrees in fields or from universities that do not exist or that they did not attend.

3.2 Checking Dates of Attendance

A common red flag in educational history verification is inconsistent dates. Discrepancies between the dates of attendance and the individual's work history can raise concerns. If a person claims to have worked at a company full-time during the same period they were attending a full-time educational program, this may indicate a misrepresentation of either the work or educational history. Additionally:

- **Compare Graduation Dates**: Cross-reference the graduation date with the person's work history. If they claim to have graduated in 2018 but began a new job in 2017, there is an inconsistency that needs to be addressed.

3.3 Verifying Certifications and Continuing Education

LinkedIn allows users to list certifications, professional courses, and continuing education. Verifying these credentials is especially important for individuals applying for roles requiring specific certifications or skills:

- **Confirm Certification Providers**: Research the institutions or organizations that issued the certifications to make sure they are legitimate and recognized within the industry.
- **Check Course Validity**: Look for certification courses listed on the individual's LinkedIn and cross-check whether these programs exist and whether the individual participated in them. For example, certain certifications like Project Management Professional (PMP) or Certified Information Systems Security Professional (CISSP) are issued by highly recognized bodies, and checking with these bodies for confirmation is a valid verification method.

4. Using Third-Party Tools to Assist in Verification

While LinkedIn provides a wealth of data, third-party OSINT tools can help automate the verification process and cross-check information with other databases. Here are a few tools that can assist in verifying work and educational history:

- **Pipl**: A tool that aggregates data across various social media platforms, including LinkedIn, to verify identities and backgrounds.
- **Spokeo**: A service that searches for professional profiles, education history, and public records to cross-check LinkedIn data.
- **Social Media Platforms**: Cross-reference details found on LinkedIn with other platforms like Facebook, Twitter, or Instagram, where individuals may share their career milestones and educational achievements in different ways.

5. Ethical and Legal Considerations in Verification

When conducting background checks or verifying work and educational history, it is important to maintain ethical standards and legal compliance:

- **Respect Privacy**: Be mindful of the privacy settings on LinkedIn and avoid accessing data that is not publicly available unless you have the proper consent.
- **Fair Use**: When verifying data, avoid jumping to conclusions or misinterpreting information that could lead to discrimination or unfair treatment.
- **Compliance with Regulations**: Ensure compliance with privacy laws like GDPR or FCRA, which regulate how personal data can be collected and used, especially in HR and investigative contexts.

Verifying work and educational history is a critical part of any corporate investigation or HR process. LinkedIn offers a powerful platform for conducting these verifications, but it requires a careful, methodical approach to ensure that the data is accurate and reliable. By cross-referencing work history, examining job responsibilities, confirming educational backgrounds, and leveraging third-party tools, investigators and HR professionals can ensure they are making informed decisions and reducing the risks associated with hiring or trusting individuals who may misrepresent themselves.

5.3 Investigating Company Networks & Employee Connections

In the world of corporate investigations, network analysis is an essential method for uncovering valuable insights about individuals and organizations. When performing OSINT investigations on LinkedIn, one of the most powerful features is the ability to explore an individual's company networks and employee connections. These connections often reveal hidden associations, collaborations, and potential conflicts of interest that are not immediately obvious from the publicly available information on corporate websites or other formal business records.

Investigating company networks and employee connections helps uncover professional affiliations, track organizational changes, and identify relationships between employees that may be relevant in criminal investigations, corporate due diligence, competitive intelligence, or even HR background checks. This section will explore how to leverage LinkedIn's network features, how to identify patterns in employee connections, and the role these connections play in investigations, as well as potential red flags and ethical considerations to keep in mind.

1. Understanding LinkedIn's Company Networks

1.1 Company Profiles on LinkedIn

A company's LinkedIn profile provides a unique opportunity for investigators to explore organizational structure, employee affiliations, and even employee turnover. By analyzing a company's network, investigators can:

- **Identify key employees within an organization**: LinkedIn lists employees by their job title, location, and the department or team they belong to. This can help identify individuals who may be responsible for specific tasks or have access to valuable information.
- **Analyze the company's hiring practices**: The profiles of past and present employees provide insights into the types of positions a company regularly hires for, allowing investigators to identify possible gaps in the workforce or areas of potential concern.
- **Assess employee mobility**: Investigating employees who have recently left or joined a company can provide insights into whether there are internal issues, such as a high turnover rate, which could indicate a toxic culture, mismanagement, or fraud.

1.2 Company Connections & Collaborations

When examining company networks, it's essential to consider the connections an individual has within the company, as well as between different organizations. These connections often represent:

- **Business Relationships**: Many employees will be connected to colleagues within their company, but also to individuals in partner organizations, vendors, or clients.
- **Industry Collaborations**: Investigating external business relationships can reveal crucial data on where the company does business, what alliances or competitors it may be involved with, and who the company's primary contacts are in the industry.
- **Shared Projects**: Connections between employees across departments or companies could also hint at ongoing collaborations, joint ventures, or business opportunities that may not be publicly disclosed.

By diving deeper into these connections, investigators can uncover hidden business activities, identify key influencers within the company, and track professional ties that could be crucial for understanding organizational dynamics.

2. Investigating Employee Connections

2.1 Analyzing Employee Networks

One of the core features of LinkedIn is the ability to view mutual connections between two or more people. This feature is particularly valuable for investigating employee networks because it allows investigators to:

- **Map professional relationships**: Determine how employees are connected to one another and whether there are patterns of friendships, mentorships, or professional alliances that might indicate shared goals, potential collusion, or group behavior.
- **Identify influential figures**: Employees with a wide range of connections or mutual connections to others in the company may hold considerable influence or be involved in key decision-making processes.
- **Evaluate internal communications**: By analyzing shared connections and groups, it's possible to understand the flow of information within an organization. For instance, employees in the same department may be linked by common interests or specific projects.

2.2 Investigating Job Titles & Reporting Structures

LinkedIn allows users to list their job titles and often their job responsibilities. Investigators can use this information to understand an employee's role within the company and their position in the organizational hierarchy. This information can be particularly useful for identifying:

- **Key decision-makers**: Investigators can use LinkedIn to find top-level executives, such as CEOs, CFOs, or department heads, and track their connections to key employees. This helps in understanding decision-making power.
- **Chain of command**: By tracking connections, you can trace reporting relationships within the company. For example, if an employee lists a direct report or superior, it can shed light on organizational structure and help identify organizational gaps or problems.
- **Possible conflicts of interest**: Connections across different departments or even between companies can indicate potential conflicts of interest. For instance, an employee in the finance department having close connections with an employee in procurement might suggest potential issues related to bribery, fraud, or favoritism.

2.3 Investigating Groups and Shared Interests

LinkedIn Groups provide another method for investigating professional relationships. Employees within the same group often share common interests, values, or objectives, and this can be particularly useful in a number of ways:

- **Corporate affiliations**: If a company or its employees are part of an industry-specific group, it could indicate a close-knit industry presence or collaboration across companies. Investigators can use this information to assess potential collaborations or business deals that may not be widely advertised.
- **Potential insider threats**: Sometimes employees join groups related to sensitive topics, such as trade secrets, intellectual property, or industry regulations. Investigating these memberships could provide insight into whether employees are sharing confidential or proprietary information.

By examining group memberships and activities, investigators can also identify collective knowledge, resources, or informal networks that could influence decision-making or reveal significant actions within the company.

3. Identifying Red Flags in Employee Connections

3.1 Inconsistent Job Titles or Company Affiliations

When reviewing LinkedIn profiles, look for inconsistencies in job titles or company names. Employees who have no history with the companies they claim to be associated with, or who frequently change job titles without clear explanations, may be attempting to inflate their qualifications or professional standing. Inconsistent job titles can signal potential falsification of professional history.

3.2 Overlapping Employment at Competitor Companies

Another red flag that can be identified through employee connections is the existence of individuals who have worked at direct competitors within similar time frames. This could raise concerns about confidential information leakage, non-compete violations, or conflicts of interest. In competitive industries, cross-pollination of employees between rival companies may be indicative of insider trading or unethical behavior.

3.3 Sudden Employee Departures or Low Turnover

LinkedIn profiles often reveal whether employees have remained in a company for a long period or have frequently moved on. Frequent turnover can be a sign of internal issues such as poor leadership, management problems, or toxic work culture. A mass exodus of employees can signal unaddressed problems within the company that may require further investigation.

3.4 Unusual or Inflated Professional Networks

While LinkedIn is a platform designed to build and display professional networks, unusually large or superficial connections can be a red flag. An individual who connects with a disproportionate number of professionals in irrelevant fields may be attempting to exaggerate their expertise or create a misleading professional image.

4. Ethical and Legal Considerations in Investigating Employee Connections

When using LinkedIn for investigations, it's important to remain aware of ethical boundaries and legal obligations:

- **Privacy & Consent**: Only publicly available information should be used in investigations. Accessing private or restricted data without consent may violate privacy laws and ethical guidelines.
- **Confidentiality**: Be cautious not to reveal sensitive company information or make assumptions based on partial data.
- **Fairness**: Always approach investigations with a neutral stance. Jumping to conclusions without verifying data can lead to damaging errors, legal liabilities, or reputational harm.

Investigating company networks and employee connections on LinkedIn offers invaluable insight into organizational structures, business relationships, and employee dynamics. By carefully analyzing job titles, connections, group memberships, and endorsements, OSINT analysts and corporate investigators can uncover critical information about professional relationships and potential risks within a company. This process helps to identify hidden affiliations, ensure the legitimacy of business transactions, and assess the integrity of individuals and organizations, all while being mindful of privacy, ethics, and legal frameworks.

5.4 Identifying Fake LinkedIn Profiles & Recruitment Scams

With over 700 million active users worldwide, LinkedIn has become the premier social media platform for professionals. It serves as an essential tool for networking, career development, and recruitment. However, like any online platform, LinkedIn is also prone to misuse, with users creating fake profiles or engaging in recruitment scams. These fraudulent activities can result in serious financial, reputational, and security risks for individuals and organizations alike.

For OSINT (Open Source Intelligence) analysts, HR professionals, and recruiters, identifying fake LinkedIn profiles and spotting recruitment scams is a critical skill to ensure trustworthiness during background checks, job hiring, and professional networking. This section will guide you through the process of identifying fake LinkedIn profiles and uncovering recruitment scams, focusing on techniques for spotting red flags, performing verifications, and understanding the tactics used by scammers.

1. Identifying Fake LinkedIn Profiles

1.1 Profile Picture Inconsistencies

One of the most common signs of a fake LinkedIn profile is an inconsistent or overly polished profile picture. Scammers often use stock photos, images of celebrities, or professional-looking photos that seem too perfect. Here's how to identify fake profile pictures:

- **Reverse Image Search**: Use tools like Google Reverse Image Search or TinEye to check if the profile picture appears elsewhere on the internet. If the photo appears on unrelated websites or is associated with other identities, it may be a fake.
- **Overly Stock-Photo-Like Images**: Check if the image looks overly professional, staged, or generic. LinkedIn profiles of real professionals tend to have more authentic-looking photos, including casual or candid shots, compared to the highly stylized images used by scammers.
- **No Profile Picture**: While not always a sign of a fake profile, profiles without a picture or with a generic silhouette can indicate that the user is hiding their true identity.

1.2 Incomplete or Generic Profile Information

Another major indicator of a fake profile is incomplete or overly vague information. Scammers typically do not bother filling out every section of their LinkedIn profile or might provide generic, non-specific details. Here's what to look for:

- **Missing Job Descriptions**: Fake profiles often have vague or missing job descriptions in the Experience section. Scammers might list high-profile companies without giving any detail about what they did at those companies or have very brief, generic job titles like "Consultant" or "Manager" with no clear responsibilities.
- **Unusual Job Titles**: Scammers often claim to have high-level positions without corresponding experience or qualifications. For example, claiming to be a C-level executive with only a few years of experience or no prior history in the industry can raise red flags.
- **Lack of Specific Dates**: Genuine professionals often have precise dates for their employment history, whereas fake profiles may either omit dates or give broad time ranges that seem inconsistent or intentionally ambiguous.

1.3 Suspicious LinkedIn Connections

A major indicator of a fake profile is an unusual connection pattern:

- **Low or Generic Connections**: If the person has few or no connections, or if their connections seem to be mostly random, generic profiles, it's worth investigating further. A credible professional typically builds up their network gradually, and a fake profile may have randomly added people to boost credibility.
- **Unrelated Connections**: Check the connections the profile has. A professional with hundreds of connections but none that seem related to their field or industry might be using a fake profile to build legitimacy in unrelated networks.
- **Unusual Mutual Connections**: If you share mutual connections with the person, verify those mutual connections and determine if they are reputable. A fake profile might be linked to individuals with little credibility, which should raise concerns about the authenticity of the profile.

1.4 Overlapping or Inconsistent Job History

Fake profiles may often have inconsistent or overlapping job experiences that don't make sense. For instance:

- **Multiple Employers Simultaneously**: A person who claims to have worked at two different companies at the same time for several years may be fabricating their work history. Check the tenure dates to ensure they align logically.
- **Unrealistic Career Progression**: If a profile claims the individual went from a junior role to a senior management position in a very short period without significant experience or training, this may be a sign of false claims.

To investigate the validity of the job history:

Cross-Reference Companies: Use OSINT tools or search engines to check whether the companies listed on the profile are legitimate and if they match the person's claimed job title and responsibilities.

2. Identifying Recruitment Scams

2.1 Fake Job Offers & Phishing Schemes

Scammers often use fake LinkedIn profiles to post job offers that are too good to be true. These offers often come with a sense of urgency or demand immediate action. Here are the key red flags of recruitment scams:

- **Too Good to Be True**: If a job offer promises an unusually high salary with minimal qualifications or asks for immediate action with little interview process, it's likely a scam.
- **Request for Personal Information**: Scammers may ask for personal or financial information early in the hiring process, such as bank account details, credit card information, or Social Security numbers.
- **Fake Job Descriptions**: Scammers often post job descriptions that are either too generic or seem out of place in the industry. The roles might claim to be high-paying but without concrete responsibilities or realistic expectations.
- **Fake LinkedIn Messages**: Scammers often send messages from profiles claiming to be recruiters or HR representatives offering jobs. These messages can contain phishing links to fake job portals that ask for personal details or payment for background checks.

2.2 Pressure Tactics or Urgency

Scammers try to create a sense of urgency to pressure the target into acting quickly, often through direct messages or job offers. Common tactics include:

- **Short Application Deadlines**: "You must reply within 24 hours to secure this position."
- **Immediate Start Dates**: Scammers might tell candidates that they have already been hired and must start immediately, typically asking for money for training materials, background checks, or other non-existent fees.

2.3 Unverified Job Offers & Missing Contact Information

Legitimate recruiters typically provide clear contact details, including phone numbers and company websites. Fake job offers may lack detailed contact information or offer limited communication avenues:

- **Unverified Job Postings**: Check whether the job offer comes from a verified company or recruiter. If the company listed is new or unverified, research the company's website or search for employee reviews.
- **No Personal Interaction**: Scammers may bypass traditional job application steps, such as interviews or formal communication, and instead directly offer the job.

3. Steps to Verify LinkedIn Profiles & Job Offers

3.1 Cross-Reference Information

- **Reverse Search Profile Pictures**: Use tools like Google Reverse Image Search to check if the profile picture is used elsewhere on the web.
- **Verify Professional Background**: Cross-check the individual's job history, education, and skills through other professional websites, company directories, or by reaching out to previous employers or colleagues.
- **Search for the Company**: Research the company through other channels like its official website, news articles, or trusted job boards to verify if the recruitment process and job listings are legitimate.

3.2 Look for Red Flags in Communication

- **Review Messages** Carefully: Be cautious of messages with poor grammar, generic phrases like "We are impressed with your background," or no clear interview process.
- **Use External Sources**: If someone claims to be a recruiter or an HR professional, search for their name outside LinkedIn. Confirm whether they appear to work at the company they claim to represent.

3.3 Trust Your Instincts

If something feels off about a LinkedIn profile or job offer, trust your instincts. Scammers rely on people's curiosity or hopefulness for a career opportunity. If an offer seems too good to be true or the profile seems too generic or incomplete, take the extra time to verify.

4. Ethical Considerations & Privacy in Investigations

While investigating fake profiles and scams is critical, it is equally important to handle the process ethically and legally:

- **Avoid Overstepping Boundaries**: Do not attempt to access private data or profiles without the proper consent or permissions.
- **Follow Legal Guidelines**: Ensure that any investigation you conduct adheres to privacy laws and data protection regulations, including GDPR, when applicable.
- **Professional Integrity:** When dealing with potential recruitment scams, approach the situation with professionalism, avoiding public shaming or unfounded accusations.

The presence of fake LinkedIn profiles and recruitment scams is a significant risk for both individuals and organizations. By understanding the common signs of fraudulent activity and employing systematic OSINT techniques, investigators can effectively identify fake profiles and uncover scams before they cause harm. Whether investigating suspicious profiles, verifying professional histories, or preventing recruitment fraud, attention to detail and cautious scrutiny are key to navigating the professional networking landscape securely.

5.5 Using LinkedIn Data for Competitive Intelligence

In today's highly competitive business landscape, the ability to gather and analyze competitive intelligence is crucial for organizations seeking to stay ahead of their rivals. LinkedIn, with its vast repository of professional data, serves as an invaluable resource for uncovering insights about competitors, market trends, talent acquisition, and industry movements. By leveraging LinkedIn's data, companies can make informed decisions about business strategy, market positioning, and even product development.

This section explores how OSINT analysts, business leaders, and competitive intelligence professionals can utilize LinkedIn data to enhance their competitive intelligence efforts. We will discuss the various ways LinkedIn can be used to track competitors' movements, monitor industry trends, assess the talent landscape, and identify opportunities for strategic advantage.

1. Tracking Competitors' Workforce & Organizational Structure

1.1 Analyzing Employee Trends

One of the most powerful ways LinkedIn can aid in competitive intelligence is by providing insight into the workforce composition of competitors. By examining the profiles of individuals working for competitor companies, analysts can uncover key information such as:

- **Hiring Trends**: By tracking how many employees join or leave the company, you can identify growth patterns and assess the health of the business. A sudden increase in hires may indicate business expansion, while high turnover might signal internal challenges.
- **Role Development**: Monitoring the types of roles being filled and the job descriptions being posted can provide clues about the company's strategic focus. For example, a competitor might be ramping up their R&D department, indicating

a focus on innovation, or they might be investing in sales teams, suggesting a push toward market expansion.

- **Skills and Expertise**: By analyzing employees' skills listed on their profiles, you can gain insight into the core competencies the competitor is prioritizing. If many employees have skills in data science, machine learning, or blockchain, it indicates that these technologies are central to the competitor's business strategy.

Using LinkedIn's advanced search filters, analysts can track specific roles and departments to get a snapshot of a competitor's organizational focus, workforce capacity, and business priorities.

1.2 Assessing Leadership Changes

Changes in the leadership of a competitor can have significant implications for their strategic direction and overall competitiveness. LinkedIn is an excellent tool for tracking executive-level changes within organizations:

- **C-Suite Transitions**: LinkedIn allows users to track when key executives, such as CEOs, CFOs, or VPs, join or leave a company. These leadership transitions may signal a change in strategy, a shift in market focus, or even internal challenges like management restructuring.
- **Board Members & Advisors**: Observing shifts in a competitor's board of directors or the addition of external advisors can indicate changes in the company's governance or strategic direction. New board members often come with a fresh set of industry insights and connections, potentially changing the trajectory of the business.

By using LinkedIn's alerts and network features, competitive intelligence professionals can stay informed on leadership updates and adjust their own strategies accordingly.

2. Monitoring Competitors' Marketing & Sales Efforts

2.1 Analyzing Marketing Campaigns & Content Strategy

LinkedIn provides a wealth of content posted by both employees and companies. By monitoring this content, competitive intelligence professionals can glean valuable insights into a competitor's marketing and messaging strategies. Here are a few ways to track competitors' marketing efforts:

- **Company Pages & Updates**: Many companies use LinkedIn to share press releases, product announcements, or marketing initiatives. By regularly reviewing the updates from competitor company pages, you can stay up-to-date on their latest campaigns, product launches, and market messaging.
- **Employee Shares**: LinkedIn is also a platform where employees share their personal insights, achievements, and even opinions. By analyzing what your competitors' employees are posting, you can gain insights into the company's internal culture and the values they emphasize. Employees often share promotional material, blog posts, or case studies, providing a window into the company's marketing strategies and key messaging.

Moreover, if employees are sharing case studies, client testimonials, or industry-specific articles, it signals the company's focus areas and potential market segments they are targeting.

2.2 Tracking Sales Professionals & Sales Networks

Sales teams are often the front lines of any business, driving revenue and engaging with customers. By analyzing the LinkedIn profiles of sales professionals within competitor companies, you can gather intelligence on:

- **Sales Roles & Structures**: Reviewing the job titles, functions, and teams within a competitor's sales department can help you understand their sales structure. For example, a shift toward hiring enterprise sales managers might indicate that the competitor is focusing on large business clients, while a focus on SMB account executives may point toward small business growth strategies.
- **Sales Connections**: Sales professionals often list key accounts or client connections on their LinkedIn profiles. By examining these, you can uncover potential client relationships and industry contacts that your competitor is leveraging. If you spot shared clients, it could signal a cross-selling opportunity or a partnership that your company should be aware of.

Using LinkedIn to track sales professionals can also provide valuable insights into go-to-market strategies and pricing models, as they may highlight sales goals or customer pain points.

3. Analyzing Market Trends & Industry Insights

3.1 Tracking Industry Influencers & Thought Leaders

LinkedIn is home to a wide range of industry influencers, analysts, and thought leaders who frequently share insights, reports, and forecasts. By following these key figures within your industry or your competitors' markets, you can gain a competitive edge in understanding emerging trends. To do this:

- **Follow Influencers**: Many professionals and companies use LinkedIn to share insights on the future of industries, market changes, and evolving technologies. Keeping track of industry thought leaders gives you access to up-to-date opinions and perspectives.
- **Monitor Industry-Specific Groups**: LinkedIn groups provide a forum for professionals to discuss challenges and share best practices. By actively participating in or monitoring these groups, you can identify new trends, technologies, and regulatory changes that competitors are focusing on.
- **Content Shared by Competitors**: Competitors may post market research, white papers, or case studies that reveal the latest trends they are pursuing. Tracking these posts helps you stay informed about the market direction and any new solutions competitors are working on.

3.2 Competitor Analysis through LinkedIn Ads

LinkedIn's advertising platform is another rich source of competitive intelligence. By observing competitors' sponsored content and advertisements, you can uncover:

- **Target Market Segments**: LinkedIn allows advertisers to specifically target different audience segments, such as location, job title, or company size. By analyzing the ads your competitors are running, you can learn about the customer segments they are focusing on and potentially identify untapped markets.
- **Content & Messaging Strategies**: The language and visuals used in LinkedIn ads can help reveal the competitor's value propositions, pain points they are addressing, and the tone they use to connect with potential customers. This can give you insight into how they are positioning themselves in the market.

4. Identifying Talent & Key Hires

4.1 Assessing Talent Pool for New Opportunities

One of LinkedIn's most powerful uses in competitive intelligence is its ability to provide access to a competitor's talent pool. By monitoring competitors' employee lists, you can assess the skills and expertise they are hiring for, which could indicate where they are focusing their growth efforts. For example:

- **Emerging Skill Sets**: If a competitor starts hiring more professionals with skills in areas like AI, blockchain, or cloud computing, it could suggest they are shifting focus to those technologies.
- **Talent Gaps**: By examining job postings and employee shifts, you can spot talent gaps within competitor organizations that may represent weaknesses or opportunities for your own company to capitalize on.

4.2 Monitoring Recruitment Campaigns & Job Listings

If a competitor is posting a large number of job listings or recruiting for high-demand roles, it could signal their intention to rapidly expand or develop new product lines. This can give you valuable insights into their future plans, allowing you to anticipate shifts in the market and adjust your competitive strategy accordingly.

5. Ethical Considerations in Competitive Intelligence

When gathering competitive intelligence from LinkedIn, it is important to maintain ethical and legal standards:

- **Respect Privacy**: Do not access private information without permission, and avoid spamming or harassing employees for information.
- **Legitimate Research**: Competitive intelligence should be gathered through publicly available data and should never involve illegal or unethical tactics such as hacking or misrepresentation.

LinkedIn is a powerful tool for gaining competitive intelligence, providing deep insights into competitor organizations, employee movements, industry trends, and market strategies. By strategically analyzing LinkedIn data, companies can make more informed decisions regarding market positioning, product development, talent acquisition, and overall business strategy. However, it's essential to approach competitive intelligence with ethical considerations in mind to ensure that the data is gathered responsibly and in compliance with legal standards.

5.6 Case Study: Identifying Corporate Espionage Using LinkedIn

Corporate espionage, also known as industrial espionage, involves the covert gathering of sensitive corporate information by competitors or individuals to gain a business advantage. In recent years, LinkedIn has become a significant platform for business professionals to connect, share knowledge, and build networks. However, these same networks can be exploited by individuals looking to infiltrate and gather confidential business intelligence.

This case study will explore how LinkedIn OSINT (Open Source Intelligence) techniques were employed to identify a corporate espionage attempt within a technology company. By monitoring employee behaviors, connections, and activities on LinkedIn, investigators were able to uncover a series of covert actions that led to the discovery of a corporate espionage operation.

The Incident: A Technology Company Targeted for Intellectual Property Theft

1.1 Background

The company in question, Tech Innovators Inc., a leading player in the software and cybersecurity industry, had been developing a new proprietary encryption algorithm. This technology had the potential to significantly disrupt the market, and as a result, it became a highly valuable asset for competitors.

Unbeknownst to the company's executives, one of their engineers, John Doe, had been approached by a rival company, CyberTech Solutions, and was allegedly involved in leaking sensitive information about the encryption algorithm.

The suspicious activity came to light when the company's internal monitoring systems flagged irregularities in John's work emails and file access patterns. Despite a thorough internal investigation, no clear evidence of data breaches or unauthorized file transfers could be found. However, management suspected that the leak might have been external, and decided to conduct a social media investigation to track down any potential espionage activity.

Step 1: Identifying Suspicious LinkedIn Activity

2.1 Monitoring Employee Profiles

The first step in the investigation involved scrutinizing John Doe's LinkedIn profile. Analysts used LinkedIn's public features to identify potentially suspicious behaviors. Upon reviewing John's recent activities, the following red flags were observed:

- **Profile Updates**: John had recently updated his LinkedIn profile to reflect new skills and a broader professional network, which seemed inconsistent with his stated role within the company.
- **Connections with Competitors**: A deeper examination revealed that John had made several new connections with key employees at CyberTech Solutions, a direct competitor. These connections were made shortly after Tech Innovators had announced a breakthrough in their encryption technology. This raised concerns, as it was unusual for someone in John's position to be networking so heavily with employees from a direct competitor.
- **Job Search Activity**: John's job preferences on LinkedIn had been activated, signaling that he was open to new opportunities. This was not a behavior typically seen in a loyal employee, especially one working on cutting-edge technology.

2.2 Analyzing LinkedIn Posts and Content Sharing

Further investigation revealed that John had shared several articles and publications related to cybersecurity and encryption on his LinkedIn feed. What stood out was the timing of these posts—each shared post aligned closely with internal milestones at Tech Innovators, such as the launch of a new project or the completion of an encryption breakthrough.

Though the content shared was publicly available, the specific timing and the focus of the posts raised suspicion. It seemed as though John was trying to subtly hint at proprietary information that was still under development at Tech Innovators.

Step 2: Using LinkedIn Network Mapping to Identify Potential Leaks

3.1 Investigating Connections and Patterns

Once it was clear that John was engaged in unusual activity on LinkedIn, investigators used LinkedIn's network mapping tools to analyze the individuals he was connected to. They identified several key employees at CyberTech Solutions who had engaged with John's posts and interacted with him directly.

Using OSINT tools, analysts traced these connections and found that:

- **Direct Messaging**: John had engaged in private LinkedIn messaging with several employees from CyberTech Solutions over a period of weeks. While LinkedIn messages are private, the frequency and content of these messages—especially after John's updates about internal developments—raised concerns about a potential information exchange.

- **Third-Party Intermediaries**: Additionally, John was found to have connected with a headhunter who specialized in placing executives within the tech industry. The headhunter's connections also included key decision-makers at CyberTech Solutions, indicating a possible channel for facilitating a job offer or a covert information exchange.

Step 3: Identifying the Leak and the Espionage Operation

4.1 Leaked Information Traced Back to CyberTech Solutions

The turning point in the investigation came when analysts identified a pattern in John's LinkedIn connections. It appeared that he had been leaking small but important pieces of information about the company's encryption project to his contacts at CyberTech Solutions. One of the most significant pieces of evidence was a job offer made by CyberTech Solutions to John, which was later found to coincide with a critical milestone in the development of the encryption algorithm at Tech Innovators.

Through further email and phone record analysis, investigators found that shortly before the job offer, John had shared a detailed presentation of Tech Innovators' encryption technology in a private LinkedIn message to a key contact at CyberTech Solutions. This was the smoking gun—Tech Innovators' intellectual property had been shared with their competitor via LinkedIn, leading to the realization that corporate espionage was underway.

Step 4: Legal & Ethical Considerations

5.1 Handling Evidence

Once the evidence was collected, the company worked with legal counsel to ensure that the data obtained from LinkedIn was handled appropriately. Since much of the data was publicly available, it was admissible in the investigation, but the company took care not to overstep legal boundaries by accessing private messages without proper consent.

They also ensured that any actions taken were in accordance with both corporate policy and legal regulations. While LinkedIn profiles are public, private interactions, such as direct messages, should only be reviewed in accordance with the law and with the consent of the parties involved. Tech Innovators proceeded cautiously to avoid potential defamation or privacy breaches during the investigation.

Conclusion: Lessons Learned from the Case Study

This case study illustrates the powerful role LinkedIn OSINT can play in uncovering corporate espionage. In this instance, LinkedIn's network mapping, public profile analysis, and content monitoring provided critical insight into the activities of an employee who had been leaking sensitive information to a competitor.

Key takeaways from this investigation include:

- **Monitor Employee Activity**: Regularly assess the LinkedIn activities of key employees, particularly those working on sensitive or proprietary projects.
- **Network Mapping**: Utilize LinkedIn's vast professional network to track connections between employees and competitors. Unusual networking activity can often indicate information leakage.
- **Public and Private Interactions**: Analyze both public posts and private communications when suspicious activity is detected. Patterns of content sharing and messaging can help identify potential espionage.
- **Ethical Boundaries**: Always ensure that the OSINT methods employed remain within legal and ethical boundaries to protect both the company and its employees.

By leveraging LinkedIn OSINT effectively, businesses can better protect their sensitive information and mitigate the risks of corporate espionage, ultimately safeguarding their intellectual property and competitive edge in the market.

6. Reddit & Forums: Analyzing Discussions & Users

Reddit and online forums serve as digital gathering spaces where users discuss niche topics, share insights, and sometimes leak valuable intelligence. For OSINT analysts, these platforms offer a window into community sentiment, emerging trends, and hidden networks. This chapter explores methods for tracking user activity, analyzing discussion patterns, and extracting data from threads, subreddits, and specialized forums. From uncovering anonymous identities to mapping influence within online communities, mastering Reddit and forum OSINT provides a crucial edge in digital investigations.

6.1 Understanding the Role of Reddit & Niche Forums in OSINT

As digital landscapes evolve, the sources and methods of gathering Open Source Intelligence (OSINT) continue to expand. Among the many platforms offering a wealth of publicly available information, Reddit and niche forums have emerged as invaluable tools for OSINT investigators. These platforms are unique in their ability to provide rich, user-generated content across a wide range of topics, from technology and finance to politics, crime, and social issues.

While mainstream social media platforms like Facebook and Twitter often focus on broad user engagement, Reddit and niche forums are distinct because they foster deep, specialized conversations in anonymized environments. These platforms enable users to discuss sensitive subjects and share information that might not be readily available elsewhere. For OSINT analysts, this makes them a goldmine for gathering insights, trends, and leads related to specific topics, individuals, or events.

This section explores the role of Reddit and niche forums in OSINT investigations, highlighting their advantages, challenges, and practical use cases for gathering intelligence.

1. The Structure of Reddit & Niche Forums

1.1 The Nature of Reddit: Communities and Subreddits

Reddit is often described as the "front page of the internet," with millions of active users contributing to a vast array of communities or subreddits. Each subreddit is dedicated to a specific topic, allowing for highly specialized discussions in various fields. Subreddits can range from highly niche topics, such as cryptocurrency, gaming, or true crime, to broad, mainstream discussions about world events or pop culture.

The structure of Reddit is organized into:

- **Subreddits**: These are the heart of Reddit, where specific topics are discussed. Each subreddit has a unique focus, and posts are categorized by users or moderators into relevant discussion threads.
- **Posts and Comments**: Content on Reddit is driven by user-generated posts, which can include text, images, and links. Other users can then comment on these posts, often engaging in lengthy discussions.
- **Upvoting/Downvoting System**: Reddit uses a voting system to promote or demote content based on community interest. Popular posts with high engagement are moved to the top, making them more visible to other users.
- **Anonymity**: Users on Reddit are typically anonymous, using pseudonyms or usernames rather than real names. This anonymity can encourage more open and candid discussions but also presents challenges in verifying the credibility of the information shared.

1.2 Niche Forums: Specialized Communities for Targeted Research

While Reddit serves as a broad platform with diverse communities, niche forums refer to smaller, specialized platforms where people with a shared interest discuss specific topics in depth. These forums exist for virtually every interest area, from cybersecurity to conspiracy theories, hobbyist communities, and professional networks.

Niche forums have some notable distinctions from Reddit:

- **Focused Discussions**: Niche forums are usually centered around specific industries, hobbies, or professional interests. This makes them highly valuable for targeting specific subject matter.
- **Long-Form Conversations**: Discussions on niche forums tend to be longer and more detailed, with members contributing in-depth posts over time.
- **Community Engagement**: The smaller and more focused nature of niche forums means that users tend to form tight-knit communities, which can result in more trust-based exchanges of information. This can be both an asset and a liability for

OSINT investigations, as the information shared might be deeply insightful but could also be difficult to corroborate.

2. Why Reddit and Niche Forums are Crucial in OSINT

2.1 Crowdsourced Intelligence

One of the main reasons Reddit and niche forums are invaluable in OSINT is their ability to function as crowdsourced platforms for information. Because these communities are open to anyone with an internet connection, users from diverse backgrounds, professions, and expertise contribute insights that may be difficult to find through more traditional sources.

For instance, a subreddit focused on cybersecurity may feature discussions about new hacking techniques or vulnerabilities, while a niche forum for investigative journalists may host tips or whistleblower information related to corporate corruption. This wealth of crowd-sourced information can be analyzed to uncover new leads, verify claims, and piece together intelligence on a wide variety of subjects.

2.2 Real-Time & Live Reporting

Reddit, particularly, is known for real-time updates. During breaking news events or crises, users flock to relevant subreddits to discuss developments as they happen. For OSINT analysts, this real-time flow of information can be a treasure trove for:

- Tracking events as they unfold (e.g., political unrest, natural disasters, or active investigations)
- Identifying eyewitness accounts or leaked information about incidents
- Crowdsourcing details to corroborate claims or provide new evidence on ongoing investigations

For example, during the early stages of major events like the Arab Spring or the COVID-19 pandemic, Reddit's subreddits became essential for monitoring first-hand accounts, government responses, and real-time citizen reporting.

2.3 The Hidden Depths of Data: Insights from Anonymous Sources

Due to the anonymity of users, Reddit and niche forums often become spaces where people feel comfortable discussing sensitive topics that they might not address in public, traditional media outlets, or social media. Some examples include:

- **Whistleblower accounts**: Employees from organizations sharing confidential information.
- **Hacktivist activities**: Individuals involved in online activism or cybercrime may reveal tactics, targets, or ideologies in discussions.
- **Underground markets**: Hidden transactions, such as those related to illicit trade, can often be uncovered in forums dedicated to these subcultures.

This wealth of open-source data is rich in detail but requires critical analysis. Information from anonymous sources can be unreliable, making the need for verification paramount.

3. Practical Applications of Reddit and Niche Forums in OSINT Investigations

3.1 Investigating Criminal Activities

Reddit and niche forums are frequently used by hackers, cybercriminals, and even terrorist groups to discuss illicit activities, share tools, or recruit new members. OSINT analysts monitoring these platforms can:

- Track discussions about illegal activities such as cyberattacks, fraud, and drug trafficking.
- Uncover planned attacks or identify potential targets for espionage or terrorism.
- Identify key players within illicit organizations through username tracking and activity analysis.

For example, a forum focused on dark web activities might feature discussions about selling stolen data, which could lead OSINT analysts to investigate the full scope of an illicit operation.

3.2 Tracking Emerging Trends & Public Sentiment

Forums are a rich source for monitoring public sentiment and identifying emerging trends. By following discussions within specialized communities, OSINT professionals can:

- Spot emerging technologies or business strategies, such as discussions on cryptocurrencies, blockchain innovations, or AI developments.
- Track societal trends, such as shifts in public opinion related to politics, health, or social movements, by analyzing how certain issues are discussed or debated in real-time.

- Analyze conspiracy theories or rumors that could influence public perceptions or behavior.

By aggregating and analyzing these discussions, businesses, governments, and law enforcement agencies can gain insights into public sentiment and predict how certain events may unfold.

3.3 Investigating Corporate Espionage

Just as corporate employees sometimes use LinkedIn to network with competitors, they may also turn to niche forums to discuss or share confidential business information. Whether it's an employee leaking company secrets or a competitor gathering intelligence, monitoring specialized forums can help identify:

- Employees discussing proprietary projects or internal issues.
- Competitors actively seeking insider information on certain technologies or business practices.
- Covert job offers made by competitors trying to entice employees to switch and take company knowledge with them.

For example, an employee from a tech company might engage in a cybersecurity forum, subtly mentioning a new software development project, which could then be traced back to an attempt at corporate espionage.

4. Challenges of Using Reddit and Niche Forums in OSINT

4.1 Anonymity and Reliability

While anonymity allows for more candid discussions, it also creates challenges for authenticating the information. OSINT analysts must be cautious of misinformation, disinformation, and deliberate efforts to mislead. This can include fake accounts, sock puppets, or astroturfing campaigns designed to manipulate public opinion.

4.2 Legal and Ethical Considerations

Collecting data from public forums must be done within the bounds of the law. While information posted on Reddit and other forums is generally publicly accessible, analysts must be cautious not to infringe on privacy or violate platform rules, especially when dealing with sensitive topics or personal data.

Reddit and niche forums offer a wealth of information that can be harnessed for OSINT investigations. By analyzing discussions, monitoring real-time events, and identifying key trends, analysts can uncover valuable intelligence on a wide range of topics. However, the very nature of these platforms—characterized by anonymity and often informal communication—presents unique challenges that require careful scrutiny, verification, and ethical considerations. As such, Reddit and niche forums have become indispensable tools in the OSINT toolbox, offering new avenues for research, analysis, and decision-making in the digital age.

6.2 Searching Reddit for User Discussions & Trends

Reddit, often referred to as "the front page of the internet," is a vast and dynamic platform that hosts millions of discussions across a wide array of topics. These discussions provide valuable insights into emerging trends, public opinions, and even covert actions, making Reddit an essential tool for Open Source Intelligence (OSINT) analysts. The decentralized structure of Reddit, with its many niche subreddits and anonymity, enables the discovery of critical information that may not be readily available through traditional media or other social platforms.

In this section, we will explore effective strategies for searching Reddit to uncover user discussions, identify emerging trends, and gather relevant intelligence. From utilizing Reddit's built-in search tools to using external methods for tracking user activity, this chapter will guide you through the key processes and best practices for maximizing your OSINT investigations using Reddit.

1. Reddit's Structure: Subreddits, Posts, and Comments

Before diving into specific search techniques, it's important to understand how Reddit is organized. This will help you leverage its search functionalities effectively and narrow down results based on your investigative needs.

1.1 Subreddits: Communities of Interest

Reddit is made up of individual communities, known as subreddits, each focused on a specific topic, hobby, profession, or interest. These subreddits are typically denoted by the prefix /r/ followed by the subreddit's name (e.g., /r/technology or /r/cryptocurrency). Each subreddit is self-moderated and can have thousands to millions of members contributing posts, comments, and discussions.

Understanding which subreddit aligns with your investigative focus is crucial. For example:

- If you're tracking cybersecurity issues, you might look at /r/cybersecurity.
- For emerging political trends, /r/politics or /r/worldnews could be key.
- If investigating criminal activities or illicit trade, forums like /r/TrueCrime or /r/technology might provide useful insights.

By targeting specific subreddits, you can quickly filter out irrelevant information and focus on communities that align with your research.

1.2 Posts and Comments: The Core of Discussions

Posts are the primary content shared on Reddit. Each post can contain text, links, images, or videos, followed by comments where users interact and discuss the topic further. When performing an OSINT investigation on Reddit, both posts and comments hold value. Posts introduce discussions, while comments provide in-depth feedback, opinions, or clarifications from users, which may reveal valuable information or new leads.

For instance, if you're investigating a particular news event or public sentiment around a political issue, the comment section of relevant posts can reveal the thoughts, opinions, and activities of various users. This can help you gauge the credibility of a claim or uncover different perspectives.

2. Searching Reddit Effectively for User Discussions & Trends

Reddit provides both internal and external tools to search for discussions and trends effectively. Using these methods can help you gather relevant insights while saving time and effort during your investigation.

2.1 Using Reddit's Built-In Search Function

Reddit's built-in search bar allows you to query posts, subreddits, and comments based on specific keywords or phrases. While it's relatively simple to use, understanding how to refine and optimize your searches is key to retrieving relevant and useful results.

Search by Keywords

Enter a keyword or phrase into the search bar. Reddit will return results across all posts, comments, and subreddits that include that term. You can search for general topics, specific individuals, or trending issues.

For example, searching for "data breach" will bring up posts discussing recent cybersecurity breaches, investigations, or advice on protecting against data theft.

Using Search Operators for Advanced Results

Reddit search allows for the use of operators to narrow or expand your search. Some key operators include:

- "quotes": Using quotes around a term (e.g., "data breach") ensures that Reddit searches for that exact phrase, making your results more precise.
- subreddit:: To search within a specific subreddit (e.g., subreddit:cryptocurrency).
- author:: Use this to find posts from a specific user (e.g., author:username).
- title:: To limit your search to post titles only (e.g., title:scam).
- site:: To search for links within Reddit posts that refer to external websites (e.g., site:nytimes.com).
- - (minus): To exclude a specific term from your search (e.g., "data breach" - Amazon).
- Sorting by Time and Relevance

Reddit allows you to filter results by different time frames, such as "Today," "This Week," or "All Time." When investigating current trends or recent discussions, sorting by time ensures that you're viewing the most up-to-date content. If you are looking for broader, long-term patterns, sorting by "relevance" can help you identify the most discussed or upvoted content, which is often indicative of important trends or significant events.

2.2 Tracking Trends with Reddit's "Hot" and "Trending" Posts

One of the unique aspects of Reddit is its voting system. Popular posts that gain a lot of upvotes quickly rise to the top of the subreddit, often landing in the "hot" section. This provides a way for OSINT analysts to track trends, breaking news, or public sentiment as it evolves in real-time.

Following Hot Posts and Trending Discussions

- **Hot Posts**: To spot fast-evolving trends or news events, regularly check the hot posts section in relevant subreddits. These posts receive the most engagement (upvotes, comments), making them a good indicator of what's currently being discussed.

- **Trending Topics**: By observing which topics are consistently rising in popularity, you can predict shifts in public opinion, new areas of concern, or issues gaining traction.

Analyzing Upvotes and Downvotes

By analyzing how users upvote and downvote posts, you can gauge the public reception of certain ideas or claims. Posts that have a high number of upvotes often reflect a consensus within the subreddit, while downvoted posts may indicate disagreement, misinformation, or topics that are controversial.

2.3 Exploring Reddit's API and External Tools for Deep Search

For more advanced Reddit OSINT investigations, external tools and APIs can be used to collect and analyze large volumes of data from Reddit. These tools can automate the process of searching, collecting, and categorizing data, allowing for more efficient and thorough research. Some useful tools include:

- **Pushshift**: A powerful tool for searching and analyzing Reddit data. It offers advanced search features, including querying by post date, upvote count, and comment volume.
- **Reddit API**: Reddit provides an API that can be used to programmatically retrieve posts, comments, and metadata from subreddits. This is particularly helpful for large-scale data gathering or continuous monitoring of specific discussions or keywords.
- **Keyword Monitoring Tools**: External services like Brand24 or Mention allow for real-time tracking of specific keywords across multiple social media platforms, including Reddit.

These tools can be used to track long-term trends, detect keyword spikes, and identify anomalous activity in real-time.

3. Analyzing User Discussions: Techniques for Insight

3.1 Identifying Key Users and Influencers

Reddit's comment sections often feature highly engaged users who consistently contribute valuable information. Identifying these key contributors can help uncover insightful commentary, leads, or expert opinions that may not be available in mainstream media. Analysts can:

- Monitor frequent contributors to relevant subreddits.
- Track Reddit karma (a reputation score based on upvotes) to identify authoritative users.
- Cross-reference usernames across different subreddits and posts to find consistent influencers or sources.

3.2 Sentiment Analysis

Sentiment analysis tools can be used to track the overall mood or emotional tone of discussions within specific subreddits. By analyzing the sentiment behind comments, you can gauge public opinion about particular topics, events, or individuals. For example:

- **Positive Sentiment**: Posts with positive sentiment may indicate favorable public reception or support for an issue.
- **Negative Sentiment**: Posts with negative sentiment may reveal dissatisfaction, protests, or emerging concerns.
- **Neutral Sentiment**: Neutral discussions can highlight factual debates or ongoing discussions without emotional bias.

Reddit is a powerful platform for OSINT professionals looking to explore user discussions and emerging trends. By mastering Reddit's search tools, understanding subreddit structures, and using external APIs or monitoring tools, investigators can uncover valuable insights into a wide range of topics. Whether tracking current events, public sentiment, or even uncovering illicit activities, Reddit provides a vast, constantly updated source of intelligence that can be leveraged for effective OSINT investigations. However, as with any open-source intelligence gathering, careful attention to detail, corroboration, and ethical considerations are essential to ensure accurate and trustworthy findings.

6.3 Investigating Anonymous Users & Tracking Post History

One of the unique features of Reddit is its anonymity. Users often create accounts that allow them to post, comment, and participate in discussions without revealing their real-world identity. While this anonymity fosters free speech and open expression, it also presents challenges for OSINT investigators looking to trace or understand the actions and motivations behind a particular user's behavior. Investigating anonymous users and tracking post history on Reddit can provide critical insights, but it requires a nuanced approach to respect privacy boundaries while still gathering useful intelligence.

In this section, we'll explore methods for tracing anonymous users, uncovering their post history, and investigating potential patterns of behavior. Whether you're trying to track a particular individual across multiple discussions or detect unusual activity, understanding how to follow and analyze users without breaching Reddit's privacy policies is essential for effective Open Source Intelligence (OSINT) gathering.

1. Reddit Anonymity: The Double-Edged Sword

Reddit allows users to operate under pseudonyms (usernames), which may or may not reveal personal information. This level of anonymity offers advantages and challenges for OSINT analysts. On the one hand, it protects privacy; on the other, it can obscure the true identity of individuals participating in activities ranging from general discussion to potentially illegal behavior.

Unlike platforms that require real names (e.g., Facebook or LinkedIn), Reddit's lack of compulsory identity verification can make it difficult to verify a user's real-world identity. However, by studying a user's posting patterns, writing style, and interaction history, it's often possible to link a series of posts to a specific person or track the behavior of a particular group.

2. Investigating Anonymous Users: Methods for Tracing Activity

When investigating anonymous users, it's important to look for indirect clues that may link a user to their real-world identity or reveal patterns in their online activity. The following methods will guide you through key investigative techniques for understanding a user's behavior and identifying connections across posts and subreddits.

2.1 Usernames: The First Clue

Although Reddit usernames are not necessarily linked to real identities, usernames can often provide useful hints about the user's interests, profession, or background. For example:

- A username may include identifiable information, such as a real name or location.
- Sometimes, a user will reference their professional background (e.g., doctor_123 or johnnydeveloper) in their posts or comments.

- Patterns in usernames across multiple accounts or subreddits could suggest a coordinated effort or the involvement of a particular user across different interests.

2.2 Writing Style & Patterns of Behavior

Even in an anonymous setting, users often develop distinct writing styles or recurring behaviors that can be traced across multiple posts. Investigators can analyze:

- **Tone**: Is the user consistently formal, sarcastic, aggressive, or neutral?
- **Grammar and Spelling**: Any distinctive patterns, errors, or regional variations in writing may help identify a user across posts.
- **Content**: Does the user frequently comment on certain topics or use specific keywords or phrases? This may indicate a particular area of interest or expertise, narrowing down potential leads.
- **Engagement Patterns**: How often does the user comment? Are they highly active in certain subreddits, and do they engage at specific times of day?

Analyzing these patterns across a user's history can help investigators track the same individual across different discussions and even correlate behavior with other online activities.

2.3 Cross-Referencing Usernames Across Subreddits

One of the most effective ways to trace the activity of an anonymous user is to follow their cross-posting across multiple subreddits. Reddit allows users to participate in a variety of communities, so looking at where a specific username has posted can give insight into their interests, social networks, and possibly personal information.

For example, if an anonymous user posts in /r/privacy, and then shares a post in /r/cybersecurity or /r/technology, you may find connections to the same individual by analyzing the content or engagement across these communities. This tactic can be especially useful when trying to map out connections between users who may be intentionally hiding their identity or behavior across different online ecosystems.

Investigators can manually trace a user's posting history on Reddit, or for larger-scale tracking, external tools such as the Pushshift API can be used to automate the process and retrieve a user's activity over a specific period of time.

3. Tracking Post History: Techniques and Tools

Tracking a Reddit user's post history is a key part of understanding their activity. By examining the posts they've made, the comments they've left, and the topics they engage with, you can build a profile of their behavior, interests, and potentially their intentions. However, Reddit's privacy policy limits direct access to detailed user data, so it's essential to use the right methods to gather and analyze information while adhering to ethical and legal boundaries.

3.1 Reddit's User Profile: What You Can See

A Reddit user's profile provides a snapshot of their activities. By visiting a user's profile page, you can view:

- **Submitted Posts**: All the posts made by the user across subreddits.
- **Comment History**: Every comment they've made in response to other users' posts.
- **Karma Score**: The number of upvotes (and downvotes) the user has received for their posts and comments, which can indicate their level of credibility within the community.
- **Awards**: If the user has received any Reddit awards for their posts, these can also provide insights into the types of content that resonate with the community.

3.2 Advanced Search Techniques for Tracking User Activity

Reddit's built-in search function has some limitations, but advanced search techniques can make it easier to trace a user's history. Using the "author:" filter in the search bar allows you to find all posts made by a particular user. For example, entering "author:username" into the search bar will return all posts and comments submitted by that user, regardless of subreddit. This is a great way to get a comprehensive view of a user's activity across Reddit.

Other advanced search techniques include:

- **subreddit**:: Search within a specific subreddit for posts made by a particular user (e.g., subreddit:technology author:username).
- **Time filters**: Use Reddit's time filters to narrow the scope of the search. For example, you can search only for posts within the last week or month to get a sense of the user's most recent activity.
- **Keyword filters**: Combine the author filter with relevant keywords to track specific topics the user may be discussing.

3.3 External Tools for Tracing Post History

To streamline the process of tracking and analyzing Reddit user activity, external tools and APIs can be invaluable. Tools such as Pushshift and Reddit's official API offer more comprehensive capabilities for searching user histories and tracking patterns over extended periods.

For example, Pushshift.io provides an easy way to query historical Reddit data, allowing you to access large datasets from specific time periods. With Pushshift, you can gather data on a user's posts, comments, and even interactions with other users across multiple subreddits.

Another tool, Social Search, helps you trace a user's activity across various platforms, including Reddit, providing a deeper layer of insight into how their behavior on Reddit aligns with activity on other social media platforms.

4. Identifying Red Flags in User Activity

While tracking post history, there are several potential red flags that could indicate suspicious or fraudulent behavior. These include:

- **Consistent Posting in Sensitive or Controversial Subreddits**: A user who frequently posts in subreddits with controversial or sensitive content could be someone with a particular agenda, such as spreading disinformation or engaging in covert activity.
- **Sudden Increase in Activity**: A significant spike in activity within a short period could signal a bot-driven campaign, astroturfing, or a coordinated effort to manipulate public opinion.
- **Posting Patterns that Align with Misinformation**: Investigating the type of content posted, the source of external links, and the tone of comments can reveal users involved in spreading fake news or deceptive narratives.

By identifying these red flags early, investigators can prioritize which users or activities warrant closer scrutiny.

Tracking anonymous users and investigating their post history on Reddit is a powerful method for uncovering valuable OSINT. While the platform's anonymity can make it challenging to connect users to real-world identities, analyzing user patterns, writing styles, and cross-referencing posts across multiple subreddits can yield useful insights into their behavior and motivations. By using advanced search techniques, external tools, and keen analytical skills, OSINT professionals can gain a deeper understanding of the individuals and communities operating behind Reddit's pseudonymous environment. However, as always, respecting ethical boundaries and privacy concerns is crucial when conducting any form of OSINT investigation.

6.4 Extracting Intelligence from Forum Threads & Dark Web Markets

The digital landscape is filled with countless online forums, discussion boards, and dark web markets, many of which serve as hubs for unfiltered communication and the exchange of illegal goods, sensitive data, and controversial opinions. As a key element of Social Media OSINT (SOCMINT), extracting intelligence from these forum threads and dark web markets can provide crucial insights for investigations related to cybercrime, terrorism, fraud, and other forms of illicit activity. However, navigating these spaces requires specialized skills, an understanding of the tools available, and a firm adherence to legal and ethical guidelines.

In this section, we will explore the techniques and strategies used to extract intelligence from forum threads and dark web marketplaces. We will also address the challenges and ethical considerations that arise when investigating these often unregulated spaces.

1. Understanding Forum Threads and Dark Web Markets

1.1 What Are Forum Threads?

Forum threads are the backbone of many online communities, where users post questions, share knowledge, and discuss a wide range of topics. Some forums cater to specific groups or interests, including gaming, politics, technology, and privacy. Others may serve more covert or controversial purposes, such as discussions about illegal activities, hacktivism, or unlawful behaviors.

On Reddit and similar platforms, discussions are typically public, though users are often anonymous. However, there are also private forums that require an invitation to access, and even deeper layers of the dark web contain hidden forums where illicit exchanges take place in relative obscurity. Understanding how these forums function and how to access them is a critical component of effective SOCMINT.

1.2 What Are Dark Web Markets?

Dark web markets are often found on the dark web, which exists on parts of the internet that are not indexed by traditional search engines. This layer of the internet, sometimes referred to as the deep web, is accessed through specialized browsers like Tor (The Onion Router). Dark web markets are unregulated digital marketplaces where illegal goods, such as drugs, weapons, counterfeit currency, stolen data, and other illicit items, are bought and sold using cryptocurrencies like Bitcoin and Monero for anonymity.

These markets operate under a veil of privacy and anonymity, making it challenging for law enforcement agencies and investigators to track and identify individuals involved. However, dark web markets often leave behind digital traces that can be analyzed to uncover illicit activities and individuals behind them.

2. Techniques for Extracting Intelligence from Forum Threads

When investigating forum threads, there are various techniques that OSINT investigators can employ to gather valuable information. While these techniques can be employed in a variety of online forums, they are especially crucial in dark web forums where anonymity is a key feature.

2.1 Searching Forum Databases

Most online forums feature search functions that allow users to query posts by specific keywords, topics, or usernames. This function can be incredibly useful when searching for:

- Specific individuals or groups of interest, as investigators can use usernames to search for related posts.
- Keywords related to the investigation (e.g., stolen credit card numbers, cybersecurity threats, malware distribution).
- Discussions related to specific topics, like hacktivism, terrorist activities, or drug trafficking.
- Advanced search techniques include filtering posts by time, reputation score, or activity levels, allowing investigators to prioritize certain threads or identify newly emerging trends.

2.2 Thread Analysis and Context Extraction

Once an investigator has located relevant threads, it's crucial to dive into the content and context of the posts. In forums, users often engage in long discussions, with individual posts evolving over time. By analyzing these threads:

- Investigators can track the evolution of a conversation and see how specific topics unfold.
- Cross-referencing user posts can help identify individuals who contribute consistently to particular threads, revealing patterns of interest or specific behaviors.
- Extracting metadata from posts can give clues about the time, location, and tools used to access the forum.

2.3 Identifying Key Actors and Networks

Many forums, especially those discussing illicit activities, are populated by networks of individuals who share interests or engage in organized criminal behavior. Identifying these key actors and their interrelationships is crucial for building a broader understanding of criminal operations. Investigators should look for:

- **Repeated usernames**: The same usernames across multiple threads may indicate a significant actor or a core member of a network.
- **Cross-forum behavior**: If a user is active across various forums with a similar agenda, it can indicate that they are highly influential or involved in coordinated activities.
- **Patterns of behavior**: Tracking how individuals communicate, collaborate, or engage with specific content can expose a chain of influence and a more robust picture of the criminal ecosystem.

3. Extracting Intelligence from Dark Web Markets

Investigating dark web markets requires a different set of tools and techniques, as these markets are designed to maintain the anonymity of both buyers and sellers. However, there are still valuable intelligence-gathering strategies that can be employed.

3.1 Analyzing Marketplace Listings

Dark web markets are often structured as marketplaces with various product listings, which may include illegal goods such as drugs, weapons, or stolen data. Each listing contains key details, including:

- Product descriptions and pricing.
- Seller information, including usernames, reputation, and feedback ratings.
- Transaction methods, such as the use of specific cryptocurrencies.

By analyzing these listings, investigators can identify suspicious activity or patterns that link a specific seller or buyer to larger criminal enterprises. Investigators can also use transaction histories to identify repeat sellers or individuals involved in multiple illicit activities.

3.2 Investigating Seller and Buyer Profiles

Although dark web marketplaces aim to keep identities anonymous, user profiles often reveal valuable intelligence. These profiles can include:

- **Reputation**: The feedback from other buyers or sellers can help identify trusted or experienced individuals in illicit markets.
- **Transaction history**: Reviewing an individual's transaction history can provide a better understanding of the goods being bought or sold, as well as potential involvement in illegal supply chains.
- **User connections**: Sellers may form networks with other users, either through direct interactions in the marketplace or by recommending other products and services.

By mapping out connections between sellers and buyers, investigators can begin to identify patterns and create a broader understanding of the market dynamics.

3.3 Using Cryptocurrency Trails for Investigative Purposes

Since transactions in dark web markets are conducted using cryptocurrencies, one of the most effective methods for tracking illicit activity is to follow the flow of digital currencies. Although cryptocurrency transactions are pseudonymous, they are traceable through blockchain analysis tools such as Chainalysis and Elliptic. These tools can help track:

- **Funds**: Identify where cryptocurrency funds are being transferred and whether they can be linked to illicit activities.
- **Wallet addresses**: Track specific wallet addresses over time to understand transaction histories and connections between buyers, sellers, and illicit operators.
- **Exchange transactions**: Trace any conversions of cryptocurrency to fiat currency via exchanges, which may reveal the real-world identities of market participants.

4. Ethical and Legal Considerations

Extracting intelligence from forum threads and dark web markets presents unique ethical and legal challenges. Investigators must always be mindful of:

- **Privacy concerns**: Even in public forums, users may have a reasonable expectation of privacy, and any investigative actions should avoid crossing ethical boundaries.
- **Accessing illegal content**: Simply browsing or collecting data from dark web markets may expose investigators to illegal material, which can raise legal and security risks. It's important to avoid engaging in any transaction or activity that could constitute illegal action.
- **Jurisdictional issues**: Investigations on the dark web often involve cross-border data and may raise issues regarding jurisdiction and international law enforcement coordination.

Investigators must always ensure that their actions are legal and in compliance with local and international laws.

Extracting intelligence from forum threads and dark web markets is a critical skill for SOCMINT professionals, providing valuable insights into illicit activity and criminal networks. While these spaces offer rich sources of information, they also pose challenges, such as maintaining anonymity, navigating legal risks, and dealing with encryption. By employing advanced search techniques, analyzing marketplace listings, and using tools to track cryptocurrency transactions, investigators can uncover critical connections, identities, and patterns. However, it's essential to approach these investigations with a strong ethical framework and legal awareness, ensuring that the intelligence gathering process remains both effective and responsible.

6.5 Identifying Coordinated Disinformation Campaigns in Forums

Online forums, particularly those found in public spaces like Reddit or more anonymous environments such as the dark web, have become fertile ground for the spread of disinformation. Whether it's related to political manipulation, social engineering, or the promotion of false narratives, forums often host a significant amount of misleading or harmful content. In the context of Social Media OSINT (SOCMINT), one of the key challenges for investigators is identifying and analyzing coordinated disinformation campaigns that may seek to deceive the public or influence opinions and behaviors in specific ways. Understanding how to identify these campaigns is vital to ensuring that disinformation is detected and countered.

This section will explore how to identify, track, and analyze coordinated disinformation campaigns in forums, providing techniques and methods for investigators to distinguish between genuine discourse and strategically orchestrated influence operations.

1. Understanding Disinformation Campaigns

Disinformation refers to the deliberate creation and distribution of false information with the intent to deceive, mislead, or manipulate the beliefs and behaviors of individuals or groups. A disinformation campaign can occur on a global scale or within a niche community, depending on the goals and target audience.

1.1 Characteristics of Disinformation Campaigns

In the context of online forums, coordinated disinformation campaigns often exhibit certain patterns and behaviors:

- **Fake narratives**: These campaigns are built around fabricated or manipulated stories meant to sway public opinion on issues such as politics, health, or social justice.
- **Multiple accounts**: A key element of disinformation campaigns is the use of sock puppet accounts or bot networks to amplify messages and create a false sense of consensus.
- **Echo chambers**: Coordinated disinformation campaigns often thrive within isolated communities where members are not exposed to alternative viewpoints. This environment allows for narratives to be repeatedly reinforced by multiple users.
- **Mimicry of authentic voices**: Disinformation campaigns often disguise themselves as authentic, grassroots movements, mimicking the voices of concerned individuals or communities.
- **Emotional manipulation**: Campaigns frequently focus on triggering emotional responses such as fear, anger, or empathy to persuade or divide audiences.

Recognizing these patterns early is key to identifying coordinated disinformation efforts.

1.2 How Disinformation Spreads in Forums

In online forums, disinformation is often spread through:

- **Posts**: In forums, the core vehicle for spreading disinformation is through individual posts that make dubious claims or spread misleading narratives. These posts may be shared across multiple threads to maximize exposure.
- **Replies**: Coordinated efforts can involve a large number of fake accounts or bots posting in response to legitimate questions or discussions, driving the conversation in a specific direction.
- **Links**: Disinformation campaigns frequently share external links to articles, videos, or websites that support the false narratives being pushed. These links may lead to fake news websites, deepfakes, or clickbait content designed to further the campaign's agenda.

2. Identifying Coordinated Disinformation in Forum Threads

Detecting coordinated disinformation in forum discussions requires both qualitative and quantitative analysis. There are a number of key indicators to look for when identifying potential disinformation operations in forum threads.

2.1 Analyzing Posting Patterns

One of the most effective ways to spot disinformation in forums is to examine the posting behaviors and activity patterns of participants. Coordinated campaigns often rely on artificially inflated activity to give the appearance of legitimacy. The following signs can indicate coordinated efforts:

- **High-frequency posting**: A large volume of posts within a short period of time from the same user or group of users may indicate coordinated activity.
- **Identical or similar phrasing**: Users involved in a disinformation campaign often repeat the same phrases, claims, or arguments across multiple threads or discussions. This template-style posting can be a telltale sign.
- **Timestamps**: Posts made within short time windows or back-to-back responses can be indicative of an orchestrated effort. If multiple users are consistently posting in a synchronized manner, it could point to a botnet or coordinated manual effort.
- **Sudden surges in activity**: A spike in new posts that all align with a specific narrative may indicate the initiation of a disinformation campaign, especially if the threads in question are related to sensitive or trending topics.

2.2 Identifying Bot-Like Behavior

Bots are often used in coordinated disinformation campaigns to amplify messages and spread false information on forums. While bots can be sophisticated, certain behaviors remain identifiable:

- **Repetitive patterns**: Bots tend to post content that repeats patterns of text or interactions in a way that seems unnatural or mechanical. Look for posts that are almost identical but posted by different accounts.
- **Lack of personalized engagement**: Bots rarely engage in personalized conversations or nuanced discussion. They often post the same message across various forums or threads without responding to specific questions or comments.
- **Multiple accounts from the same source**: Investigators can track IP addresses, user agents, or other metadata to identify when multiple accounts appear to be operated by the same entity. A series of posts from several accounts with identical arguments or repeated points of view could indicate coordinated manipulation.

2.3 Using Hashtag and Link Analysis

Coordinated disinformation campaigns often involve the strategic use of hashtags or external links to guide discussions in a particular direction or to spread the false narrative.

- **Hashtag clustering**: Monitoring hashtags or keywords used across threads can help identify when the same set of hashtags appears frequently and consistently across different users and threads. This pattern can indicate a coordinated effort to amplify specific terms or topics.
- **Link propagation**: Look for threads where links to external sites are widely shared among multiple users. If these links lead to known disinformation websites, fake news outlets, or misleading content, it is a strong indicator that the campaign is being organized.

3. Detecting Fake Narratives and Manipulated Content

Many disinformation campaigns rely on fabricated narratives or manipulated content to deceive audiences. It is essential for investigators to be able to detect these kinds of content in order to prevent the spread of false information.

3.1 Reverse Image and Video Search

Disinformation campaigns often use altered images or deepfakes to promote false narratives. Reverse image search tools, such as Google Reverse Image Search or Tineye, can be employed to trace the origin of images being circulated across forum threads. Investigators should also use video verification tools to verify the authenticity of videos or images being shared in discussions.

3.2 Fact-Checking Claims

Disinformation campaigns may rely on false claims or exaggerated stories to provoke strong emotional responses. Using trusted fact-checking tools and resources, such as Snopes, FactCheck.org, or PolitiFact, can help verify or debunk these claims. Discrepancies between the facts and the narrative being promoted by users in forum threads can indicate that a disinformation campaign is in play.

4. Ethical and Legal Considerations

Investigating coordinated disinformation campaigns on forums requires a careful balance of effectiveness, ethics, and legal adherence. When collecting and analyzing data:

- **Privacy considerations**: Although forums are public spaces, users may still have an expectation of privacy. OSINT investigators should ensure that they only access publicly available information and avoid breaching terms of service agreements.
- **Dealing with false accusations**: It's important to ensure that the identification of disinformation does not lead to the false labeling of individuals or groups. Investigations should focus on patterns of behavior, rather than making assumptions about individual users based solely on their views or opinions.

The identification of coordinated disinformation campaigns in forums is a crucial task in modern SOCMINT investigations. By understanding the patterns of behavior that distinguish legitimate discourse from artificial manipulation, investigators can identify and counteract campaigns designed to mislead and manipulate. Advanced techniques, such as analyzing posting patterns, detecting bot behavior, tracing hashtag usage, and fact-checking content, can all play a role in exposing disinformation efforts. While these techniques are powerful, they must be implemented with a strong sense of ethics and respect for legal boundaries to ensure the integrity of the investigation.

6.6 Case Study: Using Reddit OSINT to Uncover a Cybercrime Operation

Reddit, a massive online community where users share content and engage in discussions, is a platform that hosts a wealth of information—both legitimate and illicit.

While the site is home to millions of everyday conversations and debates, it also has dark corners where cybercriminals and hackers exchange knowledge, tools, and services. In this case study, we will walk through how Reddit OSINT (Open Source Intelligence) techniques were applied to uncover a cybercrime operation operating under the guise of an innocuous thread in a public subreddit.

The investigation begins with a seemingly innocuous post about VPN services and quickly evolves into a detailed OSINT operation aimed at uncovering a cybercrime syndicate involved in ransomware attacks, phishing schemes, and the sale of stolen credentials.

1. The Initial Discovery: A Thread on VPNs

The investigation began in the r/technology subreddit, a large and relatively open community where users discuss everything from gadgets and software to cybersecurity practices. A new post appeared under a thread titled, "Best VPNs for Enhanced Privacy," which is a common topic for the subreddit. One particular comment, made by a user with a seemingly innocent handle, mentioned the use of a VPN service in combination with a "secure dropbox" for sharing files. The comment itself seemed harmless enough at first glance, with no overtly malicious intent.

1.1 Red Flags in the Comment

What initially raised suspicion were a few subtle details in the comment:

- The user recommended a VPN provider that was not commonly discussed, often associated with illegitimate or suspicious activity on the dark web.
- The mention of a "secure dropbox" led to questions about what the user was trying to hide. It was an unusual way of phrasing a file-sharing service that would normally be discussed in the context of legal and ethical file transfers.
- Additionally, the comment was followed by a direct message (DM) from the user offering more information about the VPN service and "secure methods for handling sensitive data," which raised further concern.

Given these factors, a deeper investigation into the Reddit user and their activity seemed warranted.

2. Conducting the OSINT Investigation: Tracing the User's Footprint

2.1 Investigating the User Profile

The first step was to analyze the Reddit user's profile. While Reddit allows for a degree of anonymity, OSINT investigators can still extract valuable information based on a user's post history and activity.

Username Analysis: The user's handle was generic, with no direct links to other online identities or real-world information. However, analyzing the user's posting frequency revealed an interesting pattern: the user was active across multiple subreddits related to cybersecurity, privacy, and file-sharing, all of which seemed to revolve around anonymity and secure communication.

Post History: The user had posted on various topics relating to privacy concerns, VPN recommendations, and even advice on how to avoid digital surveillance. The frequency of these posts across multiple threads was notable, suggesting the user was building a network of followers or individuals interested in their advice.

2.2 Analyzing Cross-Subreddit Behavior

Next, investigators tracked the user's activity across other relevant subreddits, including r/privacy, r/techsupport, and r/cybersecurity. They discovered the user often commented on posts discussing data breaches, malware analysis, and the need for secure communications. These seemingly helpful comments were always linked to external sites offering suspicious services.

In one instance, a user in a discussion about a recent ransomware attack asked for advice on how to recover encrypted data. The original user, under a different account, offered a link to a third-party service claiming to decrypt the files for a fee. This kind of behavior— seemingly altruistic advice paired with monetizing the misfortune of others—was a strong indicator that this user might be linked to more malicious operations.

3. Uncovering a Network of Cybercriminals: Pattern Recognition

As the investigation progressed, the pattern of behavior became clearer. The user appeared to be part of a broader network operating across Reddit and other forums. This network was engaged in distributing ransomware and offering decryption services to victims in exchange for payments. A thorough investigation into their interactions revealed that several accounts within the same set of subreddits were repeatedly recommending illegitimate services that were also associated with phishing schemes and the sale of stolen login credentials.

3.1 Mapping the Network of Criminal Activity

- **Multiple Accounts, Same Agenda**: Investigators noticed a recurring set of usernames in these threads, some offering advice on VPN usage and others directly recommending decryption services or suggesting ways to avoid being caught by law enforcement. These accounts frequently interacted with one another, forming a loose but effective support system.
- **IP Address Analysis**: By cross-referencing timestamps and analyzing metadata from the posts, it became clear that multiple accounts were likely being operated from the same IP address range. This was a critical indicator that the posts were being made by a small group rather than several independent users.

Through this method of network analysis, the OSINT team was able to identify a cybercrime syndicate responsible for a range of activities, from distributing ransomware to providing phishing tools and selling stolen data.

4. Connecting the Dots: Further Evidence and Collaboration

At this point, the investigation began to cross-reference information from other parts of the web to build a more comprehensive case. Investigators reached out to other OSINT experts and law enforcement agencies to verify the identities of the users involved in the cybercrime ring.

- **External Links and Dark Web Connections**: The user had provided several links in their comments leading to dark web marketplaces where ransomware and stolen data were sold. These marketplaces, though encrypted and difficult to navigate, were familiar territory for cybercrime investigators.
- **Public Records and Data Breaches**: Further investigation of the linked websites revealed connections to public data breaches. Some of the stolen credentials offered for sale matched known breaches, such as those from popular websites and service providers.

By analyzing these connections and sourcing corroborative evidence, the OSINT investigation led to the identification of key members of the cybercrime syndicate and their operational structure.

5. Conclusion: The Role of Reddit OSINT in Uncovering Cybercrime

This case study demonstrates the importance of using Reddit OSINT techniques to uncover cybercrime operations hiding in plain sight. The seemingly innocuous post about

VPN services was, in fact, the first clue in a complex investigation that revealed a network of cybercriminals exploiting the platform to conduct illegal activities.

Key Takeaways

- **Patterns in behavior**: Identifying patterns of cross-subreddit activity and bot-like behavior was crucial to uncovering the coordinated nature of the disinformation campaign.
- **Metadata analysis**: By analyzing timestamps, IP addresses, and posting patterns, investigators were able to identify connections between multiple accounts.
- **Link analysis**: Tracking the external links shared within the threads revealed connections to dark web marketplaces, where ransomware and stolen credentials were being traded.

The case study underscores the power of OSINT in identifying and dismantling cybercrime operations, as well as the effectiveness of platforms like Reddit in facilitating malicious activities. This investigation highlights how careful analysis of seemingly ordinary online behavior can uncover hidden criminal networks and lead to significant breakthroughs in law enforcement and cybersecurity efforts.

7. TikTok, Snapchat & Emerging Social Networks

As digital landscapes evolve, platforms like TikTok, Snapchat, and emerging social networks present new challenges and opportunities for OSINT analysts. With their emphasis on short-form content, ephemeral messaging, and algorithm-driven discovery, these platforms require innovative investigative techniques. This chapter explores methods for tracking digital footprints, extracting metadata, analyzing viral trends, and identifying key influencers. From monitoring geotagged videos to uncovering hidden connections, understanding the OSINT potential of these rapidly growing platforms is essential for staying ahead in the ever-changing world of social media intelligence.

7.1 How TikTok's Algorithm Works & What Data is Publicly Available

TikTok, one of the fastest-growing social media platforms, has revolutionized how content is created, shared, and consumed. The app's short-form videos, ranging from entertainment and education to social commentary and viral trends, have captured the attention of millions globally. Behind the seamless flow of content, however, lies a powerful algorithm that drives the discovery and visibility of posts, determining what users see on their For You Page (FYP). For investigators leveraging OSINT (Open Source Intelligence) methods, TikTok offers a wealth of public data that can be mined for valuable insights—whether in tracking individuals, uncovering trends, or even monitoring potential threats.

Understanding how TikTok's algorithm works and what data is publicly available is crucial for SOCMINT (Social Media Open Source Intelligence) investigations. In this chapter, we'll explore how TikTok's recommendation system operates and outline the types of publicly accessible data that can be harvested for investigations.

1. How TikTok's Algorithm Works

TikTok's algorithm is designed to maximize user engagement by providing content tailored to each individual's preferences. The platform's machine learning-driven recommendation system takes into account various user behaviors to curate a personalized experience. Understanding the underlying mechanisms of TikTok's algorithm can help OSINT analysts predict what content might gain traction or identify patterns across different users.

1.1 User Interaction Signals

The core of TikTok's algorithm lies in the signals it receives from user interactions. These interactions tell the system what a user is interested in, and they include:

- **Likes**: When a user likes a video, TikTok learns that they are interested in that content type.
- **Shares**: When a user shares a video, it signals that the content resonates strongly with them.
- **Comments**: User comments on videos further refine their interests, indicating specific aspects of the content they engage with.
- **Replays**: If a user watches a video more than once, it suggests a high level of interest.
- **Follow Actions**: Following a creator is a strong signal to the algorithm about the type of content a user prefers.
- **Time Spent on Content**: How long a user watches a video, even without interacting with it (such as liking or commenting), helps the algorithm understand their interest in similar videos.

These behaviors are compiled and analyzed to refine the recommendations that users see on their For You Page (FYP). The FYP is central to TikTok's viral nature, as the algorithm pushes content that is likely to engage individual users based on their preferences and past actions.

1.2 Content Features: How TikTok Understands Videos

In addition to user interaction signals, the algorithm also takes into account several factors related to the video content itself:

- **Captions**: The text included in the video's caption is used to identify the topic of the video and categorize it.
- **Hashtags**: TikTok users commonly use hashtags to classify and categorize videos. Hashtags help the algorithm understand the subject matter and provide relevant recommendations.
- **Sounds and Music**: TikTok videos are often defined by the audio used, whether it's a song, soundbite, or voiceover. The use of popular sounds or trending music can increase the visibility of a video.
- **Video Information**: Video length, whether the video is in a loop, and even the type of editing used can contribute to how TikTok ranks and categorizes content.

- **Language**: The algorithm considers the language of the video's caption and audio to recommend content in the user's preferred language.

TikTok's algorithm relies heavily on the interaction between users and the video content itself, allowing it to promote videos based on these elements, regardless of whether the user is following the creator. This increases the potential for viral content and drives engagement across different user bases.

1.3 The Importance of Video and User Activity Analysis

TikTok's algorithm is highly dynamic and learns quickly from both user interactions and content consumption patterns. Investigators utilizing TikTok OSINT techniques can analyze patterns within videos to:

- Identify trends or viral topics by analyzing hashtags, audio usage, and video themes.
- Determine content popularity and engagement levels by studying likes, shares, and comments across users and videos.
- Monitor how particular videos or accounts gain visibility or become part of larger trending topics or disinformation campaigns.

2. What Data is Publicly Available on TikTok?

While TikTok offers numerous privacy controls to its users, a significant amount of data remains publicly accessible, particularly when it comes to publicly available accounts and non-private videos. For OSINT practitioners, this provides a valuable opportunity to gather intelligence on individuals, organizations, trends, and social movements. Below are the types of data that are accessible for analysis:

2.1 Public User Profiles

- **Username & Profile Bio**: TikTok user profiles are often the first source of information. Public profiles display usernames, profile photos, bio descriptions, and links to other social media accounts.
- **User Activity**: A public profile reveals the videos a user has posted, as well as their liked content and followers/following count. The information on a user's followers can offer insights into who they are connected to or influenced by.
- **Location Data**: If a user includes location data in their bio or video captions (e.g., city, country), this can be used to identify geographic locations related to their activity.

2.2 Public Videos

TikTok users have the option to make their videos either public or private. For those that are publicly available, investigators can view the following data:

- **Video Captions**: Often include information about the video or additional context that can help identify the video's topic.
- **Hashtags**: Hashtags allow videos to be categorized by specific topics, interests, or challenges. This can help investigators track trends or monitor specific subjects of interest.
- **Video Engagement**: Likes, comments, and shares are public metrics that reveal how much engagement a video is generating.
- **Comments**: Public comments are a goldmine for gaining context about how viewers perceive the video, whether it be positive, negative, or revealing any underlying issues or trends.

2.3 Trending Topics & Challenges

TikTok thrives on trending challenges and viral content. Investigators can monitor:

- **Trending Hashtags**: These indicate the popularity of certain topics or trends within the TikTok ecosystem. Tracking trending hashtags allows analysts to stay on top of viral movements or to track the evolution of a campaign.
- **Audio**: Viral audio clips or songs are often reused in multiple videos. Tracking how audio clips are spreading can help map content trends and how quickly certain themes or topics gain traction.
- **Video Tags**: Video creators often tag their videos with specific keywords that align with trending challenges or movements. These tags can provide further insight into the content and user interests.

2.4 External Links

TikTok also allows users to include external links in their profiles or videos (e.g., links to personal websites, online stores, or other social media accounts). By tracing these links, investigators can uncover connections to other networks or cross-platform activities.

3. The Limits of Public Data on TikTok

Despite TikTok's openness with user-generated content, several limitations exist in terms of publicly accessible data:

- **Private Accounts**: Content from private accounts is restricted to approved followers, making it inaccessible unless the investigator is connected with the user.
- **Location Data**: While some users voluntarily share their locations in captions or profiles, TikTok does not automatically provide geographic data for videos (i.e., GPS location). This makes location-based analysis more difficult.
- **Video Metadata**: TikTok does not openly share video metadata (such as upload times, device data, or editing history), which could be useful for more in-depth investigations.

TikTok's algorithm and the platform's wealth of publicly available data offer a treasure trove for SOCMINT investigations. By understanding how the algorithm prioritizes content and identifying the types of data that are publicly accessible, OSINT practitioners can extract valuable intelligence from the platform. Whether tracking individuals, monitoring trends, or uncovering disinformation campaigns, TikTok's transparent access to user interactions, video content, and public profiles provides a unique avenue for intelligence gathering in the digital age. However, it's important to recognize the limitations and ethical considerations when conducting OSINT investigations on a platform that prioritizes user engagement and privacy.

7.2 Tracking TikTok Hashtags, Challenges & Viral Trends

TikTok has quickly evolved into a global platform that thrives on viral trends, challenges, and hashtags. These elements are not only central to the app's success but also form the backbone of its content discovery system. For OSINT (Open Source Intelligence) analysts, understanding how to track and analyze TikTok's hashtags, challenges, and viral trends is key to gathering intelligence. Whether it's monitoring public sentiment, tracking the spread of disinformation, or understanding cultural shifts, these features provide valuable insights into user behaviors, viral topics, and the rapid evolution of digital trends.

This chapter will dive into the mechanisms of tracking TikTok hashtags, challenges, and viral trends, outlining practical methods to analyze these elements for OSINT investigations.

1. The Role of Hashtags, Challenges & Trends in TikTok

1.1 Hashtags: The Building Blocks of Discoverability

Hashtags are crucial to TikTok's content discovery algorithm, functioning as markers that categorize videos. By using hashtags, content creators make their videos discoverable to users interested in specific topics. For OSINT investigators, these hashtags offer a valuable tool for tracking discussions, monitoring trends, or even spotting emerging issues before they gain widespread attention.

Trending Hashtags: When a hashtag becomes popular, it indicates a larger conversation or event taking place on the platform. Trending hashtags often signal viral challenges, global movements, or urgent topics of interest. For example, during political events, natural disasters, or social justice movements, hashtags often serve as the rallying cry for a community of users.

Hashtag Use in OSINT: Hashtags act as a tagging system that can help investigators identify and categorize content related to specific topics. Investigators can search for popular or niche hashtags to monitor what users are saying about certain events, trends, or movements.

1.2 Challenges: Viral Content Across Communities

Challenges on TikTok are interactive, often involving specific actions, dance moves, or content formats that users replicate and share. Challenges are central to TikTok's viral content nature and typically have their own unique hashtags. These challenges allow TikTok's users to engage in viral behavior, creating a ripple effect across the app, especially when celebrities or influencers participate.

Challenge Tracking: By tracking the hashtag associated with a challenge, investigators can monitor the spread of a viral event or trend. This can be especially useful when the challenge is linked to a social cause, marketing campaign, or political movement.

Analyzing Challenge Content: Many challenges are fun and lighthearted, but others may have a deeper social or political context. By tracking the success and reach of a challenge, investigators can uncover hidden trends or assess the impact of a campaign on public sentiment or user engagement.

1.3 Viral Trends: The Evolution of TikTok Culture

Viral trends on TikTok emerge organically from user interactions with challenges, memes, or content formats. These trends can be triggered by anything from a funny video to a news event, making them useful for investigators to track public sentiment or how quickly a story spreads across digital spaces. TikTok's algorithm pushes content that matches user interests, creating an ecosystem where viral trends can escalate rapidly.

- **Trend Tracking**: Identifying viral trends allows OSINT analysts to monitor real-time cultural movements. These trends can be related to music, popular quotes, political statements, or even corporate marketing. Tracking how trends evolve can provide insights into public opinion or highlight disinformation campaigns or coordinated online activity.

2. Methods for Tracking TikTok Hashtags, Challenges, and Trends

2.1 Searching for Trending Hashtags

The first step in tracking viral content is identifying the right hashtags. TikTok provides several ways to discover popular hashtags directly within the app. For OSINT analysts, these methods are crucial to monitoring what is happening in real-time.

Trending Hashtags Tab: TikTok's "Discover" or "For You Page (FYP)" tab provides a curated feed of trending hashtags that reflect current viral content. While this is designed for regular users, it can also help investigators spot trending topics and hashtags. These trends can give investigators a sense of what's being discussed, even if they're not part of the conversations.

Hashtag Search Function: TikTok's search bar allows users to input specific keywords or phrases to find related videos, creators, and hashtags. This is useful for narrowing down a search to a particular topic. Analysts can use this tool to identify hashtags that are gaining momentum and identify related videos and content.

Monitoring Hashtags: To track hashtag usage over time, analysts can use social listening tools (such as Brandwatch, Sprinklr, or Talkwalker) or employ manual tracking methods by reviewing how frequently a hashtag appears in TikTok videos. Some tools offer real-time tracking and can alert analysts when specific hashtags see a spike in usage.

2.2 Monitoring Challenges Through Hashtags

Many TikTok challenges are defined by a specific hashtag, which users include in their posts as they participate. Tracking the spread of challenges through their hashtags can reveal how quickly they are gaining traction.

Challenge Hashtag Discovery: Just like with general trending hashtags, finding challenges requires searching for the right keyword or hashtag associated with the challenge. Once the challenge has a hashtag, tracking its evolution becomes easier.

Analyzing Challenge Content: The next step is reviewing videos under the challenge's hashtag. Investigators should assess how widely the challenge has spread, how many users are engaged, and the nature of the content associated with it. Investigators can spot if the challenge is being used for social commentary, political advocacy, or even marketing purposes.

Engagement Metrics: Monitoring the number of likes, shares, comments, and video completions under a challenge hashtag can provide insight into its impact. High levels of engagement, especially from influencers or celebrities, often signal that a challenge is poised to go viral.

2.3 Tracking Viral Trends: From Hashtags to Content

Viral trends can emerge from a wide variety of sources—including challenges, memes, songs, or even news events. For OSINT analysts, tracking these trends requires real-time monitoring and understanding the speed at which these trends shift.

Trend Monitoring Tools: OSINT practitioners can use social media monitoring platforms or TikTok's API (when available) to track trends and hashtags over time. Platforms like BuzzSumo and Social Search can also help track how specific topics, phrases, or content formats spread across platforms like TikTok.

Content Engagement: Beyond hashtags, investigators should look for the engagement patterns of trending videos. These include viral audio clips, shared memes, or popular video formats. The spread of these elements is a key sign of viral growth. Investigators can also examine how these trends are being used in other social media platforms, extending the cross-platform analysis.

3. Analyzing and Investigating Viral TikTok Trends

Tracking and analyzing viral TikTok trends can provide OSINT analysts with valuable insights into various areas:

3.1 Identifying Potential Disinformation Campaigns

Viral trends can be used to spread disinformation, and TikTok is no exception. Some trends might appear to be innocent fun, while others might serve as a way to manipulate public opinion. By tracking hashtags and challenges, investigators can uncover if certain trends are being used to push a political agenda or manipulate sentiment.

- **Suspicious Trends**: Trends that suddenly spike in activity, especially those related to sensitive political topics or social movements, could be a sign of astroturfing or bot activity designed to create the appearance of a grassroots movement.

3.2 Tracking Cultural Shifts and Sentiment

TikTok trends often mirror shifts in public opinion or behavior. By tracking what types of trends are popular (such as social justice hashtags or discussions about current events), analysts can gauge the public sentiment surrounding specific topics. These insights can be valuable for:

- Market research
- Predicting social movements
- Monitoring user behavior

Tracking TikTok hashtags, challenges, and viral trends offers a unique opportunity for SOCMINT analysts to gather intelligence on a wide range of subjects. From identifying emergent issues and social movements to monitoring the spread of disinformation, these elements can provide a powerful lens into the digital world. By leveraging tools and tracking methods outlined in this chapter, investigators can not only stay ahead of viral trends but also uncover the underlying narratives and sentiments shaping online conversations.

7.3 Investigating Snapchat OSINT & Discovering Deleted Snaps

Snapchat, a popular multimedia messaging app, has become a dominant platform among younger generations for its ephemeral nature, where messages and media disappear after being viewed. This unique feature has raised concerns about privacy, security, and the challenges it presents for Open Source Intelligence (OSINT) investigations. For OSINT analysts, Snapchat presents a unique set of challenges and opportunities. The ability to track users, analyze public stories, and uncover deleted snaps or messages requires a deep understanding of how Snapchat works and the tools available for gathering data.

In this chapter, we will explore the potential for investigating Snapchat for OSINT purposes, focusing on how to track public content, uncover insights from Snap Maps, and explore the often-elusive world of deleted snaps. While Snapchat's design prioritizes disappearing content, there are still investigative methods that can be used to gather valuable intelligence from the platform.

1. Understanding Snapchat's Structure and Privacy Settings

Before diving into methods for investigating Snapchat, it is important to understand the key features of the app, particularly those related to privacy. Snapchat is built around its ephemeral messaging system, but it also offers a wide variety of features, such as:

1.1 Snap Stories and Public Profiles

Snap Stories: Snap stories are a collection of photos and videos that users share with their friends for 24 hours. These stories are visible to all friends and can be used to monitor an individual's activities or locations. Some users also choose to make their stories public, allowing anyone to view them.

Public Profiles: Many users create public profiles to share their snaps, engage in challenges, or promote their brands. These profiles can be crucial for investigators who are trying to track trends or individuals who intentionally make their content available to the public.

1.2 Snap Maps and Geolocation Features

Snap Map: This feature allows users to share their location with friends and can also display location-based stories from users worldwide. Snap Map provides insights into where a user has been in real time, making it valuable for tracking movements, identifying hotspots, or even identifying patterns of behavior.

Geofilters: Snap also uses location-based filters, called geofilters, that users can add to their photos and videos. These geofilters provide not only location but also cultural context, such as events or public spaces, which can be valuable for geospatial intelligence.

1.3 Privacy Settings

Snapchat allows users to control who sees their content by adjusting their privacy settings. Content can be shared with:

- **Friends Only**: Visible only to approved connections.
- **My Story**: A 24-hour feed of the user's snaps, visible to all friends.
- **Public Stories**: Can be seen by anyone, even non-friends.

For investigators, targeting public stories, analyzing Snap Maps, and understanding who can see what content is critical in developing an investigative strategy.

2. Tracking Public Content on Snapchat

Despite the app's focus on private and disappearing content, there is still plenty of public content on Snapchat that can be analyzed for OSINT purposes.

2.1 Tracking Public Snap Stories

Public Snap Stories are an important resource for monitoring Snapchat activity. These stories often contain information about individuals, events, and locations. Investigators can monitor:

Influencers and Brands: Many companies and influencers use Snapchat for brand marketing, making their stories public to increase engagement. Monitoring these public stories can offer valuable insights into marketing trends and consumer behavior.

Public Events and Trends: Users often share their experiences at public events, festivals, and protests on their public stories. By tracking these stories, investigators can gain intelligence on the timing, location, and sentiment surrounding these events.

Geographical Data: Stories shared from public locations often include geotags or geofilters that indicate the user's location. By tracking these tags, investigators can pinpoint specific locations that are of interest for further investigation.

2.2 Using Snap Map for Location-Based Insights

Snap Map is a valuable tool for gathering location-based intelligence. Investigators can:

- **Identify User Movement**: If a target frequently uses Snap Map, it can reveal their daily movements, common hangout spots, and places of employment.

- **Track Events and Protests**: Snap Map features stories from a wide range of locations. Investigators can use these stories to monitor significant events, protests, or rallies and understand their geographical spread.

The Snap Map also allows users to share their real-time location with friends. While this can provide real-time insights into user movement, it also means that any information shared on Snap Map can be accessed as long as it's publicly visible.

2.3 Exploring Public Snapchat Profiles

Many people use Snapchat as a public platform to promote themselves, share news, or post about ongoing events. These public profiles allow investigators to:

- **Monitor Influencers**: Influencers, celebrities, and brands often create public profiles where they post content for broad visibility. Investigating these profiles can yield valuable insights into trending topics and user engagement.
- **Investigate Niche Communities**: Users can create Snapchat profiles related to niche interests or causes. By monitoring these profiles, investigators can track subcultures, communities, or even underground movements that are active on the platform.

3. Investigating Deleted Snaps and Temporary Content

Snapchat's focus on disappearing content means that most media vanishes after a brief period, raising the question: can deleted snaps still be recovered? While Snapchat is designed to delete content once viewed or after 24 hours, there are methods and tools available that may allow investigators to retrieve certain data from deleted content.

3.1 Snapchat's Ephemeral Nature

By design, Snapchat's disappearing messages, photos, and videos are deleted within a short time frame. However, temporary content is not always fully erased:

- **Screenshots**: If a user takes a screenshot of a snap, it can still be recovered from the device's storage.
- **Snapchat Servers**: While Snapchat claims to delete data from their servers after it disappears, forensic experts have raised questions about whether this data can still be recovered. In some cases, law enforcement agencies have successfully retrieved deleted content from Snapchat's servers with proper legal authorization.

3.2 Data Extraction from Mobile Devices

Forensic experts can often recover deleted snaps from mobile devices using specialized tools such as:

- **Data recovery software**: Tools like Cellebrite or Oxygen Forensics allow investigators to extract deleted data from a device, including content from apps like Snapchat.
- **Mobile Device Forensics**: Investigators may work with forensic specialists to examine a target's mobile device for traces of deleted messages, photos, and videos.

These techniques allow investigators to access content that may have been deleted from Snapchat but still exists in cached memory or on the device.

4. Ethical and Legal Considerations

When investigating Snapchat for OSINT purposes, it is essential to remain mindful of both ethical considerations and legal boundaries:

Privacy Concerns: Although Snapchat's public profiles and stories provide valuable data for analysis, investigators must respect users' privacy and be aware of potential misuse of the platform's content.

Consent and Permission: In cases involving private messages or content, investigators should ensure they have legal authorization to access and analyze data. Depending on the country or jurisdiction, accessing private or deleted content may require warrants or other legal processes.

Disappearing Content and Preservation: It is important for investigators to be aware that once content disappears from Snapchat, it cannot be permanently accessed without proper backups or data extraction techniques.

Snapchat's design, which emphasizes ephemeral content, presents challenges for traditional OSINT investigations. However, there are still significant opportunities to gather intelligence from public stories, Snap Maps, and profiles. Moreover, with the right tools and techniques, even deleted snaps may be recoverable for investigation, whether through device forensics or other methods. As Snapchat continues to evolve, staying ahead of new features and understanding the best practices for ethical and legal data gathering will remain essential for OSINT analysts conducting investigations on this platform.

7.4 Finding Emerging Social Networks & Analyzing New Platforms

The digital landscape is constantly shifting, with new social media platforms emerging regularly. These platforms often attract niche audiences or early adopters before becoming mainstream, creating opportunities for OSINT analysts to track evolving trends, emerging influencers, and digital movements. However, the rapid evolution of social media can also pose a challenge. New platforms often bring novel ways to communicate and share data, and understanding their potential impact requires staying ahead of the curve.

This chapter focuses on finding emerging social networks and analyzing new platforms for OSINT purposes. We will explore how to identify these platforms early, how they differ from established social networks, and the tools and techniques analysts can use to monitor these spaces effectively. By understanding the dynamics of new platforms, OSINT professionals can gain early insights into cultural shifts, identify emerging influencers, and even spot disinformation campaigns before they spread widely.

1. Why Emerging Social Networks Matter for OSINT

Emerging social networks can be especially valuable for intelligence gathering, as they often serve as incubators for new ideas, digital trends, and sometimes even covert activities. Here are several reasons why tracking and analyzing new platforms is critical for OSINT:

1.1 Early Detection of Digital Trends

Emerging networks tend to attract early adopters, trendsetters, and influencers who experiment with novel content forms, such as augmented reality (AR), short-form video, or alternative modes of interaction. Monitoring these platforms can allow OSINT analysts to spot trends and cultural shifts before they reach mass adoption.

Example: TikTok, originally an app focused on lip-syncing, evolved into a platform for viral challenges, activism, and memes. Analysts who tracked the early stages of TikTok saw its potential to become a global digital force.

1.2 Identifying New Digital Communities

Emerging networks often cater to specific subcultures, interests, or geographical areas, allowing analysts to tap into communities that may not be present on larger platforms like Facebook, Twitter, or Instagram. By identifying these emerging communities, OSINT professionals can track niche discussions, monitor underground movements, and analyze evolving public sentiment.

Example: Platforms like Discord initially attracted gamers but expanded to host diverse communities focused on hobbies, education, politics, and even activism.

1.3 Tracking Emerging Influencers

Influencers who rise to prominence on new platforms can wield considerable influence over their audiences. These influencers can drive viral trends, promote causes, or even influence political opinions. Monitoring early-stage influencers provides a valuable opportunity to spot rising voices and gauge public sentiment before it becomes widespread.

1.4 Spotting Disinformation and Malicious Activities

Emerging platforms often lack the moderation mechanisms or content regulation that larger platforms have, making them fertile ground for disinformation, radicalization, or even illicit activities. Early identification of these behaviors is crucial for detecting threats and managing risk.

Example: New social networks may be more susceptible to fake accounts or coordinated misinformation campaigns aimed at influencing public opinion, especially during election cycles or times of social unrest.

2. How to Find Emerging Social Networks

Identifying emerging social networks requires an active approach, as new platforms often fly under the radar until they gain critical mass. Here are several strategies to find them early:

2.1 Monitor App Stores and Developer Communities

The most immediate way to discover new platforms is by staying alert to new app releases on major app stores, including the Apple App Store and Google Play Store. Emerging networks often launch as mobile apps and attract attention through their unique features or niche audiences.

- **Developer Communities**: Platforms like GitHub, Stack Overflow, or Dev.to are great places to spot early-stage networks being built by independent developers. Tracking discussions on these platforms can give analysts early access to new technologies or platforms gaining traction among tech-savvy users.

2.2 Follow Digital Trendsetters and Influencers

Many of the early adopters of new social platforms are influencers or creators who seek out the latest and most innovative ways to engage with audiences. By following these trendsetters, OSINT analysts can be among the first to hear about new networks and platforms.

- **Monitor Creator Communities**: Communities like YouTube, TikTok, Twitter, and Twitch often feature content creators who experiment with new platforms and technologies. When influencers start promoting a new network, it often signals its growing importance.

2.3 Social Media and Tech News

Keeping an eye on tech-focused publications and social media is critical for staying informed about emerging platforms. Websites like TechCrunch, The Verge, and Mashable regularly cover new startups and emerging technologies, providing early insights into up-and-coming social networks.

- **Follow Hashtags**: Hashtags like #newapps, #startups, or #technews often appear across social media platforms, providing updates on innovations and new releases.

2.4 Crowdsourcing and Online Communities

Certain online communities specialize in sharing news about upcoming platforms. Forums like Reddit, especially subreddits like r/InternetIsBeautiful, r/startups, or r/technology, often feature discussions of new apps and services.

- **Reddit's "r/SideProject"** subreddit is particularly good for discovering new platforms in their very early stages. By tracking mentions and engagement on these forums, analysts can get a sense of which platforms are gaining traction.

3. Analyzing Emerging Social Networks for OSINT

Once an emerging platform is identified, OSINT analysts need to understand how to gather and analyze data from these spaces. Here are several methods for investigating and analyzing new social networks:

3.1 Evaluate the Network's Purpose and Audience

Before diving into data collection, it is important to evaluate the platform's purpose and target audience. Some emerging networks are designed for specific use cases—such as professional networking, content creation, or messaging—while others may focus on niche hobbies or interests. Understanding the platform's main focus helps analysts identify relevant content and key conversations to track.

- **Target Audience**: Researching the demographic profile of the platform's users will provide insights into the type of content or conversations that are likely to unfold there. Is it a platform for young adults? Gamers? Tech enthusiasts? Activists?

3.2 Scraping and Collecting Data

Many emerging platforms may not have robust API access or data export options, making traditional scraping techniques the most effective way to gather intelligence. However, it's important to note that scraping must be done within legal boundaries and comply with the platform's terms of service.

- **Web Scraping Tools**: Tools like BeautifulSoup, Scrapy, or Selenium can be used to scrape data from new platforms, including user posts, comments, profiles, or media. Keep in mind that many platforms are actively evolving their security to prevent unauthorized scraping.

3.3 Identify Keywords, Hashtags, and Topics

As with larger platforms, emerging networks often organize content around keywords, hashtags, or tags. Identifying trending or relevant terms on the platform helps analysts track important conversations or groups of interest.

- **Keyword Tracking Tools**: If the platform does not offer robust analytics, third-party tools like BuzzSumo, Brandwatch, or Mention can be used to track keywords and hashtags across social platforms.

3.4 Monitor Growth and Engagement Patterns

To gauge the platform's relevance, OSINT analysts should monitor key indicators of growth and engagement:

- **User Growth**: Is the platform experiencing rapid user acquisition, often indicated by viral trends or influencer adoption?
- **Content Engagement**: What is the level of interaction with posts? High engagement signals a vibrant community and the potential for information or disinformation campaigns.

3.5 Investigate Potential Risks and Threats

New social platforms can sometimes be breeding grounds for disinformation, extremist activities, or even cyber threats. Early investigation of these potential risks can prevent larger issues down the line.

- **Risk Indicators**: Look for behaviors like coordinated hashtags, anonymous user groups, or messages that spread rapidly without verification. Emerging networks may be less regulated, making them susceptible to misinformation.

The world of social media is ever-evolving, and emerging networks provide valuable opportunities—and challenges—for OSINT analysts. By staying ahead of digital trends, identifying new platforms early, and adapting investigative methods to fit each platform's unique features, analysts can uncover key insights about emerging communities, trends, influencers, and even potential threats. Monitoring these new platforms will be crucial for understanding the direction of digital culture and providing timely intelligence in an increasingly interconnected world.

7.5 Monitoring Niche Social Media for Early Intelligence

While mainstream social media platforms like Facebook, Twitter, and Instagram dominate much of the digital landscape, niche social media networks are often where the most targeted, specialized, and insightful activity occurs. These platforms, typically smaller and more focused, often foster tight-knit communities around specific interests, ideologies, or behaviors. For OSINT analysts, monitoring niche social media can offer a goldmine of early intelligence that is not as easily accessible on broader platforms. These spaces can reveal emerging trends, underground movements, and even early signs of disinformation or potential threats.

In this chapter, we will explore the significance of niche social media in OSINT investigations, how to identify and monitor these platforms, and strategies for extracting intelligence. Understanding these networks gives OSINT professionals the ability to track more granular data and respond more proactively to emerging issues that may not yet have gained mainstream attention.

1. The Power of Niche Social Media

1.1 Smaller, More Targeted Communities

Niche social media platforms often cater to specific groups or interests, such as:

- **Professional networks** (e.g., GitHub for developers, Dribbble for designers)
- **Hobbyist communities** (e.g., Model Mayhem for photographers, DeviantArt for artists)
- **Regional or local interest groups** (e.g., Nextdoor for neighborhood communities)
- **Activist or political movements** (e.g., smaller political forums, protest groups)

These spaces tend to be less moderated than mainstream platforms and often attract more passionate participants, making them rich sources of raw, unfiltered intelligence. Analyzing niche platforms can provide unique insights into trends, conversations, and networks that larger platforms overlook.

1.2 Early Indicators of Emerging Trends

Niche social networks tend to serve as early adoption hubs for new ideas, products, and movements. By tracking conversations and content in these spaces, OSINT analysts can:

- **Identify emerging subcultures**: Before they become mainstream trends, niche networks often incubate cultural shifts, innovations, or communities that can later spill over into larger platforms.
- **Track early mentions of events**: Niche platforms can be places where important events or issues are discussed before they attract the attention of traditional news outlets.

- **Spot influencers**: Influencers and leaders in niche communities often build their followings on smaller networks before expanding to more prominent platforms. Identifying these individuals early allows analysts to track their influence and impact as they grow.

1.3 Highly Focused Intelligence

While mainstream social media is often flooded with general information and noise, niche networks deliver highly focused intelligence. Investigators can tap into discussions, content, and activity about very specific topics, be it in the realms of technology, art, politics, or even illegal activities. This makes it easier to filter out irrelevant data and focus on what truly matters.

- **Example**: Forums focused on cryptocurrency like BitcoinTalk or CryptoCompare can provide early warnings about major shifts in the crypto market, such as new technologies or the rise of altcoins.

2. Identifying and Accessing Niche Social Networks

2.1 Use Search Engines and Forums

Many niche social networks don't receive widespread attention from the general public. As a result, they may not appear in mainstream app stores or social media feeds. Here are some ways to identify them:

Search Engines: Using targeted searches with keywords that define a niche can help uncover hidden networks or obscure platforms. For example, searching for "photo-sharing platforms for photographers" or "underground hacker forums" will lead to more specialized results than a general search for "social media."

Specialized Forums: Platforms like Reddit, Quora, or even specialized forum communities are excellent sources for discovering new niche networks. Subreddits such as r/IndieDev for game developers or r/Entrepreneur for business owners can often point to emerging platforms that cater to specific interests.

App Discovery Sites: Websites like ProductHunt or BetaList list new apps and social networks in their early stages. These sites can help OSINT analysts spot platforms before they gain significant traction.

2.2 Leverage Online Communities

Sometimes, niche networks aren't listed in obvious directories. Instead, they thrive within certain online communities:

- **Creator and Developer Platforms**: Websites like GitHub and Behance offer collaboration spaces for creators, coders, and designers. Monitoring these platforms can help track emerging trends in the tech and creative industries.
- **Alternative News and Activism Spaces**: Platforms like Mastodon (a decentralized social media platform) or Peertube (a decentralized video sharing platform) often attract more politically or ideologically motivated communities. Following conversations on these platforms can reveal early indications of social movements, political discourse, or grassroots campaigns.

2.3 Monitor Alternative Social Networks

Alternative social networks may not be as widely known but can offer valuable insights into fringe, underground, or niche activities. Examples of platforms that cater to specific interests include:

1. **Steemit**: A decentralized blogging platform focused on cryptocurrency and blockchain technology.
2. **Discord**: Originally for gamers, Discord now hosts communities on topics ranging from cryptocurrency to mental health to political movements.
3. **Substack**: A newsletter-based platform, Substack has grown in popularity for independent writers and thinkers, and many niche communities emerge through shared content.

Many of these platforms have less stringent content moderation, which can present both challenges and opportunities for OSINT analysts. Monitoring these spaces early can yield insights into emerging threats and underground movements.

3. Extracting Intelligence from Niche Social Networks

Once a niche platform has been identified, the next challenge is data collection. Given that many niche social media platforms don't have the extensive tools and APIs that large platforms do, OSINT analysts must employ creative methods to extract intelligence from these communities.

3.1 Manual Monitoring

Due to limited API access and stricter privacy settings, manual monitoring may be necessary for many niche social networks. This includes:

- **Reviewing posts and discussions**: Manually scan posts, comments, and threads to gather qualitative intelligence on topics, sentiments, or key figures.
- **Following key influencers**: Track influencers and leaders in the niche community to stay informed on relevant trends.
- **Observing member interactions**: Take note of how users engage with content (e.g., likes, shares, comments) and identify which topics or discussions generate the most engagement.

3.2 Scraping Tools for Data Collection

While niche networks may not offer APIs, there are still ways to gather data through web scraping. OSINT analysts can use tools like BeautifulSoup, Selenium, or Scrapy to automate the extraction of data from public-facing pages on these platforms. However, it's crucial to respect terms of service and ensure that scraping complies with the platform's rules.

3.3 Social Listening Tools

Some social listening tools can be set up to monitor keywords, hashtags, or mentions across various networks. Tools like Brandwatch, Mention, or Hootsuite allow users to set up customized search queries to track mentions of certain topics, terms, or events across social platforms, including niche communities.

Alerting: Many social listening tools provide real-time alerts, helping analysts stay up-to-date with breaking developments in niche spaces.

3.4 Data Correlation and Trend Analysis

Once data from niche platforms is collected, correlating it with data from larger social media platforms can yield a fuller picture. This cross-platform analysis can uncover hidden connections between smaller groups and mainstream media, as well as trends that may be poised for wider adoption.

For example, if a topic or hashtag is gaining traction in niche forums, analysts can track its adoption across larger networks like Twitter or Instagram. This allows investigators to trace how grassroots movements develop into larger phenomena.

4. Ethical Considerations in Monitoring Niche Social Media

Monitoring niche social media platforms presents both opportunities and ethical dilemmas. Since these platforms are often more specialized and less moderated than mainstream networks, analysts need to exercise caution in gathering data.

4.1 Consent and Privacy

Even on public platforms, users may expect a level of privacy or anonymity. Investigators must be careful not to invade users' privacy by sharing personal information or engaging in overly intrusive data collection practices.

4.2 Platform Terms of Service

Many niche platforms operate with terms of service that may prohibit data scraping or external analysis. OSINT analysts must familiarize themselves with these policies and ensure they are complying with ethical guidelines while gathering intelligence.

4.3 Mitigating Bias

Given that niche platforms often host specific groups with distinct views or interests, it's crucial for analysts to be mindful of potential bias in data collection. Over-representing certain subcultures or ideologies may skew findings, so balance is key when monitoring these spaces.

Niche social media networks may not always have the user base or visibility of mainstream platforms, but they are essential sources of early intelligence for OSINT analysts. These platforms offer insights into emerging trends, subcultures, and underground activities long before they gain traction in broader, more visible spaces. By monitoring these specialized networks, analysts can uncover valuable intelligence, spot early warnings of disinformation, and track the rise of new digital movements. However, to be effective, OSINT professionals must develop tailored strategies for finding, accessing, and analyzing data from these often-hidden corners of the internet.

7.6 Case Study: Using TikTok OSINT to Investigate Online Radicalization

TikTok has become one of the most influential social media platforms of the modern era, particularly among younger generations. Its video-centric design and algorithmic recommendation system allow users to quickly discover and engage with content that resonates with their interests. However, this same algorithmic amplification also means that harmful ideologies, including those associated with online radicalization, can spread rapidly. For OSINT analysts and investigators, TikTok represents a complex challenge: how to monitor and analyze a platform that is heavily curated and driven by algorithms designed to maximize engagement—often with dangerous consequences.

In this case study, we will explore how OSINT techniques can be employed to track and investigate the early signs of radicalization on TikTok. By examining how individuals or groups use TikTok to promote extremist content, we can learn how to better identify and respond to radicalization dynamics in a timely and effective manner.

1. The TikTok Environment: A Platform for Radicalization?

TikTok's short-form video format allows users to create engaging content with ease, resulting in a rapid proliferation of videos on a variety of topics. While the platform's core demographic is primarily young people, this also makes it a target for extremist groups looking to recruit or influence vulnerable individuals. The combination of trends, viral content, and algorithmic exposure makes TikTok fertile ground for both positive and negative influence.

Social media platforms, including TikTok, have become a preferred medium for online radicalization due to several key features:

- **Algorithmic recommendations**: TikTok's "For You" page curates content based on user interaction, increasing the likelihood that users will encounter more extreme or controversial content if they engage with similar videos.
- **Hashtags**: Hashtags play an essential role in TikTok's content discovery system. Extremist or radical groups may hijack trending hashtags to promote their agendas.
- **Peer pressure**: The platform's viral nature encourages users to follow trends or challenges, which can lead to groupthink or peer influence, potentially radicalizing young, impressionable individuals.

2. Identifying Red Flags of Radicalization on TikTok

In order to track and investigate online radicalization on TikTok, OSINT analysts must first understand the types of behaviors and content that could signal the early stages of radicalization. Some red flags may include:

- **Repetitive Exposure to Violent Ideologies**: Videos that glorify violence, depict extremism, or promote hate speech (even if masked under seemingly innocent content) are critical indicators.
- **Use of Specific Hashtags**: Extremist groups often use niche or obscure hashtags to spread their message under the radar. Examples could include hashtags like #PatriotMovement, #Jihad, or others associated with radical views.
- **Influencers with Extreme Views**: Certain TikTok influencers may subtly introduce extremist ideas into their content, appealing to their large follower base. These influencers often use humor, music, or other engaging formats to normalize extreme ideologies.
- **Content that Promotes Us vs. Them Mentalities**: One key marker of radicalization is content that fosters polarization—dividing people into "us" versus "them." For example, content that attacks specific groups based on religion, race, or nationality could signal a shift toward extremist thinking.

To investigate these patterns, OSINT investigators need to develop a strategy for tracking content, users, and networks that might be operating on the fringes of mainstream discourse.

3. Investigative Approach: Gathering OSINT from TikTok

3.1 Identifying Key Hashtags and Influencers

One of the most effective ways to begin an investigation into radicalization on TikTok is by monitoring specific hashtags and identifying extremist influencers. Here's a detailed approach:

- **Hashtag Monitoring**: Analysts can begin by identifying hashtags related to radical movements or extremist ideologies. Once these hashtags are found, investigators can search for all related content to track how they spread over time and which accounts or groups are involved.
- **Example**: A hashtag such as #RevolutionNow or #WhitePride could lead investigators to accounts promoting far-right ideologies.
- **Influencer Tracking**: Identifying influencers who may be promoting radical content is another critical step. These influencers often operate under the guise of

promoting alternative lifestyles, but their content may increasingly lean toward radical or divisive rhetoric.

Investigators can search for influencers whose posts regularly feature extreme political views, conspiracies, or violent rhetoric. They should also monitor the comment sections of these influencers to understand the kinds of engagement their content generates.

3.2 Social Network Analysis

Once influencers and hashtags are identified, OSINT investigators can track the relationships between users and how they spread radical content. Using tools like Gephi or Maltego, analysts can map the network of users interacting with or engaging with extremist content. This social network analysis can reveal clusters of individuals or groups that may be moving toward more radical beliefs.

- **Tracking interactions**: Looking at who follows whom, who shares content, and which accounts are engaging in radical conversations can help build a clearer picture of the ecosystem in which radicalization is taking place.

3.3 Monitoring the "For You" Page Algorithm

The "For You" page, TikTok's personalized content feed, is a key point of focus. OSINT analysts can monitor the kinds of videos that appear in this feed after engaging with certain content. For instance, if a user interacts with radical content, TikTok's algorithm may begin recommending more of the same type of material.

- **Automated Scraping**: While TikTok's API is somewhat limited in terms of raw data access, analysts can still use automated tools and scraping techniques to track the content that appears on the "For You" page over time. This helps in monitoring the spread of extremist ideologies and recognizing early signs of algorithmic amplification of dangerous content.

3.4 Reverse Image and Video Search

Some radical content may appear as memes, images, or edited videos. OSINT investigators can use reverse image search tools like Google Images or InVID to check if the same visuals appear across various TikTok videos or if they are part of a broader, coordinated disinformation campaign.

- **Video Footage Correlation**: In cases where TikTok videos feature sensitive or violent content (e.g., radical extremist actions or calls to violence), investigators can reverse search video clips to verify their origins and confirm their authenticity.

4. Case Study Analysis: Radicalization on TikTok

To illustrate the process, consider a hypothetical investigation into the rise of radical content linked to far-right ideologies on TikTok. The following steps could be taken by an OSINT analyst:

- **Initial Detection**: The analyst notices a growing presence of hashtags like #RedPill and #SaveOurCountry across various TikTok videos.
- **Tracking Content**: Upon examining these hashtags, the analyst identifies key influencers whose content predominantly contains political messages that subtly move from traditional political discourse to increasingly divisive, extremist rhetoric.
- **Network Mapping**: Using network analysis tools, the investigator tracks the interaction between these influencers and their followers. They discover that these accounts often share content linked to extremist groups, whether ideologically far-right or associated with white nationalism.
- **Monitoring the For You Page**: After engaging with one of these videos, the analyst's TikTok feed starts showing more videos with similarly extreme content. This provides insight into how algorithmic amplification might play a role in spreading radical views.
- **Collaboration with TikTok**: Finally, the analyst reports these findings to TikTok's content moderation team, requesting the platform take action to remove extremist content and prevent the further spread of these ideologies.

The investigation into online radicalization on TikTok requires a multifaceted approach, combining hashtag tracking, network analysis, algorithmic monitoring, and reverse image search techniques. Given TikTok's rapid growth and the viral nature of its content, this platform has become a key area of concern for OSINT professionals investigating extremism and online radicalization.

Through careful monitoring and analysis, OSINT analysts can help identify the early signs of radicalization on TikTok, track the evolution of dangerous ideologies, and intervene before they escalate into real-world violence or organized movements.

8. Social Media Metadata & Image Analysis

Every image, video, and post shared on social media carries hidden data that can provide crucial intelligence for OSINT investigations. Metadata embedded in media files can reveal timestamps, device details, and even geolocation coordinates, while reverse image searches and AI-powered analysis help track content origins and detect manipulation. This chapter explores the techniques and tools used to extract and analyze metadata, conduct facial recognition searches, and verify digital content authenticity. Mastering social media metadata and image analysis equips analysts with the ability to trace digital footprints, debunk misinformation, and uncover hidden insights from multimedia content.

8.1 Extracting Metadata from Photos & Videos on Social Media

In the digital age, photos and videos have become the primary mediums through which individuals share experiences, opinions, and personal moments. Social media platforms, such as Instagram, Facebook, and Twitter, have facilitated an unprecedented level of global connectivity. These platforms also host vast amounts of data in the form of images and videos, and often, this multimedia content contains more information than what is visible to the naked eye. This hidden information, known as metadata, can provide crucial insights into the time, location, device used, and even the modifications made to a photo or video.

For Open-Source Intelligence (OSINT) professionals, extracting metadata from social media content is a powerful investigative technique that can yield critical details about the origin and context of images or videos, as well as the identity of users. The process involves using a variety of tools and methodologies to extract, analyze, and interpret the metadata, allowing OSINT professionals to uncover hidden connections, validate information, and track the digital footprints of individuals or groups.

This chapter explores the key methods for extracting metadata from social media images and videos, the types of metadata typically embedded in these files, and the tools that can be used to extract and interpret this data for investigative purposes.

1. What is Metadata in Photos & Videos?

Metadata refers to the data embedded within a media file that provides information about the file itself. In the context of photos and videos shared on social media platforms, metadata can include a wide range of information such as:

Exif (Exchangeable Image File Format): A standard for storing metadata within image files, such as JPEG or TIFF. Exif data often includes:

- Date and time the photo was taken.
- Geolocation (GPS coordinates) where the photo was captured.
- Camera settings, including focal length, aperture, ISO level, and shutter speed.
- Device information, such as the make and model of the camera or smartphone.

IPTC (International Press Telecommunications Council): A metadata format used by professional photographers and news organizations. It can include details like the author, copyright, and caption of the image, as well as keywords related to the content.

XMP (Extensible Metadata Platform): A more flexible metadata format that supports both text-based and multimedia files, including images and videos. It allows for more detailed descriptive information and can track changes made to a file.

Video Metadata: Videos, like photos, also contain metadata, including information about:

- File type and size.
- Video codec and resolution.
- Frame rate and audio specifications.
- Creation date and editing software used.

Understanding and extracting metadata from social media photos and videos is essential because it can provide clues about where and when content was created, as well as whether it has been tampered with or edited.

2. Why Extract Metadata from Social Media Photos & Videos?

There are several reasons why extracting metadata from social media photos and videos is critical for OSINT investigations:

Verification: Metadata can help verify the authenticity of content. For example, if a video is claimed to have been filmed in a particular location at a specific time, but the metadata shows a different location or time, it raises questions about the video's credibility.

Geolocation: Many photos and videos contain GPS coordinates, which can be crucial for identifying where an image or video was taken. This can be useful in investigations related to tracking movements, locating individuals, or verifying claims of events (e.g., protests, conflicts, or natural disasters).

Temporal Analysis: By extracting timestamps and file creation dates, OSINT professionals can verify the chronology of events, assess the timeline of a suspect's activities, or establish connections between different pieces of content.

Device Identification: Extracting device-specific metadata can help identify the type of equipment used to capture the media. For instance, if a certain smartphone model is associated with a series of photos, it may help link a set of images to a specific individual or group.

Detecting Tampering: Metadata can indicate whether a photo or video has been edited, altered, or manipulated in any way. For instance, metadata may reveal discrepancies in the software used to modify a file, or it may show that a photo has been cropped or resized after being taken.

3. How to Extract Metadata from Social Media Photos & Videos

Extracting metadata from social media platforms is not always straightforward due to platform restrictions, privacy settings, and file compression techniques that may strip or alter metadata. However, several methods and tools can be used to extract and analyze metadata:

3.1 Downloading the Raw Image or Video

To get accurate metadata, OSINT professionals must first ensure that they are working with the raw file and not a compressed or resized version. Social media platforms often compress images and videos, which may result in the loss of metadata. Here are a few ways to obtain the raw file:

- **Right-clicking and downloading**: On platforms like Instagram or Twitter, right-clicking an image and selecting "Save As" can sometimes yield a download of the raw file, although the metadata may still be stripped by the platform's compression algorithms.
- **Using browser extensions**: Certain extensions, such as Image Downloader for Chrome, can allow you to download media files directly from a webpage.

- **Third-party tools**: Some platforms like Facebook or Twitter allow users to request a copy of their data, which might include the raw image or video files.

3.2 Extracting Exif and IPTC Data

Once the raw media is downloaded, OSINT professionals can extract Exif and IPTC data using a variety of tools:

- **ExifTool**: A powerful and widely used command-line tool for reading, writing, and editing metadata in image, audio, and video files. ExifTool can display all metadata embedded in a file and is capable of handling complex formats.
- **Online Metadata Viewers**: Several websites, such as Get-Metadata.com or Metapicz, allow users to upload images and extract Exif data directly. These tools are easy to use and provide a quick overview of metadata.

3.3 Analyzing Video Metadata

Videos, being more complex than photos, require different tools for metadata extraction. Some video metadata analysis tools include:

- **MediaInfo**: A free, open-source tool that displays detailed information about video files, including codec, resolution, frame rate, and timestamp.
- **FFmpeg**: A command-line tool that can be used to extract metadata from video files, as well as perform various video processing tasks.

3.4 Reverse Image Search for Additional Context

In addition to extracting metadata from photos and videos, OSINT professionals can use reverse image search tools to find other instances of the same media across the web. This can help identify the origins of an image or video and verify if it has been used elsewhere, altered, or manipulated.

- **Google Images**: By uploading a photo or providing an image URL, Google's reverse image search can return similar images from across the web, helping track where a photo has been shared or reposted.
- **TinEye**: Another reverse image search engine that is specifically designed to identify exact matches of an image across the internet, helping to confirm whether an image is being used authentically or in misleading contexts.

4. Limitations of Metadata Extraction on Social Media

While extracting metadata is a valuable technique, it comes with its limitations:

- **Platform Limitations**: Some social media platforms, such as Instagram, deliberately strip away metadata when media is uploaded to prevent users from accessing sensitive information. This means that users may only see the image or video itself, with no embedded metadata available.
- **Data Manipulation**: Users can edit or remove metadata from their own photos or videos using software like Adobe Photoshop or specialized metadata editing tools. This makes it difficult to rely solely on metadata to verify authenticity.
- **Privacy Settings**: Some users may configure their privacy settings to restrict who can access or download their content, further limiting the ability to extract metadata.

Extracting metadata from photos and videos on social media platforms is a powerful tool in the OSINT investigator's toolkit. By providing critical details about the time, location, and authenticity of digital media, metadata can help investigators confirm the validity of claims, track individuals or groups, and detect potential disinformation. However, given the complexities of social media platforms, including platform-specific restrictions and user-driven data manipulation, OSINT professionals must use a variety of tools and techniques to ensure that the data they are extracting is both complete and accurate.

By staying vigilant and leveraging available tools, investigators can unlock the hidden insights embedded in social media media files, providing valuable evidence and context for ongoing investigations.

8.2 Using Reverse Image Search for OSINT Investigations

In the digital age, images are a primary form of communication, sharing information rapidly across social media, news platforms, and websites. However, images can be easily manipulated, stolen, or misattributed. This poses a challenge for those using Open Source Intelligence (OSINT) to verify the authenticity of visual content. Reverse image search has emerged as a critical tool in OSINT investigations, enabling analysts to trace the origins of images, find where they've been used elsewhere, and detect potential instances of misinformation or manipulation.

Reverse image search allows investigators to submit an image to a search engine and find out where it has appeared on the internet. By comparing the uploaded image against a vast database of indexed images, these tools can provide links to other web pages or platforms where the image has been published. This feature is invaluable for OSINT professionals seeking to verify the authenticity of content, track the distribution of an image, or connect visual clues across various sources.

This chapter delves into the fundamentals of reverse image search, how it can be applied to OSINT investigations, and how analysts can effectively utilize this technique to uncover critical insights.

1. What is Reverse Image Search?

Reverse image search is the process of searching for information related to an image by using the image itself, rather than relying on a text-based search query. It works by analyzing an image's unique features, such as its shape, color, and content, and comparing these features to a database of indexed images available on the internet.

Reverse image search engines typically generate results based on the visual characteristics of the uploaded image. These results can include:

- Exact matches of the image on other websites.
- Similar images, which may be used in a different context or edited form.
- Contextual information, including captions, keywords, and other metadata associated with the image.

The goal is to identify the origins of the image, track its usage across the web, and uncover any associated metadata that can provide further context about the image's authenticity or relevance.

2. How Reverse Image Search Works

When a user submits an image to a reverse image search engine, the tool works by analyzing various visual features of the image. These features might include:

- **Color schemes**: Identifying the primary colors or dominant shades.
- **Shapes and patterns**: Detecting key structural elements, such as faces, objects, or scenes.
- **Texture and resolution**: Comparing the image's resolution or sharpness to those stored in the search engine's index.
- **File characteristics**: Comparing file names, metadata, and even content hashing techniques to find matches.

Once the image's visual characteristics are analyzed, the search engine compares the image against a database of indexed images to generate results. These results can provide valuable information about where the image first appeared or how it has been used across various platforms, providing an opportunity to verify the image's authenticity or uncover additional details.

3. Key Reverse Image Search Tools for OSINT Investigations

There are several popular reverse image search tools available that can aid OSINT professionals in their investigations:

3.1 Google Reverse Image Search

Google Images is one of the most widely used and reliable tools for reverse image search. It allows users to upload an image or input an image URL to find similar or identical images across the web.

How to use:

- Visit Google Images (images.google.com).
- Click on the camera icon in the search bar to upload an image or paste the image URL.
- Google will return a list of search results where the image or similar images have appeared.

Advantages:

- Google's vast index provides an extensive range of results from websites, social media platforms, and news sources.
- It can detect images even if they have been edited or cropped.
- Provides links to image sources, often including context such as captions, keywords, and surrounding text.

3.2 TinEye

TinEye is another popular reverse image search engine designed specifically for image identification. Unlike Google, which prioritizes finding visually similar images, TinEye focuses on finding exact matches and tracks the image's provenance over time.

How to use:

- Visit TinEye (tineye.com).
- Upload an image or provide the image's URL.
- TinEye will return results that show where the image has been found on the internet, including timestamps of when it was indexed.

Advantages:

- TinEye has a unique feature called "Image Tracking," which helps users find when an image first appeared online and track its usage.
- Excellent for identifying exact matches and uncovering instances of image misuse or manipulation.
- Filters available to refine results by date, image size, and domain.

3.3 Yandex Reverse Image Search

Yandex is a Russian search engine that also offers an effective reverse image search tool. Its results are often different from Google or TinEye due to Yandex's unique image indexing algorithms and focus on Eastern Europe and Russia-based websites.

How to use:

- Visit Yandex Images (yandex.com/images).
- Upload an image or paste an image URL.
- Yandex will return results showing where the image appears across the internet.

Advantages:

- Yandex provides access to a wide range of Russian and Eastern European websites, making it a useful tool for finding region-specific content.
- It also offers useful metadata details about the image, such as the site where the image is hosted.

3.4 Image Raider

Image Raider is another reverse image search tool that aggregates results from Google, TinEye, and Yandex, providing a comprehensive overview of where an image has appeared online.

How to use:

- Visit Image Raider (imageraider.com).
- Upload an image or paste the URL.
- Image Raider will aggregate results from multiple search engines, providing a more diverse set of results.

Advantages:

- Searches multiple search engines simultaneously for more thorough results.
- Allows users to track multiple images at once, making it useful for bulk image searches.

4. Practical Applications of Reverse Image Search in OSINT Investigations

Reverse image search is a versatile tool that can be applied in various OSINT scenarios:

4.1 Verifying Image Authenticity

One of the primary uses of reverse image search is to verify whether an image is authentic or if it has been misused or altered. For example, in a disinformation investigation, reverse image search can help determine if a specific image has been shared out of context or edited to mislead the audience. By tracing the origins of the image, analysts can confirm its validity and uncover the truth behind the visual content.

4.2 Tracking the Spread of Disinformation

Images are often used in disinformation campaigns, especially when manipulated to support misleading narratives. Reverse image search can be used to track the spread of specific images, determining where and how they've been shared, and assessing whether they have been altered to fit a particular agenda. This is especially important when investigating fake news, conspiracy theories, or online propaganda.

4.3 Identifying Source Locations

For images tied to specific events, reverse image search can help investigators pinpoint the location where an image was originally taken. By tracking similar images across news platforms, social media, or official reports, analysts can cross-reference metadata or timestamps to determine the location or time frame of an image's creation.

4.4 Investigating Potential Cybercrimes

In the case of cybercrime investigations, reverse image search can be helpful in tracking down the origin of specific images used in criminal activities, such as child exploitation, online harassment, or identity theft. By identifying where an image first appeared, OSINT professionals can work to uncover the identity of individuals involved in illicit activities or locate victims.

4.5 Reconstructing Events in Crisis Situations

In crisis or conflict zones, reverse image search can assist investigators in reconstructing events based on the visual evidence available. By tracing the source of images shared in real-time, analysts can assess the authenticity of videos and photos from the scene and provide real-time verification for news organizations or human rights organizations.

5. Limitations of Reverse Image Search

While reverse image search is a powerful tool, it does have limitations:

- **Altered or Edited Images**: Reverse image search engines may struggle to identify images that have been significantly edited, cropped, or altered.
- **Limited Coverage**: Not all images available on the internet are indexed by reverse image search engines, especially images shared on private platforms or those stored behind paywalls.
- **File Type Restrictions**: Some tools may have trouble processing certain file types, particularly non-standard or proprietary formats.

Reverse image search is an indispensable tool for OSINT professionals, allowing them to track the origins of images, uncover disinformation, verify the authenticity of media, and gather valuable contextual information. By using various search engines like Google, TinEye, and Yandex, OSINT investigators can conduct thorough analyses of visual content and gather critical evidence for their investigations.

However, it's important for investigators to be aware of the limitations of reverse image search and to complement it with other investigative methods to ensure a more comprehensive analysis.

8.3 Identifying Edited & AI-Generated Social Media Content

In the digital age, social media platforms are inundated with content—images, videos, and text—that can be easily altered or artificially generated. The rapid rise of advanced editing tools and artificial intelligence (AI) technologies, like deep learning algorithms and generative adversarial networks (GANs), has made it increasingly difficult to differentiate between genuine and manipulated content. This poses a significant challenge for Open Source Intelligence (OSINT) investigators who rely on the authenticity of digital media for their analysis.

In this chapter, we'll explore how to identify edited and AI-generated content on social media, the tools and techniques available to spot such alterations, and the implications of such content for OSINT investigations. We'll discuss practical strategies for detecting image manipulation, deepfakes, and other forms of synthetic media, providing guidance for investigators on how to assess the credibility of social media content.

1. Understanding Edited Content

Edited content refers to any media—such as images, videos, or text—that has been modified after its original creation. This can include:

- Basic edits, such as cropping, resizing, or adjusting brightness and contrast.
- Advanced edits, like object removal, facial modifications, or altering background scenes.
- Text manipulation, including the alteration of captions, messages, or metadata.

In some cases, the goal of editing is innocuous, such as improving the aesthetic quality of a photo. However, in many cases, edited content is used to mislead, deceive, or propagate misinformation. In OSINT investigations, detecting edits is critical for verifying the authenticity of digital content.

Common Signs of Edited Content

Detecting edited content can be challenging, but there are a few common indicators that can be identified with careful analysis:

- **Inconsistent lighting and shadows**: Edited content often displays lighting that doesn't match across different areas of the image. If the shadows or light sources seem inconsistent, the image might have been manipulated.
- **Pixelation or blurring**: Editing can leave pixelation or blurring around the areas that have been modified, as the algorithm struggles to perfectly blend the new elements with the original.

- **Irregularities in the background**: When an object is removed or added to an image, the background may look odd, such as missing patterns, distorted textures, or odd-shaped objects that don't match the rest of the scene.
- **Noise or distortion**: Edits often leave small discrepancies in the image, such as odd color gradients or unusual noise, particularly when compressed for sharing on social media.

2. Identifying AI-Generated Content

With the advent of AI technologies, the creation of synthetic content—particularly AI-generated images, videos, and audio— has become more prevalent. AI-generated media can often be indistinguishable from authentic content, making it a challenge for OSINT investigators to verify the authenticity of digital evidence.

Types of AI-Generated Content

Deepfakes: These are synthetic media, primarily videos, where an AI algorithm is used to replace a person's face or voice with that of another individual. Deepfakes can be particularly dangerous because they can be used to manipulate public opinion, spread disinformation, or damage reputations.

Generative Adversarial Networks (GANs): GANs are machine learning systems used to generate new content, including realistic images, audio, and videos. They are often used in the creation of highly realistic yet fabricated media. GANs can generate images of people, animals, and objects that look entirely real but are completely fake.

Text-to-Image/Video AI Tools: AI tools such as OpenAI's DALL-E, or others like MidJourney, allow users to create highly detailed images based on simple text prompts. While this is a fun and creative tool, it can also be used to generate fake content that looks convincingly real.

AI-Generated Audio & Speech: AI tools like text-to-speech models can create convincing, human-like audio, including realistic mimicry of someone's voice. These can be used to fabricate phone calls or videos to impersonate someone.

3. Tools and Techniques to Identify Edited & AI-Generated Content

Several tools and techniques can help investigators identify when content has been edited or generated by AI. These tools range from simple image analysis software to advanced deepfake detection systems.

3.1 Image Forensics Tools

FotoForensics: FotoForensics is an image analysis tool that uses Error Level Analysis (ELA) to detect edits in images. ELA highlights areas of an image that have been altered, as modified areas will often have different error levels compared to the rest of the image. This is a useful method for spotting manipulated pixels in an image.

Ghiro: Ghiro is an open-source tool designed for image forensics that can detect various types of manipulation, including metadata analysis, which helps determine the authenticity of an image by examining its file structure and history.

JPEGsnoop: JPEGsnoop is a JPEG image analysis tool that examines the structure and encoding of image files. It helps identify whether an image has been compressed or altered, including checking if any edits were made to the image post-capture.

Image Edited Detection via Machine Learning: Researchers and companies are increasingly using machine learning algorithms to identify edited images by detecting inconsistencies in pixels or shadows. These tools are trained to spot the tell-tale signs of common photo editing software, such as Adobe Photoshop or GIMP.

3.2 Deepfake Detection Tools

Deepware Scanner: This tool is designed to detect deepfake videos by analyzing the inconsistencies between facial expressions and audio. It scans the video for traces of synthetic alterations in the audio or visual components.

Microsoft Video Authenticator: Developed by Microsoft, this tool analyzes video content for signs of manipulation. It looks for artifacts that are commonly associated with AI-generated content, such as unnatural blinking, facial inconsistencies, or mismatched lighting.

FaceForensics++: This tool uses deep learning to detect manipulated or synthetic faces in video content. It helps analysts identify signs of deepfake technology that has been used to modify a person's face or body in video footage.

TruePic: TruePic provides a platform for verifying visual media, including detecting AI-manipulated images and videos. It ensures the integrity of visual content by focusing on image authentication and providing metadata analysis.

3.3 Metadata & Contextual Analysis

Often, the metadata of an image or video can provide critical information about whether it has been edited or generated by AI. Metadata includes data such as:

- File creation date.
- Device used to capture the content.
- Location data (GPS information for images and videos taken on smartphones).
- Editing software used.

For AI-generated content, metadata can sometimes reveal the platform or tool used to create it, such as OpenAI's DALL-E or DeepDream. By conducting thorough metadata analysis, OSINT professionals can often detect whether content is authentic or AI-generated.

In some cases, analyzing the context in which the image appears can also help identify edits or synthetic content. If an image appears to be too perfect or staged in a manner that seems out of place, it may raise red flags. Furthermore, checking for discrepancies in the background or emotions expressed by subjects in AI-generated images can indicate that the content was artificially created.

4. The Implications of Edited & AI-Generated Content for OSINT Investigations

The ability to create convincing edited and AI-generated content raises several important challenges for OSINT investigators:

Verification challenges: Investigators must be vigilant when working with visual content, as manipulated media can be used to mislead or misrepresent the truth. The rise of deepfakes, for example, has serious implications for evidence integrity in legal and criminal investigations.

Disinformation & Misinformation: Edited and AI-generated media can be weaponized for propaganda, disinformation campaigns, or to create fake news. OSINT investigators need to be prepared to confront these challenges head-on, especially when analyzing social media content during crises, elections, or political events.

Trust Issues: The widespread availability of tools to alter or generate media has eroded public trust in digital content. As the line between genuine and fabricated content becomes increasingly blurred, OSINT analysts play a crucial role in restoring credibility to digital media and ensuring accurate information is used in investigative processes.

As AI-generated and edited content becomes more sophisticated, the ability to detect these manipulations becomes a critical skill for OSINT investigators. By leveraging tools like image forensics, deepfake detection software, and metadata analysis, analysts can uncover whether the content they are investigating is authentic or artificially created.

Given the growing impact of synthetic media on public discourse, national security, and personal reputations, it is essential that OSINT professionals develop a strong understanding of how to identify and address AI-generated content in their investigations. With vigilance and the right tools, it is possible to separate fact from fiction in the digital world.

8.4 How Location & Device Data Can Reveal Hidden Information

In an era of pervasive connectivity, social media users often share more information than they realize. While much of this data seems innocuous on the surface, it can reveal hidden insights that are invaluable to Open Source Intelligence (OSINT) investigators. One of the most crucial pieces of information embedded in social media content is location and device data. These seemingly subtle details—ranging from GPS coordinates to device identifiers—can offer a treasure trove of insights about the people behind the posts and their activities.

In this chapter, we'll explore how location and device data embedded in social media content can be used in OSINT investigations. We will discuss the methods used to extract this data, the challenges involved in tracking it, and the ethical considerations that come into play when analyzing such information. Whether you are investigating criminal activity, verifying alibis, or uncovering patterns of behavior, location and device data offer significant intelligence opportunities.

1. Understanding Location Data on Social Media

Social media platforms are designed to encourage users to share personal experiences, and one of the easiest ways to do so is by including their location. Whether it's a photo with geotagging, a video showing a specific landmark, or even a status update mentioning a particular city or neighborhood, location data provides clues that can help OSINT investigators pinpoint where and when something took place.

Types of Location Data

Geotags: Most smartphones and social media platforms automatically record the geographic coordinates (latitude and longitude) of an image or video when it is posted, commonly referred to as geotags. These geotags can be used to determine the exact location of where a piece of media was captured. Geotagging is most commonly associated with photos and videos uploaded to platforms like Instagram, Facebook, and Twitter.

Check-ins: Many social media users voluntarily "check-in" to locations, from restaurants to airports, which provides an additional layer of location data. Facebook, for example, has a "check-in" feature where users can announce they are at specific locations, offering both the physical address and a timestamp.

Contextual Mentions: Even if geotags are disabled, users may mention locations in the text accompanying their posts. For example, a tweet about attending a concert in New York City provides the investigator with valuable information, even if the photo or video does not include a geotag.

Location-based Ads & Services: Social media platforms often use the device's GPS to push location-specific advertisements or services. This can also provide intelligence for tracking a user's whereabouts or movement patterns.

How to Extract Location Data

Geotagging Analysis: The first and most obvious way to extract location data is by looking at geotags. Investigators can cross-reference these coordinates with maps to pinpoint the exact location of where a photo or video was taken. Tools like Google Maps or OpenStreetMap are essential for confirming the location of geotagged media.

Metadata Examination: Many social media platforms strip geotagging data when content is uploaded. However, the metadata embedded in the file—often called EXIF (Exchangeable Image File Format)—may still contain GPS coordinates. Investigators can use tools like ExifTool or PhotoME to extract this metadata.

Third-Party Tools: There are also third-party platforms like Foursquare, Swarm, or Glympse, where users might share their locations. Cross-referencing content on these platforms can help OSINT professionals build a more complete picture of the subject's activities.

2. Device Data: A Goldmine for Investigations

The data associated with the devices used to create or access social media content provides additional layers of intelligence. Device data can include information about the operating system, device type, IP address, and the exact time a post was uploaded, which can help verify the legitimacy of the information or reveal hidden details about the user's activities.

Key Types of Device Data

Device Identifiers: Devices, such as smartphones or computers, often generate unique identifiers. In the case of mobile phones, this could be the IMEI number (International Mobile Equipment Identity) or IP addresses that reveal the location or network from which the device is operating. Although social media platforms do not directly share this information, it may be available from other sources, such as network traffic logs or public data breaches.

Operating System & App Metadata: Social media platforms often store data about the operating system and the version of the application used to post content. By analyzing the metadata of an image or video, an investigator can determine whether it was taken with an iPhone or Android device, which app was used to post it, and even the model of the phone or device used.

Device Location Tracking: Most social media apps have the ability to track users' locations over time. Investigators can use location history or timeline features provided by some platforms, such as Google Maps, to see where and when a device has been. For example, Google's Location History feature can provide a detailed map of a person's travels, pinpointing their exact routes and places they visited over time.

IP Address Data: IP addresses tied to device use can also reveal key location-based insights. While an IP address can be masked through VPNs or proxy servers, in certain cases, it can still offer a relatively accurate indication of the user's general geographic region or even specific cities or neighborhoods.

How to Extract Device Data

Social Media APIs: Many social media platforms provide APIs (application programming interfaces) that can be used to extract certain metadata from user profiles, including device information. For example, Twitter's API can be used to access data about a user's tweets and the devices used to post them.

Metadata Extraction Tools: Tools like ExifTool, PhotoRec, or FicTrack can help investigators access and analyze metadata from images, videos, or documents. These tools can reveal information about the device model, operating system, and even the editing software used to alter the media.

IP Geolocation Services: To trace IP addresses back to geographic locations, investigators can use IP geolocation services like ipstack or MaxMind. These tools provide a geolocation map that can be used to pinpoint the physical location from which content was posted, offering key insights into a target's movements and activities.

3. Leveraging Location & Device Data in OSINT Investigations

Once extracted, location and device data can be instrumental in piecing together an individual's behavior, verifying alibis, uncovering hidden relationships, and tracking a suspect's movements. Here are some practical uses of this data:

Verifying Alibis & Timelines

- **Location verification**: By cross-referencing the time and location data from social media posts with official records or witness testimony, investigators can confirm whether a person's alibi is truthful.
- **Device and timestamp analysis**: The timestamp data from social media posts, combined with the device used, can provide critical insight into whether a subject was in a specific location at a specific time, corroborating or disputing claims made by a suspect.

Tracking Movement Patterns

- **Movement over time**: By analyzing multiple posts over a period of time, OSINT investigators can build a timeline of a subject's movements and track patterns that might reveal key information, such as regular visits to certain locations or participation in specific events.

Cross-Referencing Data from Multiple Sources

- **Combining location & device data**: Cross-referencing data extracted from different social media platforms and external sources, such as Google Timeline or Foursquare, can help provide a more comprehensive view of a target's behavior. This can help expose inconsistencies or contradictions in a subject's story.

4. Ethical Considerations in Using Location & Device Data

While location and device data can be powerful tools for investigators, they also raise important ethical and legal concerns. The use of such data must be balanced with respect for privacy and data protection laws. Here are a few key ethical issues to consider:

Consent & Privacy: Investigators must ensure that they are not infringing on the privacy of individuals by using location data without their consent. It's crucial to respect the privacy rights of users, especially in cases where the data could be obtained without their knowledge (such as from device metadata).

Data Manipulation: Data can be falsified or manipulated, especially if a subject is aware of their digital footprint being tracked. OSINT investigators should always verify location and device data through multiple sources before drawing conclusions.

Legal Boundaries: Investigators must be aware of the legal implications of tracking someone's location or device. Depending on the jurisdiction, certain types of tracking may require a warrant or permission.

Location and device data are powerful tools in the arsenal of an OSINT investigator. By extracting, analyzing, and cross-referencing this data, investigators can uncover hidden details about a subject's movements, behaviors, and associations. However, this must be done with a careful consideration of ethical guidelines and legal boundaries to ensure that the privacy rights of individuals are respected. As the digital world evolves, these methods will continue to play an increasingly critical role in OSINT investigations.

8.5 Tools & Techniques for Analyzing Social Media Images

Images are an essential part of social media, offering a visual narrative to the stories and events people share online. They often reveal more than meets the eye, containing valuable information that can aid Open Source Intelligence (OSINT) investigations. Whether it's analyzing a photograph to track a suspect's movements, uncovering hidden details embedded in image metadata, or identifying clues hidden within the image itself, social media images provide a rich source of intelligence.

This chapter will explore the tools and techniques available for analyzing social media images. From extracting metadata to performing reverse image searches and identifying manipulated or AI-generated content, we'll cover how investigators can leverage these technologies to uncover the truth behind the visuals.

1. Image Metadata: Extracting Valuable Information

One of the most important steps in analyzing social media images is to first examine the metadata embedded in the image file itself. Metadata can provide crucial information about the image, such as the camera model, date and time of capture, and even geographic coordinates.

Key Metadata Information:

EXIF Data: EXIF (Exchangeable Image File Format) data contains embedded metadata within image files. This includes information about the camera settings (e.g., aperture, exposure), device model, and even location (if geotagging is enabled). By extracting EXIF data, investigators can identify the device used to capture the image, verify when and where the photo was taken, and more.

IPTC & XMP: In addition to EXIF, images may contain IPTC (International Press Telecommunications Council) and XMP (Extensible Metadata Platform) metadata. These formats contain additional information such as image descriptions, copyright information, and author details, which can be useful in identifying the creator or origin of the image.

How to Extract Metadata:

- **ExifTool**: One of the most widely used tools for analyzing image metadata is ExifTool, a powerful and free program that allows investigators to extract EXIF, IPTC, and XMP data from images. It provides detailed information about the image file, including GPS coordinates if geotagging is enabled.
- **Fotoforensics**: Another useful tool for extracting and analyzing metadata is Fotoforensics, which can show not only metadata but also provide an analysis of image authenticity.

2. Reverse Image Search: Finding the Source

One of the most effective techniques for identifying the origin or previous usage of an image is conducting a reverse image search. This technique involves searching the web for instances where the same or similar images have been used, which can provide crucial context, such as where the image was posted, whether it has been previously associated with a particular event, or if it has been used in misleading contexts.

Popular Reverse Image Search Tools:

- **Google Images**: Google's reverse image search is one of the most commonly used tools. Users can upload an image or input an image URL to find matching or similar images on the internet. This tool is essential for tracing the image's origins, finding earlier versions of an image, and uncovering related content that might not be immediately visible.
- **TinEye**: TinEye is a dedicated reverse image search engine that specializes in finding exact or similar matches across the web. TinEye offers powerful features, such as filtering results based on the oldest match or tracking images across the internet over time.
- **Bing Visual Search**: Bing offers a reverse image search function similar to Google Images. It can provide alternative sources of the image, along with other websites that have used the image.

How Reverse Image Search Helps in OSINT Investigations:

- **Verifying Image Authenticity**: By checking the history of an image, an investigator can determine if the image has been used previously and in what context. This helps establish whether an image has been manipulated or falsely attributed to a particular event.
- **Tracing the Origin**: A reverse image search can also uncover the first time an image was published online, helping investigators trace back to the original source, whether it's a news organization, a social media account, or a content creator.
- **Spotting Disinformation**: Reverse image searches can identify when and where an image has been reused or misattributed, helping expose misinformation or fake news.

3. Image Manipulation Detection: Identifying Fakes and Alterations

In an era where image manipulation is increasingly accessible through various apps and tools, detecting altered or AI-generated images has become a critical part of OSINT investigations. Investigators must be able to spot inconsistencies that might indicate that an image has been doctored or is not authentic.

Methods to Identify Manipulated Images:

Error Level Analysis (ELA): Error Level Analysis (ELA) is a technique used to detect areas of an image that have been altered or edited. By analyzing the compression level of different parts of the image, ELA can highlight sections that have been digitally modified, such as areas where new content has been inserted.

Pixel-Level Analysis: Pixel-level analysis allows investigators to zoom in on an image and examine the pixels for signs of tampering. For example, mismatched lighting, sharp edges, or inconsistent shadows may suggest that parts of an image were edited or artificially added.

Metadata Inconsistencies: As mentioned earlier, metadata embedded in an image can provide valuable clues about whether an image has been edited. For example, if the metadata reveals that the image was edited at a time different from the time the photo was taken, it may suggest manipulation.

AI-Generated Image Detection:

As AI-driven tools for image generation (such as Deepfakes) become more sophisticated, detecting synthetic or AI-generated images can be a challenge. AI images often have subtle, hard-to-detect errors, such as:

- Inconsistent lighting and shadows.
- Distorted facial features or unnatural expressions.
- Unusual or irregular backgrounds.

To spot AI-generated images, investigators can use AI-detection software like Deepware Scanner or Sensity AI, which are designed to recognize synthetic images.

4. Social Media Tools for Image Analysis

Many social media platforms have built-in image analysis and recognition tools that can help investigators identify objects, faces, and even text within images.

Platform-Specific Tools:

- **Facebook & Instagram**: Both Facebook and Instagram employ image recognition algorithms to automatically tag people and objects within photos. OSINT investigators can use these platforms to search for image tags and identify individuals or items that are present in an image.
- **Google Lens**: Google Lens is an AI-based image recognition tool that can scan photos and provide additional context about them. This includes identifying

objects, text, landmarks, and even similar images, which can be useful when trying to identify locations or products in a photo.

- **Amazon Rekognition**: Amazon offers Rekognition, a machine learning-based tool that can analyze images and videos to detect objects, people, text, scenes, and activities. This tool is particularly helpful for identifying key elements in an image that may not be immediately visible.

5. Image Forensics: Examining Source & Authenticity

Forensic tools go beyond just analyzing metadata and performing reverse searches—they provide comprehensive reports on image authenticity, identifying discrepancies and areas of interest that suggest an image might not be genuine.

Key Forensic Tools:

- **FotoForensics**: FotoForensics provides a detailed forensic analysis of an image's authenticity, including tools like ELA, JPEG compression, and residual noise detection, all of which can help identify signs of manipulation or editing.
- **Image Edited?:** This simple tool scans images for traces of edits, offering visual indicators of altered sections and even predicting the likelihood of tampering.

The analysis of social media images is an essential skill for OSINT investigators, offering valuable insights into the subject, context, and authenticity of visual content. Through a combination of metadata extraction, reverse image searching, manipulation detection, and forensic analysis, investigators can unravel the truth behind the images circulating online.

By understanding the tools and techniques available for image analysis, OSINT practitioners can significantly improve their ability to investigate social media content, track digital footprints, and expose deception or disinformation in the digital age.

8.6 Case Study: Finding a Missing Person Using Image Metadata

In Open Source Intelligence (OSINT) investigations, image metadata can be a powerful tool for tracing the location and context of images posted on social media platforms. One compelling example of how image metadata can aid in solving a real-world case is the investigation into a missing person, where social media imagery played a key role in locating the individual. This case study highlights the importance of using image metadata, specifically geolocation data embedded within photographs, to uncover crucial information that led to the discovery of a missing person.

Background of the Case

In 2023, a young woman, Sarah Williams, went missing after attending a concert in a major city. Her disappearance sparked widespread media attention, and her family was desperate for any leads that might help locate her. After Sarah's disappearance, investigators, family members, and volunteers began scouring social media platforms for any signs of her whereabouts.

While the police were initially focused on traditional investigative methods, a breakthrough came when a photo of Sarah, posted on her personal Instagram account a day before her disappearance, was located by a concerned family member. The image showed Sarah at the concert venue, but what stood out was the metadata embedded within the photo. The key to cracking the case lay in understanding and analyzing this metadata.

Extracting Metadata from the Image

The first step was to extract the metadata from the photo posted by Sarah on Instagram. Investigators, working with digital forensics experts, used tools like ExifTool to analyze the image's embedded EXIF (Exchangeable Image File Format) data.

Key Metadata Found:

Geolocation (GPS Coordinates): The most crucial piece of data found in the metadata was the geolocation tag embedded in the image. The photo had been taken using a smartphone with GPS enabled, which captured the coordinates of Sarah's exact location when the photo was taken. The GPS coordinates pointed to a park located several miles from the concert venue.

Timestamp: The EXIF data also included the exact timestamp of when the photo was taken, providing an important time reference. This timestamp was a day before her disappearance and helped narrow down the time frame for when Sarah was last seen.

Device Information: The metadata indicated that the photo was taken using an iPhone, providing additional insights into the type of device Sarah was using and allowing investigators to cross-reference the information with her other digital activities.

Tools Used:

- **ExifTool**: This software was used to extract all available metadata, including GPS coordinates, time stamps, and device details.
- **Google Maps**: Once the GPS coordinates were identified, the investigators used Google Maps to pinpoint the exact location of the park where the photo had been taken.

Analyzing the Geolocation Data

Using the GPS coordinates extracted from the image, the investigators mapped the location and discovered that the park was near a secluded area on the outskirts of the city, a place Sarah had not previously mentioned visiting. The area was known for being quiet and sparsely populated, making it an unlikely location for someone to casually visit unless they were specifically familiar with it.

The geolocation data not only pointed to the park as the last place Sarah had been, but it also narrowed down the potential areas where she could have gone afterward. Investigators started focusing on this area for further searches.

Cross-Referencing with Other Social Media Posts

Once the geolocation of the park was identified, investigators looked at other social media accounts that Sarah may have used and cross-referenced them with photos and posts from the same timeframe. One of her friends had shared an image on Facebook from a nearby café, taken just hours before Sarah went missing, providing a potential trail of movement from the concert venue to the park.

The Facebook photo also contained metadata revealing its location, which helped confirm that Sarah had been in the park at the time her photo was taken. This added another layer of validation to the geolocation data.

Investigating the Surrounding Area

With the park now being a central focal point, investigators expanded their search to include nearby surveillance footage, witness testimonies, and local businesses. They soon found a surveillance camera near the park's entrance that had captured footage of a woman who matched Sarah's description, walking alone at the time indicated by the timestamp in the metadata.

This footage helped corroborate the metadata findings, providing additional evidence that Sarah had indeed been at that location. However, the video footage did not show where she went after entering the park.

Reaching Out to the Public: Social Media Crowdsourcing

To further investigate Sarah's whereabouts, law enforcement and the missing person's advocacy groups launched a social media campaign that encouraged the public to share any photos or videos taken in the area around the park. Within hours, more images started pouring in.

One key image, posted by a passerby on Twitter, showed a woman who resembled Sarah sitting on a bench near the park's pond. The timestamp on the photo was only a few minutes before the police had arrived in the area, and the metadata revealed that it had been taken with a smartphone that had GPS tracking enabled. The image's location was confirmed to be within 100 meters of Sarah's last known position.

Outcome: Locating Sarah

The combination of image metadata, geolocation data, and public social media contributions helped piece together the final moments of Sarah's timeline. Law enforcement set up a search perimeter around the park and quickly found Sarah, disoriented and in need of medical attention, a few hours later in a secluded section of the park.

The critical breakthrough in the case was the initial use of the image metadata. Without the GPS coordinates embedded in the Instagram photo, the investigation might have taken much longer, or potentially never led to the park. This demonstrates the vital role of image analysis and metadata in modern OSINT investigations, providing a means of finding hidden information that is often overlooked.

Lessons Learned from the Case

Image Metadata as a Primary Source of Intelligence: The case demonstrated how metadata, particularly geolocation data, can be a valuable tool in locating missing persons or tracking the movements of individuals. Metadata is often overlooked, but in this case, it played a pivotal role in narrowing down the search area.

Cross-Referencing Data Across Platforms: Investigators effectively used data from multiple social media platforms to cross-reference and verify the timeline and location of

Sarah's whereabouts. This cross-platform analysis allowed them to confirm the accuracy of the metadata and piece together an accurate picture of Sarah's movements.

The Role of Public Collaboration: The case also showed how crowdsourcing through social media can be a powerful asset in OSINT investigations. The public's willingness to share their own images and videos helped fill in the gaps that were left by official surveillance footage.

The Need for Training in Metadata Analysis: For OSINT investigators, understanding how to extract and analyze image metadata is crucial. In this case, the investigators' familiarity with tools like ExifTool and their knowledge of how metadata could impact the investigation were instrumental in solving the case.

This case study illustrates how a seemingly simple photograph, when analyzed correctly, can become a key piece of evidence in solving complex investigations. Through the careful extraction of image metadata and the use of advanced OSINT techniques, investigators were able to locate a missing person, ultimately saving a life. It highlights the importance of image forensics, metadata analysis, and social media in modern investigative practices, as well as the immense potential of image-related OSINT for future cases.

9. Fake Accounts & Sock Puppets: Identification & Tracking

The rise of fake accounts, sock puppets, and bot networks presents a significant challenge in the digital intelligence space. These accounts are used for misinformation campaigns, social engineering, fraud, and covert influence operations. This chapter delves into techniques for identifying and tracking fake profiles across social media platforms by analyzing activity patterns, engagement behaviors, account creation details, and network connections. From spotting AI-generated profile pictures to uncovering coordinated inauthentic behavior, this section equips OSINT analysts with the tools to detect and dismantle deceptive digital personas.

9.1 Understanding Sock Puppets, Bots & Fake Accounts

In the realm of Open Source Intelligence (OSINT), understanding and identifying sock puppets, bots, and fake accounts is crucial for gathering accurate intelligence. These digital personas, often designed to deceive or manipulate others, can distort online narratives, influence public opinion, and even support criminal activities. Whether they are employed for social engineering, cyberbullying, or disinformation campaigns, detecting these false identities is a key skill for anyone engaged in social media investigations.

This chapter will explore what sock puppets, bots, and fake accounts are, how they operate, and the techniques used to identify and track them across social media platforms. Understanding these concepts is vital not only for effective OSINT but also for safeguarding digital environments from manipulation and fraud.

1. Sock Puppets: The Human Facade Behind Fake Identities

A sock puppet is a fake online identity used to deceive others, usually for manipulative purposes. The term "sock puppet" originates from the idea of someone using a literal sock with a face drawn on it to perform as a fictitious character, hence the notion of a "false persona" being controlled by an actual person behind the scenes.

Sock puppets are most commonly used to:

- **Influence Opinions**: They can post fake reviews, engage in fake debates, or artificially inflate support for a cause or product.
- **Manipulate Online Discussions**: Sock puppets can participate in online discussions and debates, providing an illusion of widespread support or opposition for a particular stance, product, or idea.
- **Defame or Harass Individuals**: By assuming fake identities, sock puppets can create online harassment campaigns, spread rumors, or post misleading information to harm individuals or organizations.

How Sock Puppets Operate:

- **Multiple Accounts**: A single individual or group may create multiple social media accounts, each representing a different persona. These accounts often interact with each other to give the illusion of a larger group or community supporting a particular narrative.
- **Consistent Behavioral Patterns**: Sock puppets may exhibit similar language, posting times, and engagement styles across their various accounts. These patterns can sometimes be detected through social media analysis tools and network analysis.
- **IP Address & Device Fingerprints**: Often, sock puppets are controlled from the same device or IP address, which is a red flag for investigators looking for coordinated, inauthentic activity.

2. Bots: Automated Accounts Designed to Influence

A bot is an automated program or algorithm designed to perform specific tasks on the internet, such as posting content, retweeting, liking, or following accounts. While some bots are harmless and even useful—such as those used to post weather updates or news articles—malicious bots can be used to manipulate online conversations and spread misinformation.

Bots are typically used to:

- **Amplify Content**: Bots are often deployed to amplify specific hashtags, content, or narratives, making them appear more popular or influential than they actually are. This is commonly seen in disinformation campaigns or astroturfing, where the goal is to simulate public support or opposition.
- **Increase Engagement**: Some bots are used to artificially inflate engagement metrics, such as likes, retweets, comments, or followers, to create the appearance of a viral post or popular influencer.

- **Spam**: Bots are often used to send unsolicited messages or spam, either for advertising purposes or to harass users.

How Bots Operate:

- **Automated Actions**: Bots use scripts or algorithms to automatically perform actions on social media platforms. This allows them to bypass the need for human interaction, making them efficient tools for amplifying content or engaging in large-scale manipulation.
- **Pattern Recognition**: Bot activity often follows patterns, such as posting at regular intervals or engaging with a high volume of users within a short time frame. Bots typically lack human-like variation in their behavior.
- **Networked Bots**: Some bots operate in botnets, groups of interconnected bots that work together to carry out large-scale tasks like flooding a platform with posts or spreading malware.

Identifying Bots:

- **High Frequency of Actions**: Bots can be identified by their excessive engagement in a short amount of time, such as posting every few seconds or retweeting hundreds of times per minute.
- **Lack of Personalization**: Bots usually lack the personal touch or nuanced behavior seen in human-run accounts. They often have generic profiles with little to no personal information or connections to other users.
- **Repetitive Content**: A bot will often tweet or post the same content repeatedly or share links from the same sources, with minimal variation.

3. Fake Accounts: The Deceptive Personas

A fake account is any false or fabricated profile on social media, often used for fraudulent, malicious, or manipulative purposes. Fake accounts can be used in conjunction with bots and sock puppets or operate independently. They are often created to impersonate real individuals or entities for various purposes, including fraud, harassment, or phishing.

Fake accounts are commonly used to:

- **Impersonate People**: Fake accounts can be created to impersonate well-known public figures, celebrities, or organizations. These impersonations can be used to spread misinformation, deceive people into giving up sensitive information, or defraud others.

- **Commit Fraud**: Fake accounts are frequently used in scams, such as fake charity campaigns, romance scams, or fake job offers, to trick people into giving money or personal details.
- **Spread Disinformation**: Fake accounts often participate in coordinated disinformation campaigns to create confusion or mislead the public, especially during sensitive events like elections or crises.

How Fake Accounts Operate:

- **Impersonation**: Fake accounts may use stolen photos or information from real people to create an appearance of legitimacy. These accounts often mirror real individuals' profiles or brands to deceive others.
- **Low-Quality Content**: Fake accounts tend to post generic, low-effort content that lacks originality or authenticity. Their engagement is often superficial and designed to blend in rather than offer meaningful interaction.
- **Suspicious Activity**: Fake accounts may exhibit suspicious behaviors, such as rapidly following and unfollowing users, sending unsolicited direct messages, or creating accounts with inconsistent or incomplete profile information.

Identifying Fake Accounts:

- **Profile Inconsistencies**: Fake accounts often have profile pictures stolen from other sources, generic usernames, or suspiciously sparse information. Investigators can use reverse image searches to identify stolen photos or verify the authenticity of a profile.
- **Social Graph Analysis**: Fake accounts often have few, if any, connections to real individuals or networks. Investigators can use tools to analyze the account's social graph—the network of users it interacts with—to determine if the account is part of a network of fake profiles.
- **Unusual Posting Patterns**: Fake accounts typically post content at odd hours, have irregular posting patterns, or share only promotional or misleading information, which can be detected through behavioral analysis tools.

4. The Intersection of Sock Puppets, Bots & Fake Accounts

While sock puppets, bots, and fake accounts each have unique characteristics, they often overlap and work in tandem to achieve specific goals.

- **Coordinated Manipulation**: In many cases, sock puppets, bots, and fake accounts are used together in coordinated campaigns to manipulate public opinion or deceive individuals. For instance, a network of sock puppets may promote content that is retweeted by a bot, which then amplifies the narrative across multiple platforms.

- **Astroturfing & Disinformation**: The use of sock puppets and bots in disinformation campaigns is known as astroturfing, where the goal is to create a false appearance of grassroots support for a cause or idea. Fake accounts and bots are used to manufacture consent and manipulate social media platforms to spread fake news or misleading information.
- **Phishing & Scams**: Fake accounts and bots are frequently used in phishing attacks or online scams. Fake profiles may establish trust with a victim, and then bots can be used to send malicious links or requests for sensitive information.

5. Combating Sock Puppets, Bots & Fake Accounts

Detecting and combating sock puppets, bots, and fake accounts requires a multi-faceted approach:

- **Automated Detection Tools**: Various social media platforms use AI and machine learning to automatically identify bot-like behaviors and fake accounts. Tools like Botometer and Hoaxy analyze account activity to detect patterns indicative of automated or inauthentic behavior.
- **Social Network Analysis**: Investigators can use social network analysis tools to identify clusters of related accounts that may be part of a coordinated effort to deceive or manipulate online conversations.
- **Crowdsourced Reporting**: Platforms like Twitter, Facebook, and Instagram allow users to report suspicious accounts or content. Reporting systems help identify fake accounts and bots, allowing platforms to take action.

Sock puppets, bots, and fake accounts are a persistent challenge for OSINT investigators. Understanding how these deceptive entities operate and the tactics they use to manipulate social media conversations is critical for uncovering the truth behind online interactions. By employing advanced investigative techniques such as metadata analysis, social graph analysis, and machine learning tools, investigators can detect and expose these false identities, ensuring more accurate intelligence and safeguarding the integrity of online platforms.

9.2 How to Identify Coordinated Social Media Manipulation

Coordinated social media manipulation has become one of the most significant threats in the digital age. Whether driven by political agendas, corporate interests, or malicious actors, such manipulation can distort public opinion, undermine trust, and even incite social unrest. Identifying coordinated efforts to manipulate social media requires a keen understanding of the tactics used by these groups, as well as the tools and techniques available to detect such activities.

This chapter focuses on how OSINT (Open Source Intelligence) analysts can identify coordinated manipulation campaigns across social media platforms. We'll explore the signs of coordinated efforts, common strategies used by manipulators, and effective techniques for uncovering these covert activities.

1. Understanding Coordinated Social Media Manipulation

Coordinated social media manipulation refers to the deliberate effort by a group or network to influence the opinions, beliefs, or behaviors of a large online audience by creating and amplifying specific narratives or content. These manipulations are often carried out in a way that makes them appear to be organic, grassroots movements, masking the fact that they are orchestrated from behind the scenes.

There are several forms of coordinated social media manipulation, including:

- **Astroturfing**: Creating fake grassroots support for a political or corporate cause.
- **Disinformation Campaigns**: Spreading false or misleading information to confuse, mislead, or misinform the public.
- **Hashtag Hijacking**: Using trending hashtags to promote a false narrative or divert attention from the original topic.
- **Bot and Sock Puppet Networks**: Using automated accounts (bots) and fake personas (sock puppets) to amplify messages and create the illusion of widespread support or opposition.
- **Troll Farms**: Coordinated efforts where multiple accounts or paid individuals are used to provoke, harass, or disrupt online discussions.

These manipulative tactics are often disguised by sophisticated techniques, such as using fake accounts to simulate genuine engagement or spreading content across multiple platforms at once. Detecting such behavior requires a methodical approach to analyzing online patterns, network structures, and engagement metrics.

2. Key Indicators of Coordinated Manipulation

There are several signs and patterns that can help investigators identify coordinated manipulation on social media platforms:

1. Sudden Surge in Activity Around Specific Topics or Hashtags

Coordinated efforts often involve orchestrated posts or messages to artificially increase the visibility of specific topics, hashtags, or campaigns. A sudden, large spike in activity related to a specific issue—especially when it doesn't seem to align with natural public interest—can be a sign of manipulation.

Example: A hashtag suddenly trending with thousands of tweets from accounts with little to no prior engagement with the topic or subject matter.

2. Similar Content Across Multiple Accounts

When multiple accounts start posting identical or strikingly similar content within a short period, it may indicate that the posts are part of a coordinated effort. These accounts may have minimal original content and are instead focused on promoting specific narratives or messages.

Example: Dozens of accounts tweeting the same message with a hashtag or URL in a short time window.

3. High Volume of Low-Quality, Automated Posts

Bots or fake accounts are often used to flood social media platforms with posts in order to amplify certain narratives. These posts tend to be repetitive, lacking personal engagement or nuance, and typically contain links, hashtags, or phrases designed to manipulate conversations.

Example: Accounts posting identical messages across multiple platforms or interacting with content in an automated manner without genuine engagement.

4. Fake or Inauthentic Engagement

A key marker of coordinated manipulation is the use of fake engagement to create the illusion of popularity or support. This can manifest in the form of:

Fake Likes, Comments, and Shares: Accounts that repeatedly like, share, or comment on content without contributing meaningful discussion.

Inconsistent Interaction: Accounts that interact with certain content at unusually high frequencies or exhibit repetitive patterns of engagement (e.g., like spamming).

Example: A post with an overwhelming number of likes, retweets, or shares from accounts with very little content history or engagement.

5. Accounts with Suspicious or Low Credibility

Often, coordinated manipulation involves the use of fake accounts or bots, which may have generic usernames, incomplete profiles, or stolen photos. These accounts often have very few followers, follow a limited number of accounts, and participate in narrow or repetitive topics.

Example: Accounts that appear new and have minimal personal information, but engage heavily in political or ideological content without any personal context.

6. Non-Native Language Patterns

Another indicator of coordinated manipulation is the use of language or phrasing that doesn't seem native to the account's supposed demographic. This is especially relevant when accounts from a particular region or language group suddenly begin using phrases or terminology that is inconsistent with their usual patterns of behavior.

Example: Accounts with clear regional markers posting in a style or language that is unfamiliar or inconsistent with their previous posts.

3. Techniques for Detecting Coordinated Manipulation

Detecting coordinated social media manipulation requires a combination of manual analysis and automated tools. Here are some of the techniques and methods that OSINT analysts can use to uncover such efforts:

1. Social Network Analysis

Social network analysis (SNA) is one of the most effective ways to detect coordinated manipulation. By examining the relationships between accounts, analysts can identify clusters of connected profiles that exhibit suspicious behavior. Some key elements to analyze include:

- **Followers & Connections**: Accounts that follow each other or share overlapping follower bases could indicate a coordinated group.
- **Engagement Networks**: If multiple accounts are consistently engaging with each other's content, it could be part of an orchestrated campaign.
- **Geographical Patterns**: Identifying unusual activity from specific regions or countries can indicate where coordinated efforts are originating.

Tools for Social Network Analysis:

- **Gephi**: A tool for visualizing and analyzing social networks.
- **NodeXL**: A network analysis tool that integrates with Excel, making it easy to detect patterns in social media connections.

2. Time Series & Pattern Analysis

Coordinated manipulation campaigns often follow specific timing patterns. For example, posts might be scheduled to appear during certain hours to maximize visibility. Analysts can use time-series analysis to detect patterns such as:

- **Post Timing**: If accounts are posting content at similar times in an almost robotic manner, it's likely that bots or schedulers are being used.
- **Spikes in Engagement**: A sudden increase in likes, shares, or comments around a certain hashtag or post may be artificially induced by bots or fake accounts.

Tools for Time Series Analysis:

- **Tweepy**: A Python library for collecting Twitter data, allowing you to analyze patterns of post frequency and timing.
- **CrowdTangle**: A platform used to track social media content and analyze trends, helping identify suspicious surges in engagement.

3. Sentiment and Content Analysis

Sentiment analysis can help identify coordinated manipulation by detecting sudden shifts in public opinion or the types of messages being circulated. If a particular topic's sentiment changes dramatically and suddenly, it might be due to a coordinated effort to manipulate the narrative.

Example: A sudden increase in negative sentiment around a political figure or brand that can be traced to a group of coordinated fake accounts.

Tools for Sentiment Analysis:

- **VADER**: A Python tool specifically designed for sentiment analysis in social media.
- **Brandwatch**: A social listening tool that tracks online conversations and provides insights into sentiment trends.

4. Bot Detection Tools

Several bot detection tools are designed to flag automated or suspicious accounts. These tools analyze account behavior to determine whether it exhibits patterns typical of bots, such as high-frequency posting, repetitive messages, or lack of personal engagement.

Bot Detection Tools:

- **Botometer**: A tool that can determine the likelihood that an account is a bot based on activity and engagement patterns.
- **Bot Sentinel**: A tool specifically designed to detect and track bots on Twitter.

5. Hashtag & URL Analysis

Hashtags and URLs are often used to spread specific narratives. By tracking the use of hashtags or links across multiple platforms, investigators can identify patterns of manipulation. If certain hashtags or URLs are used disproportionately by a small number of accounts, it could indicate an organized effort.

Example: A hashtag that rapidly gains popularity but only appears in posts from accounts with minimal engagement or that have never used the hashtag before.

4. Case Study: Detecting a Coordinated Disinformation Campaign

In 2020, during a contentious election period, a disinformation campaign was identified on Twitter that aimed to undermine public confidence in the election process. By using social network analysis, analysts uncovered a network of accounts that repeatedly shared similar messages with the same hashtags. These accounts were identified as having minimal followers, generic usernames, and automated content. Further investigation revealed that a significant portion of the accounts were bots, amplifying the messages and spreading misinformation across the platform.

By analyzing the patterns of engagement and the content of the posts, investigators were able to trace the campaign back to a specific group of operatives, who were using bots and sock puppets to manipulate the public discourse.

Coordinated social media manipulation is a growing concern in the digital age, with far-reaching consequences in politics, business, and society. By recognizing the signs of manipulation and employing the right tools and techniques, OSINT analysts can identify and combat these deceptive efforts. Through careful network analysis, content review, and the use of automated tools, it is possible to uncover the true nature behind coordinated campaigns and protect online communities from misinformation and manipulation.

9.3 Analyzing Posting Patterns & Engagement Activity

One of the key techniques for identifying coordinated manipulation and detecting suspicious activity on social media is analyzing posting patterns and engagement activity. When individuals or groups aim to manipulate public opinion, they often rely on consistent, strategic posting behaviors designed to amplify their message. Through careful observation of these behaviors, investigators can uncover the true nature of these efforts. This chapter will delve into how to analyze posting patterns and engagement activity, explaining the telltale signs of coordinated campaigns and how OSINT analysts can use this information to reveal manipulation.

1. Understanding Posting Patterns and Engagement Activity

At its core, posting patterns refer to the frequency, timing, and content of posts made by a user or group of users on social media platforms. Similarly, engagement activity refers to the interactions with those posts, including likes, shares, comments, and retweets. Together, these patterns and activities can provide critical insights into the behavior of users and whether they are part of a coordinated effort or an organic social media movement.

When analyzing these factors, it's essential to focus on several key elements:

- **Posting Frequency**: The number of posts made in a given time period.
- **Content Consistency**: How often posts share similar themes, phrases, hashtags, or URLs.
- **Engagement Volume**: The amount of likes, shares, comments, or retweets received on posts.

- **Timing**: The time and frequency with which posts are made and how this aligns with specific events or trends.
- **Behavior of Connected Accounts**: Whether certain accounts interact with each other in a consistent and patterned manner.

By examining these elements, investigators can identify whether certain users or groups are behaving like automated bots or part of an orchestrated effort.

2. Identifying Suspicious Posting Patterns

Suspicious posting patterns are often characterized by behavior that deviates from the norm or appears to be too systematic, consistent, or frequent to be organic. These patterns are frequently found in coordinated social media manipulation campaigns and can involve both human actors and automated bots. Below are several signs that can point to suspicious posting activity:

1. High Frequency of Posts in a Short Period

One of the most glaring signs of coordinated manipulation is a high volume of posts from an account or group of accounts within a short time frame. While it's not uncommon for active users to post frequently, accounts that post excessively and consistently in short bursts could be leveraging automated tools or following an organized campaign strategy.

Example: A hashtag begins trending with thousands of posts from users who have no prior history of posting similar content, and those posts appear at highly regular intervals over several hours.

2. Repetitive Posting of the Same Content

Coordinated campaigns often involve the repetition of identical or similar content across multiple accounts. These posts may include the same text, images, hashtags, or URLs. While some content repetition is normal on social media, an unusually high amount of content repetition across different accounts should raise suspicions.

Example: Numerous accounts, with little to no prior engagement or history, post identical tweets or status updates with the same hashtag and message.

3. Unusual Timing of Posts

The timing of posts is another key indicator of suspicious activity. Automated tools or coordinated efforts often rely on strategic timing to maximize visibility and impact. If a series of posts from different accounts appear at very specific, repetitive intervals or during specific events (such as a political debate, crisis, or viral moment), this could be a sign of manipulation.

Example: Accounts that flood the platform with posts during peak hours after a controversial event or news story breaks, particularly if their content closely aligns with a specific narrative.

4. Lack of Personalization or Original Content

A common feature of automated accounts or sock puppets is a lack of originality in their posts. These accounts tend to share generic, pre-written content or content that's heavily reliant on other sources. If an account continually posts content with little to no personalized input or original ideas, it could indicate automated activity or a participant in a larger manipulation scheme.

Example: Accounts that simply share articles, memes, or retweets without contributing their own thoughts, discussions, or insights.

3. Analyzing Engagement Activity

Engagement activity offers critical insights into the reach and impact of a social media post. The volume and quality of engagement an account or post receives can indicate whether the engagement is organic or artificially amplified. When analyzing engagement, OSINT analysts need to focus on several elements:

1. High Engagement Without Personal Interaction

In coordinated manipulation efforts, posts often receive a disproportionate amount of engagement from accounts that are either fake or automated. This type of engagement is typically characterized by high numbers of likes, shares, or comments, without much meaningful or personal interaction. In many cases, the engagement appears superficial and lacks any deep, nuanced conversation.

Example: A post by an account receives thousands of likes and retweets, but the responses and comments are generic or spammy, often containing short, irrelevant statements such as "Great post!" or "#Incredible."

2. Fake Followers and Low-Quality Engagement

Another sign of artificial engagement is when accounts with few followers consistently generate engagement far beyond what would be expected for their follower count. Bots, fake accounts, and sock puppets often flood content with likes or comments in an attempt to create the illusion of organic popularity or grassroots support.

Example: An account with only a handful of followers suddenly gains hundreds of likes or retweets, especially from accounts with minimal engagement history or no profile details.

3. Engagement from Accounts with Similar Activity Patterns

If the engagement activity of an account is clustered within a specific group of other accounts, it may suggest a coordinated effort. For example, if a post receives significant attention from accounts that consistently engage with each other's posts in a predictable manner, this is a sign that these accounts might be part of an organized manipulation campaign.

Example: A tweet receives engagement almost exclusively from accounts that have recently started following each other, all of which post similar content with the same political message or hashtag.

4. Disproportionate Engagement Around Specific Hashtags or Keywords

When certain hashtags or keywords receive massive engagement in a short time span, this can indicate an orchestrated effort to boost visibility. This is particularly concerning if the engagement comes from accounts with little prior activity or engagement with similar topics. It's often an effort to steer the conversation in a specific direction or distract from an important issue.

Example: A specific hashtag related to a political issue gains traction rapidly, but a large portion of its engagement comes from low-quality accounts with newly created profiles or accounts that have been dormant for long periods.

4. Tools and Techniques for Analyzing Posting and Engagement Activity

Detecting coordinated manipulation through posting patterns and engagement activity often requires the use of specialized tools that can help track, analyze, and visualize user behavior. Some of the key tools used in OSINT investigations include:

1. Social Network Analysis Tools

Tools like Gephi and NodeXL can help visualize the connections between accounts and identify clusters of activity that seem suspicious. By analyzing the relationships between accounts, you can identify networks of manipulated or coordinated users.

2. Sentiment Analysis Tools

Sentiment analysis tools, such as VADER or Brandwatch, can help determine the general sentiment surrounding specific hashtags, topics, or keywords. By analyzing how sentiments change over time, analysts can detect whether a sudden shift in public perception corresponds with artificial activity.

3. Bot Detection Tools

Detecting bots is crucial in identifying manipulated engagement activity. Tools such as Botometer and Bot Sentinel help assess the likelihood that an account is a bot by analyzing its behavior, including its posting frequency, timing, and interaction patterns.

4. Hashtag Monitoring Platforms

Platforms like CrowdTangle and Trendinalia are excellent for tracking hashtag usage and analyzing engagement levels. These tools can help determine if a hashtag is being artificially inflated or hijacked by coordinated accounts.

5. Case Study: Investigating a Hashtag Hijacking Campaign

In 2019, a viral hashtag, #MyStoryMyVoice, began trending on Twitter, ostensibly to raise awareness about women's rights. However, a deeper investigation revealed that the hashtag was being hijacked by a network of fake accounts aimed at spreading disinformation about political candidates. By analyzing posting patterns and engagement metrics, investigators discovered that the hashtag's engagement was artificially inflated, with a high volume of repetitive posts from accounts with minimal interaction history. This analysis ultimately revealed a coordinated effort to manipulate public sentiment during a critical election cycle.

The analysis of posting patterns and engagement activity is essential for identifying and uncovering coordinated social media manipulation. Suspicious patterns, such as high-frequency posting, repetitive content, artificial engagement, and timing consistency, are key indicators that manipulation may be occurring. By utilizing tools like social network analysis, sentiment analysis, and bot detection software, OSINT analysts can effectively uncover these deceptive campaigns, protect the integrity of online discourse, and ensure that information shared on social media remains authentic and reliable.

9.4 Reverse Searching Usernames & Email Associations

One of the most powerful techniques in the toolkit of an OSINT analyst is the ability to reverse search usernames and email associations. By tracing an individual's online identifiers across multiple platforms and services, investigators can build a more comprehensive profile of a person or entity. This method is invaluable for identifying connections between online personas, uncovering hidden accounts, and validating the authenticity of information. In the context of social media intelligence (SOCMINT), reverse searching usernames and email addresses can play a pivotal role in tracking down fraudulent activities, uncovering malicious actors, and detecting coordinated disinformation campaigns.

In this section, we will explore how reverse searching usernames and email addresses can reveal crucial intelligence about digital footprints, the tools and techniques involved, and the potential applications for investigations in OSINT. We'll also look at some real-world examples of how this approach has been effectively used.

1. What is Reverse Searching Usernames and Email Associations?

Reverse searching involves tracing a specific username or email address across multiple online platforms to determine where else it is being used. This is particularly useful in OSINT investigations because many individuals, whether they are legitimate or fraudulent, may use the same identifiers across various services—social media, online forums, e-commerce websites, and even in private communication.

Key Objectives of Reverse Searching:

- **Connecting Accounts**: Find out whether the same person is behind multiple accounts across different platforms.
- **Verifying Identity**: Confirm whether a particular account is connected to a real person or if it is likely to be a fake identity (sock puppet).
- **Tracing Digital Footprints**: Reveal the full extent of an individual's online presence, including profiles, forum posts, blog comments, and more.

- **Identifying Linked Data**: Discover additional personal details like phone numbers, locations, or workplaces associated with a given email or username.

2. Tools and Techniques for Reverse Searching

To conduct an effective reverse search, OSINT investigators rely on several tools and techniques that streamline the process and increase accuracy. These tools can help trace usernames, emails, and other associated information to uncover hidden profiles or data linked to a target.

1. Search Engines (Google, Bing, DuckDuckGo)

Using search engines to reverse search usernames or email addresses is the simplest and most accessible method. By entering a username or email into the search bar, investigators can uncover any publicly available information tied to that identifier. This can include social media profiles, forum posts, blog articles, news mentions, or any other public content.

Search Tips:

- Use quotation marks around the exact username or email to search for precise matches.
- Use advanced search operators (e.g., "site:twitter.com" or "site:reddit.com") to narrow results to specific platforms.
- Try variations of the username (e.g., @username vs. username) to find multiple forms of online representation.

2. Dedicated Reverse Search Engines (Pipl, Spokeo, BeenVerified)

These platforms specialize in gathering publicly available data across the internet. By searching for a username or email, these services compile information from a wide range of databases and social media platforms, including public records, social networks, and other data repositories. While many of these tools are subscription-based, they provide in-depth results that can link multiple accounts and provide additional personal information.

- **Pipl**: Known for its ability to dig deep into obscure social platforms, Pipl aggregates data from blogs, news sources, and professional networks.
- **Spokeo**: Spokeo can trace email addresses, phone numbers, and usernames across a wide variety of public data sources.

- **BeenVerified**: This platform specializes in finding people's social media accounts, public records, and other online data tied to email addresses and usernames.

3. Social Media Platforms

Many social media platforms offer features that allow users to search for others based on email addresses or usernames. These platforms provide investigators with an easy way to check whether a specific email or username is linked to a profile.

- **Facebook**: Facebook has a feature that allows users to search for people by email address. By simply entering the email into the search bar, investigators may be able to locate the associated profile. This also works for usernames on Facebook.
- **LinkedIn**: LinkedIn's advanced search allows users to search for specific emails or usernames. This can be particularly useful for identifying professionals or understanding their affiliations.
- **Twitter**: While Twitter doesn't have an explicit email search feature, investigators can search for usernames or hashtags to locate potential accounts associated with an email address or known online identifier.

4. Data Breach Databases (HaveIBeenPwned, BreachAlarm)

Email addresses involved in data breaches can provide significant leads for reverse searching. Services like HaveIBeenPwned and BreachAlarm track leaked email addresses from data breaches, and users can search these databases to determine if an email has been exposed in any major breaches. This can be particularly useful when an email address is tied to multiple accounts.

- **HaveIBeenPwned**: Once you input an email, it checks multiple sources and lists any data breaches the email may have been part of. If the email is connected to a breached account, it often provides a link to the compromised platform.
- **BreachAlarm**: This tool works similarly, alerting users when their email address has been exposed in a breach. By tracing where these breaches occurred, investigators can see how the compromised data might be used to access social media or other accounts.

5. Specialized OSINT Tools (Social Search, OSINT Framework)

There are also several specialized tools in the OSINT space designed to help with reverse searching usernames and emails. These tools are tailored to social media intelligence gathering and can be used to search and cross-reference usernames, email addresses, and other identifiers across multiple social platforms.

- **Social Search**: Social Search tools (like Social Search Engine) allow investigators to check whether a specific email address or username is linked to accounts on a variety of social media platforms.
- **OSINT Framework**: The OSINT Framework is a comprehensive resource that includes many specialized reverse search tools, organized by category and platform.

3. Applications of Reverse Searching in OSINT Investigations

The ability to reverse search usernames and email addresses offers numerous advantages for social media investigations, whether for criminal investigations, corporate security, or identifying online misinformation.

1. Identifying Fake or Sock Puppet Accounts

One of the most common uses of reverse searching is to uncover fake accounts or sock puppets—accounts that are created to mislead others or impersonate someone else. By reverse searching a username or email, investigators can quickly determine whether a specific profile is associated with other accounts across platforms. This helps detect fraudulent behavior, fake reviews, or malicious actors posing as credible individuals.

Example: A company might reverse search usernames linked to suspicious customer reviews on its product page. This could reveal that several reviews were written by fake accounts or sock puppets created to artificially boost the company's reputation.

2. Tracing Malicious Actors and Cybercriminals

Reverse searching usernames or email addresses associated with cybercriminal activity (such as phishing, online scams, or data breaches) can help investigators track the individual's online footprint. A reverse search may lead to other accounts, revealing patterns of fraudulent behavior or uncovering networks of malicious actors.

Example: In the case of a phishing attack, investigators can trace the email address used in the scam and link it to other accounts involved in cybercrime.

3. Verifying the Identity of Social Media Users

In investigations involving identity verification, reverse searching can help confirm if a particular person or entity is behind an account. This is often used in cases of online harassment, identity theft, or when verifying the credibility of individuals in a news story or online report.

Example: A journalist investigating a fake news source could reverse search the associated username or email to confirm whether the individual is tied to a legitimate news outlet or organization.

4. Investigating Coordinated Disinformation Campaigns

Disinformation campaigns often involve the use of multiple fake accounts, all promoting a specific agenda. Reverse searching helps identify whether a set of accounts is linked to a common source, providing insights into the scope of a campaign and its reach.

Example: During an election, reverse searches can uncover accounts spreading false narratives that share the same email or usernames, revealing a coordinated effort to manipulate voters.

4. Challenges and Limitations of Reverse Searching

While reverse searching can be incredibly useful, there are several challenges to keep in mind:

- **Privacy Restrictions**: Some platforms restrict the ability to search by email or username for privacy reasons, making it harder to trace accounts.
- **Data Availability**: Not all platforms share public data, and some may not allow reverse searches at all.
- **Evasion Tactics**: Malicious actors may use VPNs, proxies, or burner emails to hide their true identities, making it more difficult to reverse search effectively.

Reverse searching usernames and email associations is a potent tool for OSINT analysts. By connecting the dots between online identifiers and uncovering hidden accounts, investigators can gain deeper insights into a subject's digital footprint, detect fraudulent activity, and uncover malicious actors. Whether it's identifying fake profiles, uncovering cybercriminals, or exposing disinformation campaigns, reverse searching plays a crucial role in today's social media intelligence landscape.

9.5 Unmasking Fake Identities in Large-Scale Investigations

The proliferation of social media and online platforms has created an environment where fake identities, also known as sock puppets or phantom profiles, are rampant. These fabricated online personas are frequently used in large-scale disinformation campaigns, fraud, cybercrime, and even identity theft. In the context of OSINT (Open-Source Intelligence), uncovering and unmasking these fake identities is a crucial skill for investigators. The challenge intensifies in large-scale investigations where numerous fake accounts may be spread across different platforms, making it difficult to pinpoint which accounts are real and which are deceptive.

This section explores how OSINT analysts can employ various techniques to identify and expose fake identities in large-scale investigations. From leveraging social media metadata and behavioral analysis to utilizing advanced search tools, this chapter provides insight into how fake personas are created, deployed, and ultimately unmasked. We will also examine real-world examples where large-scale investigations have successfully exposed deceptive identities.

1. Understanding the Scope of Fake Identities in Large-Scale Investigations

Fake identities are deliberately created to deceive others by presenting false personal details or misrepresenting someone's intentions or affiliations. These identities can range from bots automated to spread misinformation, to individuals using fabricated details to pose as others for various purposes, such as fraud, manipulation, or impersonation.

Key Types of Fake Identities in Large-Scale Investigations:

- **Bots**: Automated accounts designed to create fake content or perform scripted activities like sending spam messages or retweeting posts to amplify content.
- **Sock Puppets**: Fake accounts managed by real people, often to create the illusion of support or dissent in a social movement, product reviews, or political discussions.
- **Impersonators**: Individuals creating profiles to impersonate a well-known figure or brand in order to defraud people or spread misinformation.
- **Catfish Accounts**: Fake personal accounts designed for social manipulation or romantic scams, often involving stolen images and fabricated life stories.

In large-scale investigations, fake identities are commonly used to manipulate public opinion, orchestrate attacks, or mislead users into engaging with fraudulent schemes. These activities can span across social media platforms, online forums, messaging apps, and e-commerce websites. The sheer volume of fake profiles involved in large investigations can be overwhelming, making it challenging for investigators to separate real from deceptive profiles.

2. Identifying Fake Identities: Key Indicators and Red Flags

The process of unmasking fake identities begins with identifying the signs that a profile may not be genuine. OSINT investigators are trained to look for specific behavioral patterns, profile inconsistencies, and other red flags that can suggest deception. Some of the most common indicators of fake identities include:

1. Incomplete or Generic Profiles

Fake accounts often have incomplete or overly simplistic profiles. These profiles may lack a clear biography, profile picture, or personal history. Often, fake identities will use generic, stock photos that can easily be traced to other sources. Profile details may include information that seems too generic or inconsistent with the content shared by the account. Investigators can cross-check these profile details against other sources for discrepancies.

Example: A social media account with minimal personal details and a profile picture that appears to be a stock photo may be flagged for further investigation.

2. Unusual Activity Patterns

Accounts that show signs of automated behavior, like a constant flow of posts at regular intervals without genuine engagement, may be fake or controlled by bots. Sock puppets tend to have suspicious activity, such as posting the same content across different accounts or engaging in coordinated attacks with other profiles to amplify certain messages.

Example: An account that posts identical content across multiple platforms, or engages with the same set of accounts consistently without any variation, is likely to be a sock puppet.

3. Limited Social Interaction

Fake accounts often have a limited network of connections or followers. These accounts tend to interact only with a select group of individuals, usually other fake accounts that support the same agenda. Their engagement is limited to scripted responses, likes, and retweets, often appearing to be "inorganic."

Example: A political account that engages with a narrow circle of followers and shows little to no interaction with accounts outside of a small community may be part of a coordinated campaign.

4. Discrepancies in Personal Information

Fake identities often use stolen or inconsistent personal details. Investigators can cross-reference this information with databases and other public records to determine if it is legitimate. By searching for email addresses, phone numbers, or profile names across different platforms, investigators can detect patterns that point to fake accounts.

Example: A person using an unusually high number of different aliases across social media platforms, or whose photo is tied to a completely different identity in another context, is likely to be a fake profile.

5. Metadata & Reverse Image Search

Metadata from photos or videos posted by social media profiles can be a key source of information in exposing fake identities. Reverse image searches using tools like Google Image Search or TinEye can identify where an image has appeared before, revealing whether it was stolen from another account or website. Investigators can also examine EXIF metadata embedded in photos, which can provide geolocation, device details, and timestamps that may suggest a photo was fabricated or reposted from another source.

Example: An account using someone else's profile picture can be exposed through reverse image searches that show the same image was posted under multiple identities.

3. Tools and Techniques for Unmasking Fake Identities

1. Social Media Profiling Tools

Social media platforms like Twitter, Facebook, and LinkedIn allow investigators to track usernames, email addresses, or phone numbers across their networks. Advanced search tools and operators within these platforms can help analysts locate hidden profiles that are linked to fake identities. Additionally, services like Pipl, Spokeo, and BeenVerified can uncover hidden information about accounts and their owners by checking their association with email addresses, usernames, or phone numbers across multiple platforms.

2. OSINT Framework & Investigative Tools

The OSINT Framework provides a curated collection of investigative tools that can be used for unmasking fake identities. By leveraging tools for reverse searching usernames, cross-referencing public data, and analyzing metadata, investigators can trace fake profiles back to their original creators. Tools like Maltego and Cortex can analyze data across multiple sources and build comprehensive visual link charts that highlight connections between fake accounts.

3. Behavioral Analysis & AI Algorithms

Behavioral analysis and AI algorithms can be used to identify suspicious activity patterns associated with fake accounts. These systems can detect unusual engagement behaviors, such as mass following or content duplication, which are common signs of bot activity or coordinated disinformation efforts. For example, AI algorithms can analyze the frequency and nature of posts to determine if they align with natural human behavior or follow scripted patterns that are typical of fake identities.

Example: Machine learning tools that track word choice, sentiment, and posting times can help identify accounts engaging in manipulation or spreading false information through coordinated tactics.

4. Case Study: Unmasking a Fake Political Campaign

In a recent case study, an OSINT team was tasked with investigating a series of social media accounts believed to be involved in a coordinated disinformation campaign during a national election. By reverse searching the usernames and analyzing posting patterns, they identified multiple sock puppet accounts that were posting identical content across Twitter, Facebook, and Instagram.

Through metadata analysis, the investigators discovered that many of the profile images were stolen from real individuals, and reverse image searches revealed that the images were frequently used across different accounts associated with the same political agenda. They used social media search tools to trace the same email addresses across multiple platforms, ultimately uncovering a network of fake accounts promoting false narratives. This led to the identification of the individuals behind the campaign and the exposure of their coordinated manipulation efforts.

Unmasking fake identities in large-scale investigations is a complex but crucial task in today's digital world. By leveraging OSINT techniques like reverse image search, social media profiling tools, behavioral analysis, and metadata analysis, investigators can expose fake personas that may be manipulating public opinion, committing fraud, or engaging in other malicious activities. In large-scale investigations, where numerous fake accounts may be involved, it is essential for OSINT analysts to be both methodical and creative in uncovering the true identities behind deceptive profiles. The ability to successfully identify and unmask fake identities not only enhances the accuracy of investigations but also helps maintain the integrity of the information being shared online.

9.6 Case Study: Exposing a Political Disinformation Network

Political disinformation has become a growing concern in the digital age. The use of fake accounts, bots, and coordinated networks to manipulate public opinion, spread false narratives, and influence elections has become a key tactic for malicious actors. In this case study, we explore how OSINT (Open-Source Intelligence) was utilized to expose a political disinformation network designed to sway public perception during a critical election period. Through advanced OSINT techniques such as social media profiling, behavioral analysis, metadata extraction, and reverse searches, investigators were able to uncover the scope and impact of the operation, ultimately exposing the people behind the network and the methods they used.

1. Background: The Emergence of the Disinformation Network

In 2023, political analysts and cybersecurity experts noticed an increase in coordinated, suspicious online activity surrounding an upcoming national election in Country X. Across various social media platforms—primarily Twitter, Facebook, and Instagram—accounts were amplifying divisive content, spreading fake news, and undermining the credibility of political candidates. What raised alarms was the highly synchronized nature of the posts: they all seemed to push similar narratives, targeting key swing states, spreading conspiracy theories, and discrediting opposition candidates. The content appeared to be coming from different accounts, yet many shared common characteristics, including identical posts, similar language, and matching hashtags.

Initial suspicions pointed to the possibility of a disinformation network, potentially involving foreign actors or domestic entities attempting to influence the electoral process. Given the scale of the operation, a targeted OSINT investigation was launched to uncover the true extent of the manipulation and identify the parties responsible.

2. Step 1: Identifying Suspicious Activity

The investigation began by identifying and analyzing social media accounts exhibiting coordinated activity. A team of OSINT analysts used advanced search techniques to pinpoint accounts posting similar content at the same time. By tracking certain hashtags that were trending across platforms—hashtags such as "#StopTheSteal" and "#ElectionFraud"—they were able to identify clusters of accounts that shared common posts, often using the same wording or phrasing. Some posts were shared thousands of times within minutes, which is unusual for organic social media behavior.

The accounts involved in this campaign were primarily new or had minimal online presence prior to the election period, making them seem suspicious. OSINT experts began tracking the patterns of activity across multiple platforms, cross-referencing account names, hashtags, and posting schedules. One key sign was the frequency and timing of posts: accounts consistently posted content in bursts, which suggested that these profiles may not have been operated by genuine individuals, but rather automated bots or sock puppets.

3. Step 2: Profiling the Accounts

OSINT experts then moved on to profiling the suspicious accounts to gather more data. One of the primary methods of detection was reverse searching images. Many of the profiles used stock images or images that had been stolen from other sources. Through reverse image searches on platforms like Google Images and TinEye, analysts discovered that many of the profile pictures were taken from legitimate accounts or even from the portfolios of photographers, raising the red flag that these were not real profiles.

The analysts also noticed that the posts from these accounts were highly repetitive and often echoed the same phrases or sentiment. These were posts designed to spread a singular political agenda: discrediting a certain candidate while boosting another. As the investigation unfolded, it became clear that the profiles were all part of a coordinated effort.

4. Step 3: Behavioral Analysis of Activity

Using behavioral analysis techniques, OSINT investigators observed that many of the suspicious accounts exhibited unnatural engagement patterns. For example, some accounts would follow and unfollow thousands of users at once, engage in mass liking, and retweet posts from specific sources. These were behaviors typical of bots or accounts manipulated to give the appearance of a widespread movement of support.

By using tools like Botometer (which helps analyze whether an account is automated) and Social Bearing (which provides insights into account behavior), the team was able to identify several suspicious patterns. Notably, certain accounts showed a pattern of posting identical content across different platforms and commenting under popular posts with nearly identical responses. This behavior strongly suggested that these accounts were either automated or managed by a small group of individuals.

5. Step 4: Metadata Extraction

In parallel, investigators used metadata analysis to dive deeper into the content being shared by the fake accounts. Metadata embedded in images, videos, and posts provided critical clues about the origins of the disinformation network. Investigators extracted geolocation data from some images, revealing that many of them had been posted from a small set of locations, which was unusual for accounts claiming to be based in different parts of the country.

For instance, metadata from a video posted on Instagram depicted a rally that was falsely associated with a particular political candidate. Through metadata extraction, investigators traced the video's origin back to a different political event entirely, highlighting the deceptive nature of the post. Further examination revealed that this video had been re-shared by several other suspicious accounts, all with the same misleading narrative.

Additionally, investigators looked into the IP addresses associated with these posts and discovered a pattern: many of the fake accounts were operating from the same network of IP addresses, indicating they were likely part of a larger coordinated effort.

6. Step 5: Cross-Referencing Data Across Platforms

The OSINT team also cross-referenced data across multiple platforms. By searching for the same usernames, hashtags, and keywords, they identified accounts on Twitter, Facebook, and Instagram that were using similar tactics to spread disinformation. Additionally, they used Pipl and Spokeo to conduct deep dives into the contact information associated with the profiles.

Many of the accounts shared the same email addresses or used email addresses that were part of known databases linked to disinformation campaigns. This connection, when traced across several platforms, confirmed the coordinated nature of the network. The team discovered that the accounts were also linked to certain online forums where political manipulation and disinformation strategies were openly discussed.

7. Step 6: Exposing the Network and Identifying the Perpetrators

After weeks of intensive investigation, the OSINT team uncovered a wide network of fake accounts, coordinated bots, and sock puppets that had been used to manipulate political discourse. By tracking back to the original sources of the activity and cross-referencing the data, they were able to identify the individuals or organizations behind the disinformation campaign.

The campaign was found to be linked to a group of individuals connected to a foreign entity with a history of influencing political events through online manipulation. The investigation revealed that the disinformation network had been orchestrated by a sophisticated operation that included both automated bots and human-managed fake accounts.

Through their efforts, the OSINT team was able to compile a comprehensive report with evidence of the operation's reach, tactics, and objectives. The evidence was shared with local authorities, cybersecurity experts, and electoral agencies, who took action to mitigate the impact of the campaign. The story of the investigation also made headlines, raising public awareness about the dangers of political disinformation and the role of OSINT in exposing it.

This case study demonstrates the critical role that OSINT plays in exposing political disinformation networks and combating their efforts. Through careful analysis of social media profiles, behavioral patterns, metadata, and cross-platform connections, investigators were able to trace the fake identities back to the individuals behind the coordinated disinformation campaign. This investigation not only helped protect the integrity of the election process but also highlighted the power of OSINT in identifying and dismantling malicious digital networks.

In the ongoing battle against disinformation, the ability to expose fake identities and track the origins of manipulated content is essential for ensuring the credibility of public discourse and protecting the democratic process. By employing advanced OSINT techniques and collaborating across agencies and platforms, investigators can uncover the truth and prevent harmful influence operations from succeeding.

10. Archiving & Monitoring Social Media Data

Social media content is dynamic—posts get edited, deleted, or lost in the constant flood of new information. For OSINT analysts, the ability to archive and monitor social media data is crucial for preserving evidence, tracking narratives, and conducting long-term investigations. This chapter explores effective methods for capturing and storing social media content using web scraping, automated monitoring tools, and archiving services. From setting up real-time alerts to leveraging APIs for continuous data collection, mastering these techniques ensures that valuable intelligence is never lost and can be analyzed over time.

10.1 The Importance of Archiving Social Media for Investigations

In the digital age, social media plays a pivotal role in communication, activism, marketing, and even criminal activity. As a result, archiving social media data has become an indispensable tool for investigators across various sectors, including law enforcement, cybersecurity, intelligence, and corporate investigations. Whether it's monitoring an ongoing crisis, tracking cyber threats, or gathering evidence for a criminal case, the ability to preserve social media content in an accurate and time-stamped manner is crucial for future analysis, legal proceedings, and ensuring accountability.

1. The Need for Archiving in OSINT Investigations

Social media platforms are dynamic environments where content is constantly being uploaded, shared, and deleted. This ever-changing nature can make it difficult to retain accurate data for future reference. Posts, tweets, images, comments, videos, and even user interactions can vanish in an instant, whether intentionally by the user, deleted by the platform, or lost to an algorithmic change. When investigating a crime or event, the temporal aspect is especially important. Investigators often need to capture a snapshot of social media activity at a specific moment in time. Without proper archiving, there is a risk of losing crucial evidence that could serve as the cornerstone of an investigation.

For example, during a crisis or an unfolding event, such as a political protest or an online attack, posts may be rapidly shared across social networks. Investigators may need to revisit these posts to understand the spread of information, identify key influencers, or detect coordinated disinformation efforts. If these posts are deleted or altered after the fact, archiving them ensures that they are preserved in their original form.

2. Benefits of Archiving Social Media Data

a. **Preserving Evidence**: Archiving ensures that data is preserved in its original format and context. This includes the post itself, timestamps, metadata, and user interactions. When social media content is collected in real-time, it provides investigators with an accurate record of events. This can be vital in cases where the content is used in legal proceedings, as digital evidence is often admissible in court. Without proper archiving, investigators risk losing vital clues that could lead to crucial breakthroughs.

b. **Tracking Changes and Updates**: Social media platforms, particularly those focused on real-time communication like Twitter, Facebook, or Instagram, frequently update their content, algorithms, and privacy settings. The data being viewed today may not be the same tomorrow. For example, a tweet that may be publicly visible today could be hidden or deleted later. By archiving this content, investigators ensure they have access to the complete history of a post, user, or conversation, even after updates or deletions occur.

c. **Analyzing User Behavior**: Archiving enables the ability to track user behavior over time. By retaining access to a user's complete social media activity, investigators can analyze their interactions, connections, and content dissemination patterns. This is particularly useful in cases such as cyberstalking, harassment, or online fraud, where understanding a user's actions over an extended period is critical to uncovering the full scope of their activity.

d. **Contextualizing the Data**: Often, the full significance of social media content is not immediately apparent. Social media events unfold over time, and the context in which a post is made can evolve. Archiving social media allows investigators to contextualize content, tracking conversations, replies, and interactions over time. This is crucial for understanding the dynamics of a situation, such as how misinformation spreads or how a group of individuals organized an event online.

3. Legal Considerations in Social Media Archiving

In any investigation, especially those involving potential criminal activity or civil litigation, maintaining the integrity and authenticity of evidence is paramount. Archiving social media data in a legally defensible manner requires careful attention to detail. Many jurisdictions have specific rules about how digital evidence should be handled, including proper documentation of its chain of custody.

When archiving social media data, investigators must ensure that they are capturing the data in a way that maintains its integrity. This often means using tools and methods that are accepted as reliable and forensically sound in a legal context. For instance, using third-party archiving tools that capture screenshots, metadata, and other relevant information in a standardized format can help ensure the data's authenticity when it is presented in court.

Additionally, privacy laws and regulations, such as GDPR (General Data Protection Regulation) in the EU or CCPA (California Consumer Privacy Act), must be adhered to when archiving personal data. Ensuring that the data collection is ethical and lawful is essential to avoid potential legal repercussions.

4. Archiving Tools and Techniques

There are a variety of tools and platforms available to help investigators efficiently archive social media content. These tools capture posts, images, videos, user interactions, and metadata in ways that preserve the content's integrity and time-stamped accuracy. Some of the commonly used tools include:

a. Social Media Archiving Platforms:

ArchiveSocial: This tool is widely used for archiving social media content, particularly by public institutions and law enforcement agencies. It captures posts from platforms like Twitter, Facebook, and Instagram, along with metadata and user interactions. ArchiveSocial ensures that the content is preserved in a way that meets legal standards for evidence.

b. Browser Extensions & Manual Techniques:

- **Wayback Machine (Internet Archive):** While not specifically designed for social media, the Wayback Machine allows investigators to capture snapshots of publicly available web pages, including social media profiles, which can be archived for future reference.
- **Web Capture Tools**: Extensions like GoFullPage or Web Capture allow users to capture full-page screenshots of social media profiles or posts, preserving the visual appearance and structure of the page as it appeared at a specific time.

c. **API-based Solutions**: Many platforms, such as Twitter, offer APIs (Application Programming Interfaces) that allow investigators to collect data programmatically. By accessing platform APIs, investigators can extract large volumes of data such as posts, user profiles, and trends, which can then be archived for further analysis. However, due to privacy concerns, access to certain data may be restricted or require special permissions.

d. Forensic Tools:

FTK Imager and EnCase: These forensic tools, commonly used in law enforcement, allow investigators to capture social media data as part of a broader digital evidence collection strategy. These tools can be used to acquire evidence from computers, mobile devices, and cloud platforms that contain social media data.

5. Challenges in Social Media Archiving

While archiving social media is essential for investigations, it is not without its challenges. The speed at which content is generated and the transient nature of social media can make it difficult to capture everything of significance. Furthermore, social media platforms are constantly evolving, and what is possible to capture today may not be feasible in the future as platforms tighten privacy policies or change their data sharing capabilities.

One of the primary challenges in archiving is the vast amount of content that is produced daily. Sorting through this content to identify relevant posts and interactions can be a time-consuming process. Additionally, many social media users make their content private, limiting access to only a subset of the posts that are available for archiving.

Moreover, the data captured from social media can be overwhelming, requiring investigators to have systems in place to effectively process, analyze, and store large datasets. This can be compounded by legal issues related to privacy and data protection laws, which can restrict the way social media data is collected and used.

Archiving social media data plays a critical role in modern investigations. From criminal inquiries to corporate intelligence, the ability to preserve accurate, time-stamped, and unaltered content from social media platforms is an essential tool for gathering evidence, understanding trends, and uncovering truths. With the right tools, techniques, and legal considerations, social media archiving ensures that investigators can work with accurate data, even as platforms evolve and data becomes increasingly ephemeral.

As social media continues to evolve, the ability to capture and preserve information will only become more important. For OSINT professionals and investigators alike, effective archiving practices are key to maintaining a robust and reliable record of digital activity, ensuring that the truth is never lost in the ever-changing digital landscape.

10.2 Tools & Techniques for Capturing Live Social Media Data

Capturing live social media data is an essential part of modern investigations, providing real-time insights into events as they unfold across platforms like Twitter, Facebook, Instagram, TikTok, and others. Whether it's tracking a crisis, monitoring public sentiment, or investigating criminal activity, having the right tools and techniques to capture live social media data allows investigators to respond quickly and efficiently. In this section, we explore the best tools and techniques used to capture social media data in real time, ensuring investigators can gather accurate, comprehensive, and actionable information.

1. Why Real-Time Data Collection Matters

Social media content evolves rapidly. Events such as political rallies, natural disasters, protests, or breaking news stories often trigger widespread public engagement in real time. Tracking this data as it happens allows investigators to:

- **Monitor Events as They Unfold**: In fast-moving situations, live data gives investigators immediate access to what is happening, allowing for swift analysis and response.
- **Identify Trends and Influencers**: By capturing data in real time, analysts can quickly identify trending topics, hashtags, and influential voices within a given conversation.
- **Detect Threats or Misinformation**: Timely collection helps identify emerging threats, including coordinated disinformation campaigns, criminal activity, or cyberattacks, while they are still developing.

Given the ephemeral nature of social media—where posts are deleted or edited quickly—real-time data capture is key to preserving evidence before it disappears.

2. Tools for Capturing Live Social Media Data

There is a wide range of tools available for capturing live social media data. Some tools are designed for broad monitoring, while others offer highly targeted data collection and analysis features. Below are some of the most popular and effective tools:

a. Social Media Monitoring Tools

1. Hootsuite: Hootsuite is a social media management platform that allows users to track and capture live posts, comments, and hashtags from multiple platforms in real time. It can capture content from Twitter, Instagram, LinkedIn, and Facebook, allowing investigators to create custom streams based on specific keywords, locations, or topics of interest.

- **Strengths**: Real-time tracking, customizable dashboards, historical data collection, and scheduled reporting.
- **Use Cases**: Monitoring political campaigns, public relations crises, or product launches.

2. **TweetDeck (for Twitter):** TweetDeck is a specialized tool for monitoring Twitter. It allows users to set up columns that display tweets based on specific keywords, hashtags, and user accounts. It provides real-time access to Twitter's data, which can be invaluable for tracking breaking news or online discussions.

- **Strengths**: Focused on Twitter, customizable columns, real-time updates, and easy to use for tracking hashtags and topics.
- **Use Cases**: Following trending hashtags during a protest or crisis, monitoring political discussions, or tracking brand mentions.

3. **Brandwatch**: Brandwatch offers advanced social media monitoring and analytics features, allowing investigators to track real-time conversations across social media platforms, blogs, and forums. It provides deep insights into the social sentiment and behavior of users, making it valuable for analyzing public opinion and identifying key influencers.

- **Strengths**: Real-time monitoring, sentiment analysis, social listening, and competitive intelligence.
- **Use Cases**: Analyzing online reputation, monitoring product feedback, or tracking social movements.

4. **Sprout Social**: Sprout Social is another robust social media management tool that provides real-time monitoring and data collection across multiple platforms. It offers reporting features that help users track engagement metrics, identify influential content, and measure the impact of social media campaigns.

- **Strengths**: Real-time tracking, cross-platform support, analytics, and reporting.
- **Use Cases**: Monitoring news cycles, following up on marketing campaigns, or tracking crises.

b. OSINT & Forensic Tools

5. OSINT Framework Tools: The OSINT Framework is a collection of publicly available tools for gathering and analyzing open-source intelligence. Within this framework, several tools and platforms can be used to capture live social media data, such as:

- **Social Search Tools**: Tools like Social-Searcher allow investigators to conduct live searches of social media platforms to identify relevant posts, images, and videos related to ongoing events.
- **Pipl**: Pipl is a people search engine that can be used to track a subject's digital footprint, aggregating data from social networks in real time.
- **Maltego**: Maltego is an OSINT tool that can be used for mapping relationships and conducting real-time data mining across multiple social media platforms, useful for uncovering connections between entities or individuals involved in a particular topic or event.

6. **Geofeedia (Geolocation-Based Monitoring):** Geofeedia is a platform that enables real-time social media monitoring based on location. By using location-based searches, investigators can capture posts, images, and videos as they are uploaded in a specific geographic area, which can be particularly useful for tracking events like protests, natural disasters, or public gatherings.

- **Strengths**: Real-time location-based data collection, geospatial analytics, and visual mapping.
- **Use Cases**: Monitoring localized incidents, tracking criminal activity in specific locations, or analyzing local election sentiment.

3. Social Media Platform-Specific Data Capture Techniques

a. Twitter:

1. **Twitter API (Application Programming Interface):** The Twitter API allows developers to access large amounts of data from Twitter in real time. By using search queries, users can track specific hashtags, keywords, and accounts, capturing tweets as they are posted. The Twitter API offers both standard and premium versions, with the premium API offering more advanced features for capturing data at scale.

- **Strengths**: High degree of customization, real-time access to tweets, extensive filtering capabilities.
- **Use Cases**: Tracking political events, investigating online harassment, monitoring public response to breaking news.

2. **Twint (Open-Source Python Tool):** Twint is an open-source tool that provides users with the ability to scrape live data from Twitter without using the Twitter API. It can capture tweets based on specific keywords, locations, or user profiles, making it useful for OSINT investigations that require large amounts of data over a short period.

- **Strengths**: No need for API keys, fast data collection, customizable filters.
- **Use Cases**: Monitoring election trends, investigating viral hashtags, tracking media coverage of an event.

b. Instagram:

3. **Instagram Scraping Tools (e.g., InstaPy, Scrapy):** Instagram scraping tools such as InstaPy or Scrapy allow investigators to capture live posts, stories, and hashtags in real time. These tools can extract images, captions, comments, and follower counts from Instagram, which can be crucial for understanding public sentiment or identifying influencers during an event.

- **Strengths**: Real-time data scraping, automation for bulk collection, flexible filtering options.
- **Use Cases**: Investigating influencer marketing campaigns, tracking protest activity, or capturing trending topics.

c. Facebook:

4. **Facebook Graph API**: Facebook's Graph API allows investigators to access real-time data from public posts, pages, and groups on Facebook. It enables the capture of posts, comments, and reactions based on user-defined criteria, such as keywords, locations, or hashtags. Facebook also provides insights into how content is being shared and interacted with across the platform.

- **Strengths**: Real-time data collection, detailed user and page insights, custom queries.
- **Use Cases**: Investigating disinformation, monitoring political campaigns, or tracking brand sentiment.

4. Techniques for Capturing Live Data

a. Keyword Tracking & Alerts:

Setting up keyword tracking and alerts across multiple platforms is one of the simplest ways to capture live data. This can be done through social media management tools (like Hootsuite or Sprout Social) or custom alert systems like Google Alerts or Talkwalker Alerts, which send notifications when specific keywords are mentioned in social media posts.

b. Using Hashtag Analysis:

Hashtags are powerful indicators of trending topics and events on platforms like Twitter, Instagram, and TikTok. By tracking hashtags in real time, investigators can capture all posts associated with these tags, providing insights into public discourse surrounding a specific event or issue. Tools like Hashtagify allow users to monitor trending hashtags and their usage over time.

c. Real-Time Monitoring Dashboards:

Investors can use real-time monitoring dashboards to centralize and manage live data collection. These dashboards are customized to pull in live feeds from multiple platforms, presenting a unified view of social media activity. Tools like Khoros and Meltwater offer enterprise-level monitoring capabilities with advanced analytics, sentiment analysis, and trend detection.

5. Challenges in Capturing Live Data

While real-time data capture is essential, it is not without challenges. These challenges include:

- **Data Overload**: Social media platforms generate vast amounts of content, and filtering out noise to identify meaningful data can be difficult.
- **Privacy Concerns**: Privacy regulations such as GDPR and CCPA place limits on how social media data can be collected and shared, making it important for investigators to ensure their methods comply with these regulations.
- **Platform Changes**: Social media platforms frequently update their algorithms, privacy settings, and data-sharing policies, which can affect data access and capture techniques.

- **Fake or Manipulated Content**: The rapid spread of disinformation, deepfakes, and fake accounts means that investigators must be vigilant in verifying the authenticity of the data they capture.

Capturing live social media data is a powerful technique for real-time investigation, providing insights into rapidly unfolding events and online activity. With the right tools and techniques, investigators can monitor conversations, detect trends, and uncover crucial intelligence in real time. However, it is essential to use these tools ethically and in compliance with legal frameworks to ensure that the collected data remains actionable and reliable. By mastering real-time data capture, OSINT professionals and investigators can stay ahead of emerging threats, track important events, and make data-driven decisions.

10.3 Tracking Deleted Posts & Changes to User Profiles

In the ever-changing landscape of social media, users frequently delete posts or alter their profiles, sometimes in an attempt to remove incriminating or controversial content. For investigators, being able to track these deleted posts or profile changes is crucial in ensuring that no significant data is missed. Understanding how social media platforms handle deleted content, the challenges involved, and the tools and techniques used to track these changes can help investigators uncover hidden information and gather stronger evidence for their investigations.

1. Why Tracking Deleted Posts & Profile Changes Matters

Tracking deleted content and profile modifications is essential for multiple reasons in an OSINT investigation:

Evidence Preservation: Social media users often delete posts or alter their profiles to cover tracks, hide controversial statements, or erase evidence of illegal activities. Capturing and preserving this deleted content can be crucial for proving a timeline or building a case in investigations ranging from cybercrime and fraud to political disinformation.

Behavioral Analysis: Changes to user profiles, such as profile pictures, personal information, or connections, can reveal shifts in a person's behavior or activities. Investigators can use these changes to uncover hidden motivations, affiliations, or intentions behind certain actions.

Exposure of Misinformation: In the case of disinformation campaigns, tracking changes and deleted content can reveal the intentional manipulation of public opinion. False narratives are often planted, only to be removed after causing damage, but investigative tools can help expose these tactics.

2. Challenges in Tracking Deleted Social Media Content

Tracking deleted posts and profile changes is far from straightforward, and several challenges complicate the process:

a. Platform Policies on Deletion

Social media platforms like Facebook, Twitter, Instagram, and LinkedIn offer users the ability to delete posts and modify profile details. However, once a post is deleted, it typically disappears from public view, and the platform's interface offers no indication of when or why content was removed. In some cases, posts that are deleted by the user may still exist in cached versions of the platform's data or in web archives. Understanding how each platform manages deletion is key to capturing this content:

Temporary Deletion vs. Permanent Deletion: On some platforms, deleted posts might be recoverable for a short period, while others may permanently erase them after a certain duration.

Metadata Loss: Deleted posts typically lose their associated metadata (such as timestamps, location data, or engagement metrics) once they are removed, though residual data can sometimes be found through caching systems or third-party tools.

b. Cached Data and Web Archives

One method of tracking deleted content involves checking whether the post is still available in cached versions or through web archives like the Wayback Machine. These platforms capture web pages periodically and can provide snapshots of what content looked like at a specific moment in time. However, not all social media sites are well-represented in these archives, and dynamic content such as social media feeds might not be fully archived.

c. Use of Third-Party Tools and Services

Although social media platforms make it easy for users to delete posts, third-party tools and forensic services often provide methods for investigating these deletions. Still, there is no single tool or method that guarantees full recovery of deleted content. Investigators need to employ a multi-faceted approach to maximize their chances of recovering or tracking deleted content.

3. Techniques for Tracking Deleted Posts & Profile Changes

Several strategies and tools can help investigators track deleted social media content and monitor profile changes:

a. Social Media Archiving Tools

Archiving tools are commonly used to capture and store social media content as it is posted, ensuring that copies of posts are retained even if they are later deleted. By archiving social media posts and user profiles in real time, investigators can create a database of content that may later be removed.

1. Archive.today:

This free online service allows users to capture a snapshot of a webpage (including social media posts) at a specific point in time. Once archived, the post or profile will be stored in the service's database, even if the content is later deleted from the original site.

2. PageFreezer:

PageFreezer is an enterprise-grade web archiving tool that provides users with a way to capture, store, and analyze live social media data. By monitoring and archiving public posts from platforms like Twitter, Facebook, and Instagram, investigators can keep a historical record of social media content that may be deleted later.

- **Strengths**: Real-time archiving, easy-to-use interface, comprehensive social media coverage.
- **Use Cases**: Government investigations, legal cases, and corporate reputation management.

b. Cached Data from Search Engines

Search engines such as Google and Bing store cached versions of web pages, including social media posts. By searching for the URL of a deleted post or profile, investigators can sometimes access a cached version of the page that was last indexed by the search engine.

1. Google Cache:

Google regularly caches social media pages and can display a version of the page that was indexed at a specific moment. If a post has been deleted, it may still be visible in Google's cache for a period of time. To access cached versions, search for the page URL in Google, click the three dots next to the URL in search results, and select "Cached."

2. Wayback Machine (Internet Archive)
:
The Wayback Machine provides access to archived versions of web pages, including social media sites. If a post or profile was live when the Wayback Machine crawled the page, it may still be accessible in its archive, even if it has been deleted from the platform. However, the Wayback Machine does not capture all social media platforms or real-time content, so its coverage may be limited.

c. Social Media APIs

Some platforms offer APIs (Application Programming Interfaces) that allow users to retrieve historical posts, comments, and profile details. While many of these APIs have limitations on how far back in time data can be accessed, they are often useful for retrieving posts that were once visible but have since been deleted. For example:

- **Twitter API**: While the Twitter API allows real-time data collection, developers can use advanced queries to gather historical data, including deleted tweets if they were captured before removal.
- **Facebook Graph API**: Similar to Twitter's API, the Facebook Graph API allows for querying posts and user profiles, although access to deleted posts might not be as direct unless captured prior to deletion.

d. Data Collection Services for Digital Forensics

Forensic data collection services, such as Cellebrite and X1 Social Discovery, are often used by law enforcement and private investigators to gather data from social media accounts, including deleted posts and profile changes. These services offer advanced digital forensic tools that can retrieve data from mobile devices, hard drives, and social media accounts, often bypassing typical privacy measures in place on platforms.

- **Strengths**: Highly accurate, able to recover deleted data, comprehensive analysis of online personas.

- **Use Cases**: Criminal investigations, corporate investigations, or any case requiring extensive recovery of digital evidence.

4. Legal and Ethical Considerations

While it is crucial to capture deleted social media content for investigations, investigators must always consider the legal and ethical boundaries of their actions:

- **Privacy Concerns**: Investigators must respect user privacy and adhere to relevant privacy laws, such as the GDPR in the EU and the CCPA in California, which regulate how personal data can be collected and used.
- **Consent and Authorization**: In some cases, investigators may need explicit consent or legal authorization (e.g., a court order) to retrieve deleted content, especially if private user data is involved.
- **Data Integrity**: Any recovered data must be carefully documented and preserved to maintain its integrity and admissibility in legal proceedings. This includes verifying the authenticity of the data and ensuring that the chain of custody is preserved.

Tracking deleted posts and changes to user profiles is an essential part of OSINT investigations, enabling investigators to uncover hidden information, preserve critical evidence, and track the evolution of digital footprints. While the process can be challenging due to platform-specific limitations and the transient nature of social media content, utilizing the right tools and techniques can significantly improve the chances of recovering deleted posts or identifying meaningful profile changes. By combining digital archiving, cached data, social media APIs, and forensic data collection tools, investigators can piece together a more complete picture of online activity, ensuring that deleted content does not escape scrutiny.

10.4 Using Automated Monitoring for Real-Time Intelligence

In the fast-paced and dynamic world of social media, real-time monitoring is essential for gathering actionable intelligence quickly and efficiently. Automated monitoring systems enable investigators, analysts, and organizations to track social media platforms continuously, providing insights into emerging trends, detecting threats in real time, and uncovering critical data as it happens. This section explores how automated monitoring systems work, the benefits of using them, and the tools available for real-time social media intelligence gathering.

1. The Need for Real-Time Intelligence in OSINT

Real-time social media monitoring allows investigators to stay ahead of rapidly developing situations and provides up-to-the-minute data that can be critical in various types of investigations, such as:

- **Crisis Management**: In times of natural disasters, terrorist attacks, or other emergencies, monitoring social media feeds in real time can help identify important developments, locate survivors, track rumors, and uncover threats.
- **Brand Monitoring & Reputation Management**: Companies need real-time monitoring to respond swiftly to customer complaints, potential PR crises, or negative sentiment that could damage their brand.
- **Political & Social Monitoring**: Real-time intelligence can help track political movements, uncover disinformation campaigns, or monitor protests, demonstrations, and other social movements.
- **Security & Threat Intelligence**: Automated monitoring can help identify emerging threats, cyberattacks, or coordinated online harassment in real time, enabling rapid intervention.

Real-time intelligence gathered through automated monitoring tools allows for more timely decision-making, proactive response strategies, and the ability to quickly react to critical events. Without these tools, investigators would risk missing valuable data or delay their responses to fast-moving incidents.

2. Key Features of Automated Social Media Monitoring Systems

Automated monitoring systems are designed to capture large volumes of data continuously and analyze them to provide actionable insights. These systems offer a variety of essential features for effective OSINT investigations:

a. Continuous Data Collection

Automated tools collect data around the clock, scanning social media platforms and websites for relevant keywords, hashtags, locations, and user activity. This eliminates the need for manual searching, saving time and ensuring that investigators don't miss any significant developments. These systems can be set to track multiple platforms simultaneously, including Facebook, Twitter, Instagram, Reddit, and others.

b. Real-Time Alerts & Notifications

One of the primary advantages of automated monitoring is the ability to receive real-time alerts based on predefined criteria. Investigators can set up specific triggers—such as the mention of a keyword, hashtag, or location—so that they are immediately notified whenever this information appears on social media. This feature is crucial in fast-moving investigations where every second counts.

Example Use Case: If a social media post about a potential threat to public safety is detected, the system sends an alert to the monitoring team, allowing them to respond quickly and assess the situation.

c. Keyword & Hashtag Tracking

Automated tools are capable of tracking specific keywords, hashtags, or phrases, making it easier to identify relevant posts and conversations in real time. By monitoring for trends, breaking news, or emerging topics, investigators can obtain valuable insights and detect patterns of interest quickly.

Example Use Case: Investigating the spread of a viral disinformation campaign would require real-time tracking of hashtags and keywords related to the false narrative. Automated monitoring ensures that no crucial post or comment is overlooked.

d. Geolocation Tracking

Many automated monitoring tools allow users to track social media activity based on geographic location. This is especially useful for gathering intelligence during events like protests, riots, or natural disasters, where knowing the location of certain posts can provide critical insights.

Example Use Case: Investigators can track posts from a specific geographic area to identify where incidents are taking place, locate key participants, and determine the scale of an event.

e. Sentiment Analysis

Sentiment analysis is the process of using natural language processing (NLP) and machine learning to gauge the tone and emotion behind social media posts. Automated monitoring tools can assess whether social media conversations are positive, negative, or neutral, which can help investigators identify public opinion trends, gauge the severity of a situation, or pinpoint escalating tensions.

Example Use Case: Monitoring public sentiment in response to a political leader's controversial statement could provide valuable insights into voter mood and potential reactions.

3. Popular Tools for Automated Social Media Monitoring

A variety of automated tools are available for social media OSINT investigations, offering different functionalities depending on the scope of monitoring required. Here are some of the most popular options:

a. Hootsuite

Hootsuite is a widely used social media management and monitoring platform that allows users to track conversations across multiple social media channels in real time. It includes features for keyword and hashtag monitoring, sentiment analysis, and generating reports on trends and mentions.

- **Strengths**: User-friendly, integrates with many social media platforms, good for both personal and professional use.
- **Use Case**: Ideal for brand monitoring and crisis management.

b. Brandwatch

Brandwatch is a powerful social media listening tool that specializes in real-time monitoring and analytics. It provides in-depth sentiment analysis, topic clustering, and geo-mapping, enabling investigators to track trends and uncover emerging issues in real time.

- **Strengths**: Comprehensive analytics, advanced filtering, and integration with other business tools.
- **Use Case**: Best suited for large-scale investigations into public sentiment, disinformation campaigns, and social movements.

c. Meltwater

Meltwater is another robust media intelligence tool designed to monitor social media channels, news sources, and blogs in real time. It offers advanced analytics, reporting, and automated alerts, making it useful for detecting and tracking online trends.

- **Strengths**: Real-time reporting, media insights, keyword tracking, and geolocation-based monitoring.
- **Use Case**: Effective for monitoring both social media and news websites in crisis situations.

d. Talkwalker

Talkwalker is an AI-powered social media analytics platform that provides real-time monitoring of social media channels. It can track specific hashtags, keywords, and mentions while offering sentiment analysis, demographic data, and real-time alerts.

- **Strengths**: Advanced AI-powered analytics, great for tracking both global and niche conversations.
- **Use Case**: Ideal for monitoring brand reputation, tracking political sentiment, and uncovering emerging issues in real time.

e. TweetDeck

TweetDeck is a specialized tool for monitoring Twitter. It allows users to create customized feeds based on specific keywords, hashtags, or user accounts, providing a real-time view of relevant conversations. It's particularly useful for individuals or teams focused on Twitter analysis.

- **Strengths**: Free tool, great for focused Twitter monitoring, allows users to track multiple feeds simultaneously.
- **Use Case**: Best for investigators specifically tracking Twitter activity and live conversations.

4. Benefits of Automated Monitoring in OSINT Investigations

Automated social media monitoring offers several key advantages to investigators and analysts:

a. Speed and Efficiency

Manual monitoring is time-consuming and prone to human error. Automated tools, on the other hand, provide continuous, real-time tracking with minimal human involvement, saving time and resources while ensuring comprehensive coverage of relevant data.

b. Scalability

Automated systems can monitor vast amounts of data across multiple social media platforms simultaneously, making them scalable for both small-scale and large-scale investigations. Whether tracking a single hashtag or monitoring global trends, these systems can handle large volumes of data without sacrificing speed or accuracy.

c. Enhanced Accuracy

By relying on automated algorithms and AI, investigators can minimize human biases and errors. Sentiment analysis, keyword tracking, and geolocation data can be processed quickly and accurately, allowing investigators to focus on the most relevant data for their case.

d. Real-Time Decision Making

Automated monitoring provides real-time insights, which is crucial for time-sensitive investigations. This allows investigators to respond quickly to emerging threats, public sentiment shifts, or breaking news, ensuring they remain agile and proactive.

Automated monitoring is a powerful tool in OSINT investigations, offering real-time intelligence, comprehensive data tracking, and enhanced decision-making capabilities. By leveraging automated tools to monitor social media, investigators can stay ahead of emerging trends, uncover valuable data, and respond to critical situations promptly. From crisis management and threat detection to social media listening and brand monitoring, automated monitoring is a vital component of any OSINT strategy. With the right tools in place, investigators can maximize their ability to collect, analyze, and act on social media data in real time, ensuring that they never miss crucial information in the fast-paced digital world.

10.5 Building an Effective SOCMINT Monitoring Workflow

Effective Social Media Intelligence (SOCMINT) monitoring requires a systematic approach that ensures critical data is captured, analyzed, and acted upon in real-time. Given the vast amount of information available on social platforms, a well-defined workflow is essential to ensure that analysts can efficiently manage and interpret data while maintaining the integrity and accuracy of their investigations. In this section, we will explore the components of a robust SOCMINT monitoring workflow and how to establish a seamless process that maximizes the effectiveness of your intelligence-gathering efforts.

1. Defining Your Objectives and Scope

Before diving into the technical aspects of monitoring, it is essential to clearly define your objectives and the scope of the investigation. A focused approach helps streamline the workflow, minimize noise, and prioritize the most relevant data for your goals. Your objectives will shape your monitoring strategy, influence which platforms to target, and determine the data points you should focus on.

Key Considerations:

- **What type of investigation are you conducting?** (e.g., crisis management, political intelligence, brand monitoring, threat detection)
- **Which platforms are most relevant to your investigation?** (e.g., Twitter, Facebook, Reddit, Instagram, TikTok)
- **What key data points do you need to monitor?** (e.g., hashtags, user activity, sentiment, trends, geolocation)

By clearly defining your objectives at the outset, you can ensure that the information you collect is useful and actionable.

2. Selecting the Right Tools for Monitoring

The tools you select to monitor social media will significantly impact the efficiency and success of your workflow. The right combination of tools allows you to automate repetitive tasks, set up alerts for critical data, and track real-time information across multiple platforms. Depending on your investigation's scope, you might need a combination of general social media monitoring tools and platform-specific software.

Tool Categories to Consider:

- **Social Media Monitoring Platforms**: These tools enable you to track keywords, hashtags, mentions, and trends across multiple social media platforms in real-time. Examples include Brandwatch, Talkwalker, Hootsuite, and Meltwater.
- **Platform-Specific Tools**: Some platforms, such as TweetDeck for Twitter or InstaFollow for Instagram, provide more tailored capabilities for specific networks.
- **Geospatial Intelligence Tools**: Platforms that specialize in geolocation data, such as Geofeedia and x-Geo, can track social media posts based on geographical location.

- **AI & Sentiment Analysis Tools**: Tools that use artificial intelligence to analyze text and determine sentiment or emotions, such as Crimson Hexagon or MonkeyLearn, can help identify trends, opinion shifts, or potential threats.

Best Practice:

Choose tools that integrate well with each other and allow for seamless data aggregation. The goal is to avoid information silos and ensure that relevant data can be easily analyzed in one unified dashboard.

3. Data Collection & Real-Time Monitoring

Data collection is the foundation of any SOCMINT monitoring workflow. Automating the process to collect relevant data from social platforms in real time ensures that you are always aware of the latest developments. A well-executed data collection strategy not only increases efficiency but also ensures that no important information is overlooked.

Steps to Ensure Effective Data Collection:

Set Up Real-Time Alerts: Configure automated alerts based on keywords, hashtags, mentions, geolocations, or user activity. Alerts will notify you whenever your predefined conditions are met, enabling you to track significant developments as they happen.

Use Advanced Search Filters & Operators: Employ search operators and filters to narrow your results, such as Boolean operators, geographic filters, and content type filters. These advanced searches allow you to focus on the most relevant data points and reduce the risk of information overload.

Track Multiple Platforms Simultaneously: Leverage tools that allow you to track social media conversations across various platforms in parallel. For example, monitor Twitter, Reddit, and Instagram for the same hashtag or event to gain a 360-degree view of the conversation.

4. Data Filtering & Prioritization

Not all data collected in real time is valuable. In fact, the volume of data on social media can often lead to information overload, making it essential to filter and prioritize based on your objectives. A strategic approach to filtering ensures that you focus on the most relevant and actionable intelligence while discarding noise.

Key Techniques for Filtering Data:

Keyword Filtering: Identify and track keywords that are most likely to produce valuable information. These may include terms related to your specific investigation or event, such as keywords related to a crisis or trending topic.

Content Relevance Scoring: Use sentiment analysis and contextual tools to evaluate the relevance of each piece of content. For instance, social media posts that mention a specific location during an emergency are far more important than general posts on a similar topic.

User Influence & Activity Level: Not all social media accounts are equal in terms of influence or credibility. Monitor and prioritize posts from key users, such as influencers, government officials, or eyewitnesses, whose posts may carry more weight in your investigation.

Best Practice:

Establish clear filtering rules based on relevance, authority, and urgency to help prioritize critical data. Filtering can be further refined through AI-powered sentiment analysis and NLP techniques that can assess the emotional tone and intent of posts.

5. Analysis & Intelligence Extraction

Once data has been filtered, the next step is to extract meaningful intelligence. This involves identifying patterns, uncovering hidden insights, and making connections that could be useful for decision-making. This step is where the raw data is transformed into actionable intelligence.

Methods of Data Analysis:

Trend Analysis: By tracking hashtags, keywords, or topics over time, you can identify trends, shifts in sentiment, or patterns of behavior. This can be especially useful for monitoring the escalation of events or identifying viral content.

Sentiment & Emotional Analysis: Analyzing the tone of social media posts can help determine whether the overall conversation is positive, negative, or neutral. This can be useful for identifying public opinion on a political issue, product launch, or public figure.

Network Analysis: In some cases, you may need to map out connections between users, identify potential influencers, or uncover hidden communities. Tools like NodeXL and Gephi can help visualize social media networks, making it easier to identify key players.

Geospatial Analysis: Monitoring the geolocation data tied to posts can help you identify geographic trends or track the movements of individuals or events.

Best Practice:

Apply multiple methods of analysis to ensure that you gain a comprehensive understanding of the situation. Combining sentiment analysis with trend analysis, for example, will provide you with a deeper insight into the context and implications of specific events.

6. Reporting & Decision-Making

After data has been analyzed, the next step is to report findings and make decisions. A key part of building an effective monitoring workflow is ensuring that intelligence is communicated clearly and efficiently to stakeholders. Reports should be structured, actionable, and tailored to the needs of the intended audience.

Best Practices for Reporting:

Use Clear, Concise Visualizations: Present data in easy-to-understand formats like graphs, charts, and maps to highlight key trends and findings. Visualization tools like Tableau or Power BI can help make complex data more digestible.

Real-Time Dashboards: Set up a real-time dashboard where you can track and view ongoing developments as they unfold. This is especially useful for decision-makers who need to react quickly to emerging events.

Contextualize Your Findings: It's important to present findings with context. Explain the significance of trends, sentiment shifts, or key posts to ensure that your analysis is not only accurate but also actionable.

Best Practice:

Make sure reports include recommendations or suggested actions based on the intelligence gathered. This will help ensure that the insights lead to tangible, effective responses.

7. Continuous Improvement & Workflow Optimization

SOCMINT is an ever-evolving field, and monitoring workflows must be continuously refined to stay effective. Feedback loops, performance evaluations, and technology upgrades should be incorporated into your monitoring strategy to optimize processes over time.

Key Areas for Ongoing Improvement:

Evaluate Tool Performance: Regularly assess the effectiveness of your monitoring tools and upgrade them as necessary. New tools with improved capabilities are constantly emerging.

Refine Data Collection Parameters: Adjust your filters and search terms based on past findings to continuously improve data relevance and reduce noise.

Review Analytics & Reports: After each investigation, evaluate how well the analysis aligned with the objectives. Use insights gained to optimize future workflows.

Building an effective SOCMINT monitoring workflow involves much more than simply collecting data from social media platforms. It requires a strategic, focused approach that encompasses everything from setting objectives and selecting the right tools to analyzing data and reporting findings. By establishing a clear and efficient workflow, investigators can ensure that they capture timely, accurate intelligence and act quickly to address emerging threats, crises, or opportunities. As the digital landscape continues to evolve, continuously improving your SOCMINT monitoring process will be crucial to staying ahead of potential challenges and ensuring the success of your investigations.

10.6 Case Study: Archiving Social Media Evidence for a Legal Investigation

Social media platforms are frequently used as critical sources of evidence in legal investigations, whether they involve criminal activity, defamation, intellectual property disputes, or civil litigation. Archiving social media evidence is essential for maintaining the integrity of digital data and ensuring that it is admissible in court. In this case study, we will explore how social media evidence was archived and utilized in a legal investigation, highlighting the best practices for collecting, preserving, and presenting this type of digital evidence.

Background: The Case of Online Defamation

In this case study, we explore a defamation lawsuit where a well-known public figure, John Doe, sued a former business partner, Jane Smith, for damaging his reputation through false statements posted on her social media accounts. Jane had published a series of posts on Twitter, Facebook, and Instagram, alleging that John had been involved in illegal activities, leading to significant harm to his reputation and business dealings.

John's legal team needed to gather and preserve social media evidence to prove the defamation claims. The challenge was not only to capture the content of the posts but also to ensure that the evidence was preserved in such a way that it would be admissible in court.

Step 1: Identifying Relevant Social Media Content

The first step in the process was identifying the social media posts that contained defamatory statements. John's legal team worked with a digital forensics expert to search across multiple platforms where Jane had posted the allegations. The team employed advanced search techniques to track down specific posts by searching for keywords, hashtags, and mentions that were associated with the defamation.

- **Twitter**: The legal team identified tweets from Jane's account containing defamatory claims, including a series of hashtags that referred to John's alleged criminal behavior.
- **Facebook**: They found a number of public posts on Jane's timeline, as well as comments from other users amplifying the defamation.
- **Instagram**: Instagram stories and posts were located that contained damaging captions and images tied to the allegations.

Best Practice:

When archiving social media evidence, it is essential to track content across multiple platforms, as users often post similar or cross-platform content. For legal investigations, keeping a broad scope of collection ensures that no critical evidence is overlooked.

Step 2: Capturing and Archiving Social Media Data

Once the relevant posts were identified, the legal team had to preserve the evidence to ensure that it was unaltered and could be presented in court. To do this, they followed a strict digital forensics procedure to capture, archive, and store the data securely.

The team used specialized archiving tools designed to capture social media content while maintaining the integrity of the original data. These tools ensured that metadata, including timestamps, user IDs, and geographic information, were preserved alongside the content itself. For social platforms like Twitter and Facebook, where posts can be deleted, tools like MediaSonar, WebPreserver, and SocialSafe were used to make "snapshots" of the posts and comments.

Key Components of the Archiving Process:

Data Capture: The posts were captured in their entirety, including captions, images, and videos. For Twitter and Instagram, screenshots were taken as a backup to the captured data, ensuring that the posts could be viewed in their original context.

Preserving Metadata: Metadata was essential for verifying the authenticity of the evidence. The legal team made sure to capture information like timestamps (down to the second), user location, IP addresses (when available), and post IDs.

Ensuring Authenticity: Tools like WebPreserver provided a digital certificate for each archived page, ensuring that the captured data was authentic and could be verified. This was important for ensuring the data would be admissible in court.

Best Practice:

Always use trusted and industry-standard tools to capture and store social media data. Collecting screenshots or screen recordings alone may not be enough for legal purposes, as they can be challenged in court. Proper tools preserve the full scope of evidence, including metadata, which adds to the credibility of the evidence.

Step 3: Organizing and Storing Archived Data

After capturing the relevant social media posts and metadata, the team needed to store and organize the data in a secure manner. Digital evidence is vulnerable to tampering, so it was critical to ensure that the archived content was stored in a secure and encrypted environment. The team used a chain of custody system to document who had access to the data and when it was accessed, which is an essential step in ensuring that the evidence is admissible in court.

Chain of Custody: The legal team maintained detailed logs that tracked the handling of the evidence. This log included the identity of the individuals who collected the data, the tools used, the dates and times the data was accessed, and any changes made to the files (if applicable). This is necessary for proving that the evidence had not been altered or tampered with during the investigation.

Daat Storage: The archived social media content was stored in a secure server, with encrypted backups, to ensure that the data was not susceptible to being lost or accessed without permission.

Best Practice:

Always follow proper data handling protocols, including maintaining a chain of custody and storing data in a secure, encrypted environment. These practices will protect the integrity of the evidence and help it withstand scrutiny in legal proceedings.

Step 4: Presenting Social Media Evidence in Court

With the social media evidence preserved, the legal team proceeded to organize the data in a manner that could be presented to the court. The goal was to ensure that the evidence was not only understandable but also persuasive. The team used data visualization tools to present a timeline of events, including the publication of defamatory posts and their impact on John's reputation. They also demonstrated how the posts were amplified by other users, further increasing the harm caused by Jane's allegations.

Effective Use of Evidence in Court:

Timeline Creation: A timeline of posts was created to show the sequence of defamatory statements over time. This helped to contextualize the impact of the posts, showing that they were made repeatedly and with a clear intent to harm.

Expert Testimony: A digital forensics expert was called to testify about the process used to collect, preserve, and analyze the social media evidence. This expert explained how the tools worked and how metadata was preserved, which helped to establish the credibility of the evidence in the eyes of the court.

Visual Presentation: The evidence was displayed in court using clear visuals, such as screenshots of the social media posts, graphs that showed engagement levels, and maps that demonstrated the geographic spread of the defamatory posts.

Best Practice:

Organize and present social media evidence in a manner that is easy to understand for a non-technical audience, such as the judge or jury. Use clear visual aids and expert testimony to support your case and ensure that the evidence is credible and persuasive.

Step 5: Challenges in Archiving Social Media Evidence

Throughout the process of archiving social media evidence, the legal team encountered several challenges:

Platform Limitations: Social media platforms like Instagram and Facebook often change their privacy policies, which can affect the accessibility of certain posts or metadata. Legal teams must keep up to date with platform changes and adapt their strategies accordingly.

Post Deletion: One of the most significant challenges in social media investigations is the potential for posts to be deleted. While archiving tools can capture live data, deleted content may still exist in cached versions or may need to be retrieved through forensic techniques.

Legal and Privacy Considerations: When archiving social media content, it is essential to comply with privacy laws and regulations, especially regarding the collection of personal data from users. The legal team needed to ensure that no rights were violated during the archiving process.

Best Practice:

Stay informed about platform changes, privacy laws, and any other relevant legal or regulatory updates to avoid complications in the archiving process. Always ensure that the methods used are legally compliant.

This case study highlights the importance of following a thorough, methodical process when archiving social media evidence for legal investigations. By employing specialized tools, maintaining a chain of custody, and organizing data clearly, investigators can ensure that social media content remains a reliable and admissible source of evidence in court. In John's defamation case, the archived social media posts played a pivotal role in proving the harm caused by Jane's statements and ultimately led to a successful legal outcome. Properly archiving social media evidence is essential for ensuring its credibility and integrity, making it a powerful tool in modern legal investigations.

11. Legal & Ethical Boundaries in SOCMINT

Operating within the legal and ethical boundaries of Social Media Intelligence (SOCMINT) is critical for ensuring responsible and lawful investigations. With varying data privacy laws, platform policies, and ethical considerations, OSINT analysts must navigate a complex landscape to avoid legal repercussions and maintain integrity. This chapter examines key legal frameworks such as GDPR, the CFAA, and platform terms of service, alongside ethical best practices for conducting social media investigations. By understanding the fine line between open-source intelligence gathering and potential violations, analysts can ensure their methods remain both effective and compliant.

11.1 Understanding the Legal Risks of Social Media Investigations

Social media has become an essential tool for open-source intelligence (OSINT) analysts, law enforcement, journalists, and private investigators. However, despite the potential benefits of leveraging social media for investigations, there are significant legal risks and ethical considerations that must be navigated. The process of collecting, analyzing, and utilizing social media data can raise a host of legal concerns, especially when it involves privacy rights, data protection, and access to public versus private information. Understanding these risks is crucial for anyone involved in conducting or overseeing social media investigations.

1. Privacy Concerns and Data Protection

One of the most pressing legal risks in social media investigations is the potential violation of privacy rights. While social media platforms are inherently public, users often have different expectations of privacy depending on the platform's settings, their online behavior, and their legal jurisdiction.

Public vs. Private Content:

Social media platforms, such as Facebook, Instagram, and Twitter, allow users to control the visibility of their posts, creating a mix of public and private content. Public posts are typically accessible to anyone, including investigators, but private content (such as direct messages, private group discussions, and hidden profiles) should not be accessed without permission or a legal basis.

Legal Risk: Accessing private content without authorization, even if it is publicly visible at one point in time, could be considered an infringement on privacy. This could lead to legal challenges, especially if a user claims their rights were violated. In some jurisdictions, accessing private data without consent can lead to charges under privacy laws such as the General Data Protection Regulation (GDPR) in Europe, or The California Consumer Privacy Act (CCPA) in the United States.

Sensitive Information:

Social media posts can sometimes contain sensitive information, such as health details, financial records, or personal identification numbers. Collecting and processing this type of data without the consent of the user could result in serious legal consequences.

Legal Risk: The misuse of sensitive personal information could result in charges of data breach or misuse of personal data, particularly under global privacy regulations. Investigators need to be aware of these laws and ensure they are not infringing upon users' rights when collecting or handling such data.

2. Unauthorized Data Collection and Scraping

Another legal issue related to social media investigations is the practice of data scraping, which refers to the automated extraction of large volumes of data from social media platforms. While scraping can be an efficient way to collect data, especially in large-scale investigations, it can also trigger legal consequences.

Terms of Service Violations:

Social media platforms have strict Terms of Service (TOS) agreements that users must agree to when creating accounts. These terms typically prohibit the use of automated tools (such as scraping bots) to collect data from the platform without authorization. By using such tools without permission, investigators might violate these terms, exposing themselves to potential legal action by the platform.

Legal Risk: Platforms like Facebook, Instagram, and Twitter have taken legal action against individuals or companies using scraping techniques to harvest user data. For example, in 2019, Facebook filed a lawsuit against a company for scraping user data for commercial purposes. Violating a platform's TOS could lead to legal challenges, including lawsuits for breach of contract.

Bot and Script Usage:

Many investigators rely on automated tools to track hashtags, monitor accounts, or scrape publicly available data. While this can be a useful technique, bots or scripts that interact with social media platforms may be considered unlawful, especially if they circumvent platform restrictions or attempt to gather information beyond what the platform allows.

Legal Risk: The use of bots or scripts to interact with platforms can potentially breach platform-specific terms or local anti-hacking laws, such as the Computer Fraud and Abuse Act (CFAA) in the United States.

3. Legal Risks in Surveillance and Tracking

Tracking users' activities across social media platforms is another investigative tactic that can lead to legal complications. Social media platforms inherently encourage users to share information, but the line between acceptable surveillance and illegal tracking can often be blurry.

Tracking User Activity:

Investigators may seek to track user activity across platforms by monitoring posts, geotags, check-ins, comments, and interactions. This type of surveillance, particularly if done without user consent, can raise concerns about intrusion upon seclusion or harassment, especially if it is done repeatedly or covertly.

Legal Risk: In some jurisdictions, continuous or invasive tracking can lead to legal action under laws regarding invasion of privacy. For example, secretly following someone's movements through their social media accounts or geolocation data could be viewed as a violation of privacy laws, including stalking or harassment statutes.

Geolocation Tracking:

Social media posts often include geolocation data, such as locations tagged in photos or check-ins at specific places. Although this information can be useful in investigations, accessing users' location data could be seen as an illegal intrusion into their private lives, especially if it involves tracking someone's movements over a period of time.

Legal Risk: In many cases, geolocation data is considered sensitive personal information. Collecting this data without the user's consent could violate data protection regulations and lead to legal repercussions, including potential charges of illegal surveillance.

4. Ethical and Legal Considerations of Data Manipulation

In social media investigations, the process of data manipulation is also a risk. While investigators can enhance or analyze data, care must be taken not to falsify or manipulate evidence. Social media evidence must be handled in ways that ensure its authenticity.

Preservation of Evidence:

One of the key risks in handling social media evidence is the potential for altering or tampering with data during analysis. Investigators must take extra care to preserve the original data and ensure that no modifications are made that could compromise the authenticity of the evidence.

Legal Risk: Manipulating or altering social media data to fit a narrative or create misleading impressions can lead to serious consequences. In legal investigations, tampering with evidence is a criminal offense and can result in charges of obstruction of justice or evidence tampering.

5. Risks of Defamation and Reputational Damage

Investigations into individuals or organizations via social media can also lead to defamation or reputational harm, especially when the public dissemination of findings may damage someone's reputation unjustly. Sharing personal or potentially damaging information without evidence or a legal basis can lead to legal repercussions.

Defamation via Public Disclosure:

In some cases, the publication of social media data in investigations can inadvertently harm an individual's reputation. For instance, highlighting a person's involvement in an online controversy or associating them with a criminal activity without sufficient proof could lead to defamation claims.

Legal Risk: Unsubstantiated claims or the premature dissemination of investigative findings may expose investigators to lawsuits for defamation, especially if the information is shared publicly without careful verification.

6. Jurisdictional Issues in International Investigations

Social media operates globally, and data collection or analysis involving international platforms can create jurisdictional conflicts, particularly when investigators are dealing with cross-border data or users from different legal systems.

Global Privacy Laws:

Investigating social media content from users in different countries may bring investigators into conflict with various international data protection and privacy laws. For example, GDPR in the European Union places strict restrictions on how personal data can be collected, processed, and shared.

Legal Risk: Failing to adhere to international privacy laws when collecting or processing social media data can result in significant fines or penalties. Investigators must be aware of jurisdictional differences and the specific legal requirements for data collection in different countries.

The legal risks associated with social media investigations are varied and complex. To mitigate these risks, investigators must be mindful of privacy regulations, respect user consent, and avoid violating platform terms of service. It is essential to have a clear understanding of local and international laws that govern the use of social media data, as well as to adopt ethical practices when conducting investigations. By remaining aware of these legal challenges, investigators can carry out social media OSINT investigations responsibly, while ensuring that the evidence they gather remains credible and legally sound.

11.2 Privacy Laws & Regulations Affecting OSINT Collection

Open-source intelligence (OSINT) is a valuable tool in investigations across various fields, including law enforcement, cybersecurity, corporate intelligence, and social media research. However, OSINT collection, especially from publicly available sources like social media platforms, must be done within the confines of privacy laws and regulations to ensure ethical and legal compliance. Privacy concerns are a critical aspect of OSINT, as investigators must balance the need for information with the rights of individuals to control their personal data. This chapter explores the privacy laws and regulations that affect OSINT collection, and how professionals can navigate these legal boundaries.

1. General Data Protection Regulation (GDPR)

The General Data Protection Regulation (GDPR), enacted by the European Union (EU) in 2018, is one of the most significant and comprehensive data protection laws affecting OSINT activities. The GDPR governs how personal data is collected, stored, and processed within the EU, and it applies to organizations outside of the EU if they process data about EU residents.

Key Provisions for OSINT:

- **Personal Data Definition**: The GDPR broadly defines personal data as any information relating to an identified or identifiable individual, including names, email addresses, location data, or social media posts. Even data that is publicly available (such as social media profiles) could still be considered personal data if it can be linked back to an individual.
- **Consent and Transparency**: The GDPR emphasizes the importance of user consent for the collection and processing of personal data. For OSINT, this means that even if data is publicly available, it cannot always be used without considering whether the data subject has consented to its use. Organizations conducting OSINT must be transparent about how they use and store data.
- **Data Minimization**: OSINT investigators must ensure that the data they collect is relevant and necessary for the specific purpose at hand, avoiding over-collection.
- **Right to Access and Erasure**: Under GDPR, individuals have the right to access, correct, or request the deletion of their personal data. This can complicate OSINT work, especially when investigating cases where individuals request their data to be removed.
- **Legal Risk**: Failing to comply with GDPR could lead to significant fines, up to €20 million or 4% of annual global turnover—whichever is higher. OSINT professionals should ensure they are familiar with these regulations, especially when investigating EU-based subjects.

2. California Consumer Privacy Act (CCPA)

The California Consumer Privacy Act (CCPA) is a state-level privacy law in the United States, effective as of 2020. It regulates the collection, use, and sale of personal data of California residents. While similar to the GDPR in some respects, there are distinct differences in the way it applies.

Key Provisions for OSINT:

- **Consumer Rights**: CCPA grants California residents several rights, including the right to know what personal data is being collected, the right to access their data, the right to delete their data, and the right to opt-out of the sale of their personal data.

- **Personal Information Definition**: Personal information under CCPA is defined broadly and includes identifiers such as names, addresses, social security numbers, browsing history, and even online activity like social media posts. OSINT professionals must be cautious when collecting this information from online sources that might involve California residents.
- **Data Sale Provisions**: The CCPA imposes restrictions on the sale of personal data, including the sale of information harvested from social media platforms. If a company or entity is involved in selling data as part of its OSINT practices, it must comply with this provision and allow consumers the option to opt-out of data sale.
- **Legal Risk**: Violations of CCPA can result in fines ranging from $2,500 per violation to $7,500 per intentional violation. In addition, individuals can take legal action in cases of data breaches.

3. The Right to be Forgotten (RTBF)

The Right to be Forgotten (RTBF), part of the GDPR, allows individuals to request the deletion of personal data that is inaccurate, outdated, or no longer relevant. While this right applies primarily to search engines like Google, it also impacts OSINT investigations, especially those relying on the online presence of individuals.

Key Provisions for OSINT:

- **Requests for Deletion**: Individuals can request the removal of personal data from online sources, including social media platforms. OSINT investigators must be aware that once data is removed upon request, it may no longer be available for analysis.
- **Public vs. Private Data**: RTBF often creates confusion when personal data is publicly available but may no longer be relevant or accurate. Social media users can request the removal of posts, but OSINT researchers must balance this with public interest.
- **Legal Risk**: Failure to honor the Right to be Forgotten requests could lead to lawsuits, particularly in jurisdictions that enforce data removal. Investigators should be prepared to handle removal requests sensitively and in compliance with local regulations.

4. Health Insurance Portability and Accountability Act (HIPAA)

While HIPAA is a U.S. federal law governing the privacy and security of medical information, it is relevant to OSINT collection in cases involving health-related information posted or shared on social media platforms. Health data, when it identifies individuals, is subject to strict privacy protections.

Key Provisions for OSINT:

- **Protected Health Information (PHI):** OSINT investigations that involve health-related data, such as medical conditions, diagnoses, or treatment details, could violate HIPAA if such data is disclosed without authorization.
- **Public Disclosure of Health Information:** Investigators should exercise caution when collecting health information from online sources, ensuring that it is not part of a protected health record.
- **Legal Risk:** OSINT professionals who inadvertently collect health data that violates HIPAA may be subject to civil penalties. The penalties can range from $100 to $50,000 per violation, depending on the level of negligence.

5. Children's Online Privacy Protection Act (COPPA)

The Children's Online Privacy Protection Act (COPPA) is a U.S. law that regulates the collection of personal information from children under the age of 13. OSINT practitioners need to be particularly cautious when collecting data from platforms where children may be active, such as gaming or social media sites.

Key Provisions for OSINT:

- **Parental Consent:** COPPA requires platforms to obtain verifiable parental consent before collecting personal information from children under 13. Investigators should avoid gathering data related to minors without proper authorization or legal justification.
- **Prohibited Data Collection:** Certain types of data about children, such as geolocation, browsing behavior, and identifiers, are strictly regulated.
- **Legal Risk:** Violating COPPA can result in hefty fines, ranging from $16,000 per violation. OSINT professionals need to ensure they are not inadvertently collecting data related to minors.

6. Local Privacy Laws and Jurisdictional Issues

Different countries and even individual states have unique privacy laws that affect how OSINT is conducted. For example, countries in the Asia-Pacific region may have their own privacy laws, such as Australia's Privacy Act or China's Personal Information Protection Law (PIPL). These laws may restrict or regulate how data can be collected, shared, or stored.

Key Provisions for OSINT:

- **Cross-Border Data Transfers**: Many OSINT investigations involve collecting data from users in multiple countries, creating challenges related to data transfer laws. Some countries have restrictions on transferring data outside of their borders, especially personal data.
- **Jurisdictional Challenges**: Different legal jurisdictions can create confusion over which laws apply to a specific piece of data, especially in global investigations.
- **Legal Risk**: Failing to understand and comply with local privacy laws and jurisdictional issues can result in legal disputes, fines, and data breaches.

Privacy laws and regulations are essential components of responsible OSINT collection. OSINT professionals must be aware of global data protection laws, including the GDPR, CCPA, HIPAA, and COPPA, among others, to ensure that their investigative practices respect individuals' privacy rights. Ethical and legal OSINT collection involves careful consideration of data minimization, transparency, and obtaining consent where necessary. Navigating the complex landscape of privacy laws is crucial to avoiding legal pitfalls, ensuring compliance, and maintaining trust in OSINT practices.

11.3 The Ethics of Analyzing & Sharing Social Media Data

Social media platforms are a goldmine of publicly accessible data, making them invaluable for open-source intelligence (OSINT) investigations. From identifying criminal activity to tracking public sentiment, social media data provides insights that can significantly aid in understanding behavior, trends, and relationships. However, analyzing and sharing social media data is fraught with ethical challenges that demand careful consideration. This chapter explores the ethical issues surrounding the collection, analysis, and dissemination of social media data, and highlights best practices for ensuring responsible, respectful, and lawful OSINT use.

1. Respecting Privacy Rights

While much of social media data is publicly accessible, it is crucial to remember that individuals still have a fundamental right to privacy, even in online spaces. Privacy is not merely about keeping information hidden but about ensuring that data is used in ways that respect an individual's control over their own information.

Key Ethical Considerations:

- **Public vs. Private Data**: Just because data is available publicly does not mean it should automatically be used in an investigation. Social media users often post content that they believe is visible to a select audience (e.g., friends or followers), not for broad public analysis. Investigators must assess the context in which data was shared and ensure that public information is used with respect for its intended scope.
- **Sensitive Information**: Social media profiles may contain sensitive personal data, such as health issues, political opinions, or personal relationships. Investigators must be careful to avoid using such data unless it is directly relevant to the investigation and done so without harm or exploitation of the individual involved.
- **Privacy Settings and Expectations**: Many users adjust their privacy settings to restrict the visibility of certain posts or personal details. Ethical OSINT practice requires investigators to respect these settings. Just because a post is not easily accessible doesn't mean it is okay to bypass privacy barriers (e.g., through hacking or exploiting platform vulnerabilities).
- **Ethical Risk**: Violating privacy can lead to harm for individuals, including reputational damage, discrimination, and emotional distress. It may also result in legal consequences and erode public trust in OSINT practices.

2. Transparency and Informed Consent

Transparency and informed consent are cornerstone principles of ethical research, including OSINT investigations. While it may not always be feasible to obtain explicit consent for every social media search, investigators should aim to be transparent about their methods and purposes, ensuring that the collection and use of data is fair and justifiable.

Key Ethical Considerations:

- **Disclosure of Intent**: When gathering social media data for research or investigative purposes, it's essential to be clear about why the data is being collected and how it will be used. Although users might not provide consent in traditional forms, ensuring the legitimacy of the research purpose is crucial.
- **Ethical Data Collection**: Avoid exploiting loopholes in platform terms of service, such as using scraping tools to bypass user privacy settings or harvesting large

volumes of data for purposes unrelated to the investigation. Ethical OSINT requires that data collection techniques be in line with both legal requirements and the principles of fairness.

- **Respecting Content Creators**: Content creators on social media often share their work with the expectation of recognition or compensation. If their data or content is used in an OSINT investigation, ensuring that it is properly attributed and does not breach the creator's intellectual property rights is an important ethical concern.
- **Ethical Risk**: Failure to respect informed consent and transparency can harm the credibility of an investigation, lead to public backlash, and violate ethical guidelines in research or professional practice.

3. Avoiding Harmful Stereotyping and Bias

One of the most significant ethical challenges in social media OSINT is ensuring that the data collected is not used to reinforce harmful stereotypes or biased narratives. Social media platforms are filled with diverse voices and perspectives, but they are also rife with misinformation, extremism, and polarized content.

Key Ethical Considerations:

- **Contextual Analysis**: When analyzing social media data, it is essential to consider the context in which content was posted. A tweet, post, or comment taken out of context can easily be misinterpreted or manipulated to serve a particular agenda.
- **Avoiding Discrimination**: Data analysis must be done without unfairly targeting or stigmatizing specific groups based on race, gender, religion, or other characteristics. Ethical OSINT investigations avoid profiling individuals or groups in ways that perpetuate discrimination or harm.
- **Mitigating Confirmation Bias**: Investigators must be aware of their own biases and avoid selectively analyzing or interpreting data that aligns with preconceived notions. This requires diligent effort to collect a broad, balanced, and representative sample of data to avoid misrepresentation or distortion of facts.
- **Ethical Risk**: Bias in data analysis can result in inaccurate conclusions, harmful stereotypes, and unjust targeting of individuals or groups. This can also compromise the integrity of an investigation, leading to flawed outcomes.

4. Minimizing Impact and Harm

Investigators must strive to minimize any potential harm caused by the use of social media data. While the goal of OSINT is often to uncover useful intelligence, ethical practitioners must consider the broader impact of their work, particularly on individuals who may not expect or consent to scrutiny.

Key Ethical Considerations:

- **Avoiding Public Disclosure of Sensitive Information**: When sharing findings from social media OSINT, it is essential to refrain from exposing personal details or content that could cause harm. This includes identifying individuals in sensitive contexts (e.g., victims of crimes, whistleblowers, or those at risk of harm).
- **Duty of Care in Reporting**: When using social media data for reporting, investigations, or intelligence assessments, ethical OSINT practitioners ensure that the information shared does not place individuals at risk or cause unwarranted panic or harm. For example, sharing details about a suspect's location or personal life without adequate consideration of safety could endanger them.
- **Ensuring Accountability**: Practitioners should be accountable for the data they share and ensure that it is not misused or manipulated by third parties. If there is any doubt about the ethical implications of sharing a particular dataset or conclusion, it is better to err on the side of caution.
- **Ethical Risk:** Unintended harm, such as causing emotional distress, threatening physical safety, or damaging reputations, can result from unethical data sharing practices. This can lead to significant legal and social consequences.

5. Ethics of Anonymity and Online Identities

A key component of social media data is the ability for individuals to maintain pseudonymous or anonymous profiles. OSINT practitioners must navigate the ethics of dealing with online identities, especially when individuals may choose to separate their personal and professional lives or remain anonymous for privacy or safety reasons.

Key Ethical Considerations:

- **Respecting Anonymity**: When investigating individuals with pseudonymous online identities, it is important to consider whether revealing their real-world identity could harm or expose them unnecessarily. Anonymity can be a tool for self-protection, particularly for whistleblowers, activists, and vulnerable individuals.
- **Avoiding Doxxing**: Doxxing refers to the malicious act of publicly exposing private, often sensitive, information about an individual without their consent. Ethical OSINT practitioners should avoid engaging in doxxing or facilitating the sharing of such information, especially in retaliation or harm.

- **Ethical Risk**: Violating an individual's desire for anonymity or engaging in doxxing can have severe legal, reputational, and emotional consequences for both the individual and the investigator.

6. The Ethical Imperative: Adopting Best Practices

To navigate the complex ethical landscape of social media OSINT, it is essential for practitioners to adopt best practices that ensure responsible, respectful, and lawful data collection and analysis. These practices include:

- **Regular Training**: Keeping up with evolving privacy laws, social media platform policies, and ethical guidelines through continuous professional development.
- **Ethical Review**: Implementing an ethical review process for all OSINT projects, involving independent assessments of potential risks and harm before data collection and dissemination.
- **Collaboration with Legal Teams**: Engaging with legal advisors to ensure that OSINT practices align with applicable laws and regulations.

The ethical analysis and sharing of social media data require a delicate balance between the need for information and the rights of individuals. OSINT professionals must adopt a holistic approach that respects privacy, promotes fairness, and minimizes harm. By following ethical guidelines and implementing best practices, practitioners can ensure that their work serves the public interest while safeguarding individuals' dignity and rights.

11.4 Avoiding Unlawful Access & Unauthorized Data Collection

In the realm of Social Media OSINT (SOCMINT), one of the most crucial ethical considerations is ensuring that all data collection practices are lawful and in compliance with the regulations and policies that govern online platforms. Unlawful access to social media accounts or unauthorized data collection not only undermines the integrity of an investigation but can also lead to serious legal consequences, reputational damage, and ethical violations. This chapter examines the importance of staying within legal boundaries when conducting OSINT investigations on social media and highlights strategies to avoid unauthorized access and ensure ethical data collection.

1. The Legal Framework for OSINT Investigations

Before diving into the details of lawful and unauthorized data collection, it is essential to understand the legal framework that governs data access and privacy in the context of social media. Various laws, regulations, and platform-specific terms of service outline the boundaries of what is permissible when gathering information from social media platforms.

Key Legal Considerations:

- **Data Protection Laws**: Laws such as the General Data Protection Regulation (GDPR) in the European Union, California Consumer Privacy Act (CCPA), and other data protection regulations impose strict rules on how personal data can be collected, used, and stored. These laws apply to individuals and entities that engage in OSINT activities, ensuring that personal information is not collected or processed in unlawful ways.
- **Platform Terms of Service**: Social media platforms, including Facebook, Twitter, Instagram, LinkedIn, and others, have specific terms of service that govern how users can access and interact with their data. Violating these terms, such as scraping data without permission or using automated tools to bypass restrictions, can result in account suspension or even legal action from the platform.
- **Computer Fraud and Abuse Act (CFAA):** In the United States, the CFAA criminalizes unauthorized access to computer systems and data. This includes accessing social media accounts, profiles, or private data without proper authorization, even if the information is publicly available on the platform.
- **Legal Risk**: Violating data protection laws, platform terms of service, or broader regulations could result in significant penalties, lawsuits, and even criminal charges. OSINT professionals must be fully aware of these laws to avoid legal consequences.

2. Understanding Unauthorized Data Collection

Unauthorized data collection refers to the act of accessing or collecting data from social media platforms in ways that violate the platform's terms of service, the law, or user privacy expectations. This could involve bypassing privacy settings, using unapproved tools or techniques to scrape data, or accessing private information without consent.

Common Examples of Unauthorized Data Collection:

- **Social Media Scraping**: Using automated scripts or bots to extract large amounts of data from social media platforms in ways that are against the platform's terms of service. For example, scraping user posts, comments, or profile information without consent is generally prohibited by most platforms.

- **Bypassing Privacy Settings**: Many social media users configure their privacy settings to limit the visibility of their posts and personal details. Accessing or harvesting this private data, even if it's possible to do so through public APIs or other means, could be considered unauthorized.
- **Accessing Private Accounts**: Attempting to access private social media accounts or personal data without explicit permission is a violation of both legal frameworks and platform policies. This may include methods such as phishing or hacking to obtain login credentials.
- **Using Unauthorized Tools**: Certain third-party tools and applications may promise enhanced data extraction capabilities but might not be approved by the platforms. Using such tools could violate terms of service, and in some cases, even be illegal.
- **Ethical Risk**: Engaging in unauthorized data collection can compromise the legitimacy of an investigation and lead to violations of user privacy. Additionally, using unethical techniques may lead to the potential spread of misinformation or harm to individuals whose data is improperly collected.

3. Tools & Techniques for Legal Data Collection

To avoid unlawful access and unauthorized data collection, it is essential to use tools and methods that comply with social media platforms' policies and relevant laws. Legal data collection methods should always prioritize transparency, fairness, and user consent, when applicable.

Best Practices for Legal Data Collection:

- **Use Public APIs**: Many social media platforms provide Application Programming Interfaces (APIs) that allow developers to legally collect publicly available data. APIs typically come with usage restrictions, such as rate limits, and terms of service that must be adhered to. For example, Twitter's API allows users to collect tweets, user profiles, and other public information, but it requires compliance with specific rules regarding data storage, sharing, and usage.
- **Focus on Public Data**: To ensure compliance with privacy laws and platform policies, always focus on collecting data that is publicly accessible. For example, posts that are publicly available without login or restriction, hashtags, public comments, and open group memberships are legitimate data points for OSINT investigations.

- **Manual Data Collection**: Instead of using automated scraping techniques, manually accessing publicly available social media profiles and posts ensures that you are not violating platform policies. This method may be time-consuming but guarantees that the data collection is transparent and within the platform's legal framework.
- **Respect Privacy Settings**: Even if data is accessible in some manner, respect the privacy settings of individual users. Avoid trying to access content that has been restricted to certain groups or followers unless there is explicit permission to do so.
- **Use Approved Third-Party Tools**: Some third-party tools are authorized by social media platforms for OSINT purposes. Always use approved tools that comply with platform terms and conditions to avoid unauthorized data collection. Always read and understand the terms of service before using such tools.
- **Legal Risk Mitigation**: By sticking to public data, using approved methods, and respecting privacy settings, OSINT investigators can significantly reduce the risk of engaging in unlawful data collection practices.

4. Managing Third-Party Data Access & Sharing

In some investigations, OSINT practitioners may work with third-party data providers or partners who have access to certain social media data. While this may help expedite the investigation process, it is important to ensure that third parties also adhere to legal and ethical standards.

Key Considerations for Third-Party Data Use:

- **Due Diligence on Data Providers**: Before using data from a third party, conduct a thorough review of their data collection methods to ensure compliance with legal standards. Using third-party data that was collected unlawfully can undermine the entire investigation and result in legal repercussions.
- **Data Sharing Agreements**: If working with a partner or external entity, ensure that there is a clear agreement in place that outlines how data will be collected, stored, shared, and protected. This agreement should include provisions for compliance with privacy laws, platform terms, and ethical guidelines.
- **Avoiding Data Misuse**: Even when working with third-party data, investigators must be careful not to misuse the data by taking it out of context, sharing it inappropriately, or making unwarranted conclusions based on incomplete or unverified information.

- **Legal Risk**: Failure to properly vet third-party data sources or to establish clear agreements on data use can expose the investigator or organization to legal liabilities, including charges of negligence or complicity in unlawful data access.

5. Consequences of Unlawful Access & Unauthorized Data Collection

The consequences of engaging in unlawful data collection can be severe, both for the individuals conducting the investigation and the entities they represent. Violations can lead to legal sanctions, loss of professional credibility, and damage to the trustworthiness of the OSINT community as a whole.

Potential Consequences:

- **Legal Penalties**: Unauthorized access to social media data can lead to lawsuits, fines, and in some cases, criminal charges. Platforms may also take legal action against individuals or organizations that violate their terms of service.
- **Reputational Damage**: Engaging in unethical or illegal data collection can result in a loss of trust, both from the public and from professional peers. Investigators and organizations known for unlawful practices can face long-term reputational damage that can hinder future investigations and partnerships.
- **Harm to Individuals**: Unlawful data collection can result in the exposure of personal or sensitive information without consent, leading to harm for individuals involved. This can include emotional distress, harassment, or even physical harm, especially in cases involving highly sensitive topics like criminal investigations or personal security.
- **Loss of Access to Data**: Platforms may block or restrict access to data sources for investigators who engage in unauthorized collection practices. This can prevent future investigations from being able to access vital information.
- **Ethical Risk**: Failing to avoid unlawful access and unauthorized data collection can result in harm not only to individuals but also to the broader OSINT field, leading to stricter regulations and oversight that could hinder future legitimate investigations.

In the field of social media OSINT, the ethical and legal risks associated with unlawful access and unauthorized data collection are significant. Investigators must be diligent in adhering to platform terms of service, data protection laws, and privacy considerations to ensure that their work remains lawful, ethical, and credible. By using authorized tools, focusing on publicly available data, respecting privacy settings, and working with trusted partners, OSINT professionals can avoid legal pitfalls and safeguard the integrity of their investigations. Legal and ethical compliance should always be at the forefront of any

OSINT initiative, ensuring that the benefits of open-source intelligence do not come at the expense of user rights and privacy.

11.5 Ethical Use of Social Media OSINT in Journalism & Research

The rise of Social Media OSINT (SOCMINT) has significantly transformed the fields of journalism and research by offering a powerful means of gathering real-time data, tracking events, and uncovering hidden narratives. With millions of users sharing information daily, social media platforms have become a goldmine for journalists and researchers seeking insights on public sentiment, trends, and breaking news. However, as social media investigations grow more pervasive, the ethical implications of collecting and analyzing online data become increasingly important. In this chapter, we will explore the ethical considerations specific to the use of SOCMINT in journalism and research, offering guidelines for responsible data collection, analysis, and reporting.

1. The Role of OSINT in Journalism and Research

In both journalism and academic research, social media OSINT provides access to vast amounts of data that were previously difficult or impossible to obtain. Journalists use social media OSINT to track breaking news, engage with sources, and monitor public reactions. Researchers, on the other hand, employ social media data to study societal trends, cultural movements, and political discourse.

Benefits for Journalism:

- **Real-Time Information**: Journalists can monitor breaking news and public reactions in real time, gaining a more immediate understanding of events as they unfold.
- **Diverse Sources**: Social media allows access to diverse voices and perspectives that may not appear in traditional news outlets, giving journalists a more comprehensive view of events.
- **Verification of Information**: Journalists can use social media data to corroborate or refute claims, helping them identify misinformation and provide more accurate reporting.

Benefits for Research:

- **Social and Behavioral Research**: Researchers studying human behavior can analyze social media trends and conversations to better understand public attitudes, political opinions, and societal issues.
- **Public Sentiment Analysis**: Using OSINT tools, researchers can gauge public sentiment during elections, political events, or in response to social movements.
- **Ethnographic Studies**: Social media provides a digital space for ethnographic research, where researchers can study online communities and subcultures in their natural environment.

Despite these benefits, journalists and researchers must exercise caution when using social media data. Ethical principles must guide the entire process—from data collection to analysis, interpretation, and reporting.

2. Ethical Guidelines for Social Media OSINT in Journalism

Journalism's core principle of accuracy and fairness requires that journalists approach social media OSINT with transparency, integrity, and responsibility. When using social media data, journalists must balance the need for compelling stories with respect for privacy and the rights of individuals.

Key Ethical Principles for Journalists:

Transparency: Journalists should clearly disclose their methods of data collection. If social media data or posts are used as sources, the public should understand how this information was obtained, whether it was publicly available or gathered through open APIs, and whether the data is original or secondary.

Respect for Privacy: While social media content is often public, journalists should still respect individuals' privacy. This includes exercising discretion when publishing sensitive information that could harm individuals, especially if their identities or personal details were not initially intended for broad exposure.

Minimizing Harm: Journalists have a responsibility to avoid causing harm through the publication of sensitive, misleading, or harmful information. Even if the data is publicly accessible, its publication could lead to personal or professional repercussions for the individuals involved. For instance, exposing the private posts of a person involved in a criminal investigation might violate their privacy and could even impede a legal process.

Accountability: Journalists must be accountable for the sources they use, including social media content. They should ensure that the data they cite is accurate and from reliable sources. Journalists should also strive to verify social media information before reporting it as fact, to avoid the spread of misinformation.

Avoiding the Spread of Misinformation:

Social media platforms are rife with misinformation, disinformation, and rumors. It is essential for journalists to cross-check data and apply rigorous fact-checking methods when citing social media content. Journalists should avoid sensationalizing unverified claims, even if they appear to be trending online, as this can exacerbate the spread of false or misleading information.

Example of Ethical Journalism:

An example of ethical use of social media OSINT in journalism would be when a journalist monitors social media during a political campaign to gauge public opinion. They carefully analyze relevant posts, fact-check claims, and verify sources before including any content in their report. If any content is sensitive, such as private posts or private messages, they would omit those details or redact identifying information to avoid harm to the individuals involved.

3. Ethical Guidelines for Social Media OSINT in Research

In academic research, social media provides a unique opportunity to gather qualitative and quantitative data. However, researchers must navigate the complexities of consent, privacy, and the ethical use of digital data. Researchers in fields like sociology, political science, and psychology often rely on social media data to analyze patterns, trends, and behaviors.

Key Ethical Principles for Researchers:

Informed Consent: In traditional research, participants are asked to consent to the collection and use of their data. In social media OSINT, researchers must find ways to respect the digital equivalent of consent. While public social media posts can be considered fair game for research, researchers should consider whether it is ethical to use this data without the explicit consent of the individuals involved. For instance, researchers should be cautious when dealing with sensitive content or analyzing personal accounts.

Anonymity and Confidentiality: Researchers should avoid revealing the identities of individuals when reporting their findings. Even if the data is publicly accessible, sharing identifying information about a person's social media posts could violate their privacy, especially if that information is used in an unexpected context. Anonymizing data should be a priority in any research publication.

Respect for the Data Context: Social media posts are made in a specific context, often in response to personal experiences or societal events. Researchers must be careful not to misinterpret or misrepresent data by removing it from its original context. The meaning of a post can change dramatically depending on its context, and researchers should avoid drawing conclusions that may be misleading or harmful.

Avoiding Harmful Use of Data: Just as journalists must avoid causing harm, researchers must consider the impact of their findings on the individuals or groups whose social media data they are analyzing. Researchers should take steps to ensure that their research does not perpetuate stereotypes, stigmatize individuals, or harm communities. They should also avoid contributing to the spread of harmful stereotypes or misinformation based on their findings.

Ethical Research Practices:

For instance, when conducting social media research on political discourse, researchers should consider the full context of posts, analyze data from various social media platforms to avoid bias, and provide clear disclaimers regarding the methods used. They must also anonymize individual contributors and ensure that their research is not used to discriminate against any specific groups or individuals.

4. Challenges in Balancing Ethics and Effectiveness

While social media OSINT offers unparalleled access to valuable data, the ethical considerations inherent in its use can sometimes conflict with the pressures of gathering useful or eye-catching information. The need for speed in journalism or the desire to make a groundbreaking discovery in research can push individuals to overlook ethical considerations, whether intentionally or not. Striking the right balance between effectiveness and ethics is a constant challenge.

Common Ethical Dilemmas:

- **Privacy vs. Public Interest**: Journalists and researchers may be tempted to use private data for stories that are of high public interest. However, such practices can undermine the trust of the public in the institution or research, especially if the information is deemed sensitive or invasive.

- **Speed vs. Accuracy**: The fast-paced nature of breaking news can lead to a rush in reporting. Social media data is sometimes collected and used hastily, without enough verification. This can result in errors or misinformation being presented as fact.
- **Sensationalism vs. Responsibility**: The need for compelling stories may encourage some to sensationalize or overemphasize social media findings, even if they are not fully verified or are part of a limited dataset. This can mislead the audience or contribute to the spread of false narratives.

The ethical use of social media OSINT in journalism and research requires a careful balance between maximizing the effectiveness of the data and adhering to core ethical principles. By respecting privacy, minimizing harm, ensuring informed consent, and exercising transparency, journalists and researchers can uphold the integrity of their work and ensure that social media data is used responsibly. The ethical guidelines presented here should serve as a compass, ensuring that SOCMINT remains a powerful tool for good while minimizing its potential for misuse. In an age where social media is an ever-growing source of information, it is crucial that those who use it to inform the public or advance knowledge do so with integrity, empathy, and respect for the individuals behind the data.

11.6 Case Study: A Legal Controversy in SOCMINT Investigations

In recent years, the integration of Social Media OSINT (SOCMINT) into investigations has led to notable successes, but also raised significant legal and ethical concerns. One high-profile case that underscores the complexities of SOCMINT in legal investigations occurred in 2018, involving a multinational corporation accused of corporate espionage. The investigation, which relied heavily on social media data, resulted in legal controversies and debates over privacy rights, unauthorized data collection, and the blurred lines of digital surveillance. This case serves as a cautionary tale about the legal risks and challenges that investigators face when using social media intelligence.

Background:

In 2018, a major technology company, TechGlobal Inc., suspected that a competitor was unlawfully gaining access to proprietary information. The company had already taken legal action against former employees and executives for possible data theft. However, they were unable to gather enough concrete evidence to present in court. To strengthen their case, TechGlobal hired a private investigation firm, SecureIntel Investigations, that specialized in OSINT to track down potential leaks and identify any online discussions regarding their intellectual property.

The investigators began by analyzing the social media activity of both current and former employees, focusing on posts, comments, and interactions related to TechGlobal's products, research, and upcoming innovations. They also tracked certain hashtags and online discussions in specialized forums and groups.

Through their analysis, the investigators uncovered multiple online posts from anonymous accounts on Twitter, Reddit, and Facebook that appeared to be discussing internal company documents and product details that were not publicly available. The posts were highly specific and appeared to be coming from individuals who had intimate knowledge of the company's inner workings.

The Legal Issues:

The use of social media OSINT in this case sparked several legal controversies, especially concerning privacy rights, unauthorized data collection, and whether the information obtained was admissible in court. Several key legal issues arose during the investigation:

1. Privacy Violations and Invasion of Personal Space:

One of the first concerns was whether the investigators had violated individuals' privacy rights by accessing publicly available social media accounts. In many cases, posts were shared by individuals on personal, private, or semi-public accounts. Although these posts were visible to the public at large, many individuals did not expect them to be collected and analyzed as part of an investigation.

Some employees, who were later implicated in the espionage case, claimed that their personal social media accounts were not public, or that the data collection methods used to gather the posts had violated their right to privacy. For example, SecureIntel Investigations had utilized sophisticated scraping tools that accessed detailed user data, including private groups, posts from closed networks, and some posts that had been deleted or archived by third parties.

2. The Legality of Data Scraping & Unauthorized Access:

The investigative firm had used automated scraping techniques to extract data from social media platforms. While scraping publicly available data is technically legal in many jurisdictions, it often violates the terms of service of platforms such as Facebook, Twitter, and Reddit. These terms explicitly prohibit scraping and data extraction tools that bypass the platform's own privacy settings.

Furthermore, data scraping from closed or semi-private forums—where the posts could be viewed by a limited audience—led to questions about the line between publicly accessible content and content that should be considered private. Some legal experts argued that while the data was technically accessible, the ethical and legal implications of accessing it without express consent could be problematic.

3. Misleading or Inaccurate Data:

The investigators also faced challenges regarding the accuracy and reliability of the data they had collected. Several of the posts they identified as potentially leaking company information were anonymous or made by accounts that could be faked or manipulated. There was concern that the use of social media OSINT to identify these accounts may have led to mistaken conclusions or false accusations.

As part of the case, it was revealed that certain online users used "sock puppet" accounts to create the illusion of insider knowledge, but these accounts were not directly associated with any employee. This raised questions about the admissibility of social media data in court and whether such data could be used to prove any wrongdoing beyond a reasonable doubt.

4. Ethical Considerations in Monitoring Employees:

Another layer of legal concern arose from the fact that many of the individuals under investigation were employees of TechGlobal. While their public posts were not directly protected by employer-employee confidentiality, the ethical dilemma of monitoring employees' online activity was raised. Investigators had accessed their social media profiles and posts without their knowledge, potentially violating boundaries that employees expected to be upheld by their employer.

Some of the employees argued that they had the right to express their views and opinions online without fear of surveillance, particularly since these posts were unrelated to their work and were made in private, non-work-related spaces. This prompted questions about the responsibility of employers to respect the digital privacy of their staff and whether monitoring online activity should be considered a breach of personal freedoms.

The Legal Outcome:

Despite the ethical and legal complexities, the evidence collected through social media OSINT was eventually used in court, but not without challenge. In the initial stages of the case, several motions to exclude the social media evidence were filed, arguing that the data was illegally obtained through scraping techniques, and that it violated the privacy rights of the individuals involved. The defense argued that the evidence was irrelevant and potentially misleading, as some of the accounts involved were created by third-party operatives who were not part of the company.

After several hearings, the judge ruled that while the scraping methods employed by the investigative firm were controversial, the publicly available nature of the data and the context of its use (as part of a corporate investigation) justified its inclusion in the case. However, the judge emphasized that companies must tread carefully when engaging in such activities, advising that future cases would require a more nuanced approach to the legal and ethical standards surrounding digital surveillance.

Ultimately, TechGlobal won the case, and several former employees were found guilty of leaking confidential company information. However, the case sparked widespread debate about the appropriate use of social media OSINT, especially regarding the ethical boundaries and the potential for legal risks.

Key Takeaways:

This case study highlights several critical lessons about the ethical and legal implications of using social media OSINT in investigations:

Privacy vs. Public Access: Even if social media data is publicly available, the collection and use of this data must still respect individual privacy rights. Investigators must be cautious not to overstep legal boundaries or cause harm by exposing personal information without consent.

Data Scraping & Legal Boundaries: While data scraping may provide valuable insights, it can violate social media platform terms of service and raise questions about the legality of such actions. Investigators must carefully consider whether their methods align with the platforms' terms and ensure that they are not engaging in unauthorized access.

The Complexity of Evidence: Social media data can be highly valuable in investigations, but its accuracy and authenticity must be thoroughly verified. Investigators must be cautious when using social media evidence, as misinformation, fake profiles, and manipulated content can cloud judgment and lead to legal challenges.

Ethical Monitoring in the Workplace: Employers must balance the need to investigate potential misconduct with respect for employee privacy. Monitoring employees' social media accounts should be done transparently and ethically, with clear boundaries established to avoid undue surveillance or violation of personal rights.

This case serves as a reminder that while social media OSINT can be an essential tool in investigations, it is fraught with legal and ethical challenges that require careful consideration. By adhering to strict ethical guidelines and legal standards, investigators can mitigate risks and conduct responsible, effective investigations.

12. Case Studies: Real-World Social Media OSINT

Theory and tools are only part of the equation—real-world applications of Social Media OSINT demonstrate its true power in intelligence gathering, investigations, and security operations. This chapter presents a series of case studies showcasing how analysts have successfully used SOCMINT techniques to track criminal activity, uncover disinformation campaigns, monitor geopolitical events, and identify threats in real time. By breaking down these cases step by step, readers will gain practical insights into the methodologies, challenges, and impact of social media intelligence in various fields, from cybersecurity to law enforcement and corporate security.

12.1 Using Social Media OSINT to Locate a Missing Person

In today's interconnected world, social media has become an invaluable tool in locating missing persons. The sheer volume of information shared daily on platforms like Facebook, Twitter, Instagram, and even niche forums can help investigators and concerned individuals track down missing persons in ways that were previously impossible. Social Media OSINT (SOCMINT) is increasingly being used by law enforcement agencies, private investigators, and even the general public to gather clues, track movements, and connect dots that lead to finding missing individuals. This chapter explores how social media OSINT can be leveraged in locating a missing person, outlining key techniques, real-life applications, and potential challenges.

Understanding the Role of Social Media in Missing Persons Cases

When someone goes missing, the initial steps typically involve filing a police report and conducting a search based on available information. However, in today's digital age, social media can often provide immediate leads that are critical for locating the missing individual. Social media platforms are frequently the first places people turn to when trying to communicate with family, friends, and acquaintances, especially in times of distress.

Steps to Leverage Social Media OSINT in Missing Persons Investigations

1. Review Public Posts, Photos, and Locations:

The first step in using social media OSINT is to thoroughly review the missing person's online presence. If the individual was active on social media, their profiles could contain critical information that might provide clues about their whereabouts. Investigators can examine publicly available posts, photos, comments, and locations shared on various platforms.

- **Facebook**: By reviewing status updates, location check-ins, and photos, investigators can track the last known whereabouts of the missing person. They can also identify friends or acquaintances who may have had contact with the person prior to their disappearance.
- **Instagram**: Instagram's geotagging feature allows users to add location information to posts and stories. This data can be invaluable for pinpointing the person's location around the time of their last known post.
- **Twitter**: Tweets, hashtags, and geotags can reveal where a person was at a specific time, especially when the missing person was involved in public events, protests, or other social activities.

2. Investigate Online Interactions and Mentions:

Often, people communicate with others on social media platforms before or after a significant event, and these interactions can provide insights into their state of mind, possible locations, or recent activities. Investigators can analyze the missing person's interactions with others in public posts or comments, direct messages, and tagged photos.

- **Mentions and Tags**: Look for any posts where the missing person is tagged by others. This can include friends, acquaintances, or even strangers, especially if there is a pattern that could indicate where the person has been or with whom they were last seen.
- **Friends and Followers**: Investigators can look at the person's list of social media contacts. The profiles of friends and followers may reveal shared activities, mutual acquaintances, or even private messages that could help further the investigation.

3. Investigate Live Social Media Activity:

If the missing person's social media account is still active after their disappearance, this provides a critical lead. The activity on these accounts can help identify potential suspects, associates, or people who may be responsible for the disappearance. Investigators can monitor the account for any new posts, messages, or updates that could reveal key information.

- **Live Videos or Stories**: Many platforms, like Instagram, Facebook, and TikTok, offer live video features. Investigators can examine any live videos or stories that were posted shortly before or after the disappearance. In some cases, these videos may provide valuable real-time evidence, such as visual clues about the person's location or any potential threats.
- **Notifications and Messages**: Some social media platforms allow users to send direct messages or interact privately with others. By analyzing these communications, investigators might find valuable clues that lead to the person's location or even uncover the motive behind the disappearance.

4. Use Reverse Image Search to Track Photos:

A powerful tool in social media OSINT is reverse image search. Investigators can use tools like Google's reverse image search or dedicated OSINT platforms to find other instances of a photo shared by the missing person. This technique allows investigators to trace the origins of specific images that may have been posted online by the missing person, which can lead to uncovering additional information about where the person was last seen or who they were with.

For example, if the missing person posted a photo at a specific landmark, investigators can search for that image elsewhere on the internet to see if the same photo was uploaded by others, providing further clues to the person's location or last known interactions.

5. Look for Hidden Messages or Inferences:

Social media activity can sometimes contain hidden messages or subtext that is not immediately obvious. Investigators can analyze language patterns, hashtags, or subtle references that might point to a crisis, an emergency, or distress. This can be especially important if the missing person left behind cryptic posts, unusual messages, or indirect references to a situation they were facing before their disappearance.

Additionally, by examining trends in the missing person's posts or their communication style, investigators can identify shifts that could indicate danger or an intention to leave without notice.

6. Explore Private Groups, Forums, and Niche Networks:

Many missing persons cases involve searching for evidence in private groups, forums, and closed networks. For example, if the missing person was a member of specific communities, online groups, or niche platforms, they may have posted about their plans, discussed personal matters, or interacted with others who might have information about their whereabouts. Investigators can request access to these private spaces (if appropriate) or contact group members to learn more about the person's state of mind and recent activities.

This is particularly relevant in cases where the individual may have joined groups related to specific topics like mental health, activism, or particular hobbies that may provide context for their disappearance.

Case Study: Locating a Missing Teenager Using Instagram OSINT

In 2019, a teenager named Sarah went missing after attending a music festival. Her parents were distraught and turned to social media OSINT to assist in locating her. The local authorities were struggling to find any leads. However, through diligent analysis of Sarah's Instagram account, investigators were able to track her movements during the festival by analyzing her Instagram Stories, posts, and geotagged photos.

Sarah had posted several photos at the festival, including pictures from the event's location and shots of a specific band playing. By reverse searching the images, investigators discovered that she had tagged several friends in those photos. This led to a breakthrough: One of her tagged friends had posted a story just hours after Sarah's last Instagram post. The location of the friend's story was close to an isolated area near the festival grounds.

Further investigation of her social media contacts led to conversations with people who had seen Sarah after she had left the festival. Using the clues gathered from these posts, along with geolocation data, the authorities were able to track down the missing teenager within a few days. This successful resolution was made possible by leveraging social media OSINT.

Challenges in Using Social Media OSINT for Missing Persons Investigations

While social media OSINT has become a powerful tool for locating missing persons, there are several challenges that investigators must consider:

- **Privacy Concerns**: The use of social media data raises privacy concerns, particularly regarding the collection of personal information without consent.

Investigators must ensure that they are acting within legal boundaries and adhering to privacy laws when using social media in investigations.

- **Misinformation & False Leads**: Social media can be rife with misinformation, and false leads can complicate the investigation process. Investigators must carefully verify any data or reports to ensure they are following the correct path.
- **Inconsistent Online Behavior**: Some missing individuals may deactivate or abandon their social media profiles during a crisis, making it difficult to track them. Others may intentionally alter their online presence to conceal their whereabouts.

Social media OSINT has become a game-changer in locating missing persons. By analyzing publicly available posts, photos, locations, and interactions, investigators can uncover critical leads that help piece together the whereabouts of a missing person. Though challenges exist, the use of social media in conjunction with traditional investigative methods continues to prove vital in bringing closure to cases that would otherwise remain unsolved. For those involved in missing persons investigations, mastering the techniques of social media OSINT is an invaluable asset.

12.2 Exposing a Large-Scale Online Scam Through SOCMINT

In the digital age, online scams have become more sophisticated, reaching unprecedented levels of scale and complexity. From fake investment schemes to fraudulent e-commerce sites, scammers have exploited social media platforms to deceive countless individuals. Social Media OSINT (SOCMINT) has emerged as a powerful tool for uncovering and exposing these large-scale scams, often before they cause significant financial or reputational damage. By tracing digital footprints, analyzing user behavior, and monitoring patterns of deception, investigators and cybersecurity professionals can dismantle these criminal operations. This chapter explores the techniques, tools, and methodologies used in exposing large-scale online scams using social media intelligence, along with real-world case studies.

The Rise of Online Scams and the Role of Social Media in Amplifying Fraud

The exponential growth of social media has brought about new opportunities for fraudsters. With billions of users actively engaging on platforms like Facebook, Instagram, Twitter, and LinkedIn, scammers now have an expanded reach to target victims across different demographics. These fraudsters leverage the trust and credibility social media offers to execute a wide range of deceptive schemes, including:

- **Investment Scams**: Fraudulent "get-rich-quick" schemes, often involving cryptocurrency or fake financial services.
- **Romance Scams**: Scammers build relationships online to manipulate victims emotionally and financially.
- **Phishing and Identity Theft**: Fraudulent links and malicious software used to steal personal information.
- **Fake E-Commerce Sites**: Online stores that sell counterfeit or non-existent products, or collect payment without delivering goods.

For investigators, these scams often appear as coordinated efforts, involving multiple fake profiles, bots, and misleading posts that encourage others to fall victim to the scam. Recognizing the signs of a large-scale online scam requires a strategic and methodical approach to social media intelligence.

Steps to Exposing a Large-Scale Online Scam Using SOCMINT

1. Identifying Red Flags Across Multiple Platforms

The first step in uncovering a large-scale scam is identifying red flags across social media platforms. By analyzing posts, comments, hashtags, and user profiles, investigators can spot suspicious patterns that indicate fraudulent activity. Key indicators to watch for include:

- **Unusual Activity on Multiple Accounts**: Scammers often create numerous fake profiles to promote their fraudulent activities, whether it's endorsing a fake investment opportunity or advertising a non-existent product. These profiles may share the same photos, similar names, or engage in coordinated posting.
- **Overly Generic or Contradictory Messaging**: Fraudulent posts and messages often rely on generic statements or contradictory claims to lure in victims. Investigators can look for inconsistencies in messaging, such as promises of too-good-to-be-true returns on investment or urgent requests for personal information.
- **Excessive Promoting of Links or Offers**: Fraudulent accounts often flood social media with links to fake websites or suspicious offers. These links may direct users to phishing sites, counterfeit marketplaces, or fake customer support channels.

By systematically scanning across social media platforms for these red flags, investigators can begin to uncover the existence of a larger network of fraudulent activity.

2. Analyzing User Behavior and Connections

Once a potential scam has been identified, investigators can examine the connections and interactions between users. Fraudsters frequently use fake profiles to build credibility and create a network of supporters who amplify their fraudulent messages.

- **Mutual Connections and Patterns of Engagement**: Investigators can analyze the relationships between accounts involved in the scam. Do these accounts have mutual followers, likes, or comments? Are they amplifying each other's posts? By identifying the fake accounts and their interactions, investigators can uncover the scale of the scam.
- **Followers and Community Analysis**: Scammers often rely on a network of "shills" or fake accounts that masquerade as satisfied customers or trustworthy promoters. Investigators can cross-reference user profiles, follower counts, and engagement patterns to identify suspicious activity.
- **Fake Testimonials and Reviews**: Many scams rely on fabricated testimonials or reviews to create a facade of legitimacy. Analyzing the consistency and authenticity of these reviews can expose scams that are built on false narratives. A large number of glowing reviews from newly created accounts with similar characteristics is a strong red flag.

SOCMINT tools can help automate much of this analysis, allowing investigators to identify clusters of fake accounts and connections, speeding up the process of uncovering large-scale fraud.

3. Using Reverse Image Search to Identify Fake Accounts

A common tactic used by scammers is to steal images or create fake profiles using stock images or stolen photos of unsuspecting individuals. By using reverse image search tools, investigators can trace the origins of these images and track down other instances of their use across the web.

- **Identifying Stolen Images**: A reverse image search can help identify if a photo used by an account is original or stolen from another source. Scammers often use the same photos across multiple profiles to create a false sense of legitimacy. By tracing the origin of these images, investigators can expose a large network of fake accounts linked to the same scam.
- **Investigating Profile Images of Suspicious Accounts**: Fake profiles often share similar or identical profile pictures. Reverse image searches can help uncover whether these images are being used across multiple accounts to amplify a scam.

In many cases, scammers create a series of fake personas using the same stolen or stock images, which is a strong indication that a coordinated fraud operation is at play.

4. Tracing Website Links and Domain Registration

Many online scams involve fraudulent websites, which may host phishing forms, fake product listings, or malicious downloads. Investigators can track the URLs shared across social media and use domain registration tools to identify who is behind the website.

- **Tracking Suspicious URLs**: Investigators can perform WHOIS searches to uncover information about domain ownership and registration. Often, fraudsters use fake or anonymous details when registering websites, which can be traced back to specific locations, payment methods, or even the fraudsters themselves.
- **Identifying Fake E-Commerce Sites**: For e-commerce scams, investigators can check whether the websites are legitimate, such as by examining product listings for inconsistencies or cross-referencing prices and shipping details. Fake e-commerce sites often have poorly written product descriptions, photos copied from other sources, and untraceable customer support channels.

By following these links and connecting the dots, investigators can expose the full extent of the scam and gather evidence that is actionable for law enforcement or public awareness campaigns.

5. Monitoring for Victim Testimonies and Public Alerts

As scammers work to expand their operations, victims often turn to social media to warn others. These victim testimonies can serve as crucial evidence in exposing a scam. Social media platforms are rife with people sharing their experiences, and investigators can monitor for posts that mention scams, fraudulent accounts, or suspicious activity.

- **Victim Complaints and Warnings**: Hashtags and posts related to fraud, scam, or warning can help investigators identify active cases of victimization. Investigators can track these mentions and determine if the scam has affected multiple individuals.
- **Crowdsourced Intelligence**: In some cases, the collective efforts of a community can aid in uncovering a scam. Victims or concerned individuals may share screenshots, payment details, and correspondence with scammers that help corroborate the investigator's findings.

Case Study: Exposing a Cryptocurrency Investment Scam

In 2021, a large-scale cryptocurrency investment scam was uncovered through the use of SOCMINT. The scam involved fake online ads promoting lucrative investment opportunities in a new cryptocurrency project. The fraudsters used fake social media accounts to spread the word, often posing as successful investors who had made substantial profits. They created a website with high-quality branding and user-friendly interfaces to lure people into depositing money.

Using SOCMINT tools, investigators were able to identify patterns in the social media activity promoting the scam. Reverse image searches uncovered that many of the accounts used for promotions were employing stolen photos of professional investors. Further analysis of their online interactions revealed that these fake accounts were all connected to the same network of fraudulent profiles.

By tracking the domain name of the website, investigators found that the cryptocurrency project was registered using fake information. Victims began to share their experiences on social media, and their testimonies provided crucial evidence. Thanks to SOCMINT, law enforcement agencies were able to shut down the fraudulent website, arrest several individuals involved, and recover a portion of the funds.

Large-scale online scams are a growing concern in the digital world, but through the use of Social Media OSINT (SOCMINT), investigators are increasingly able to identify, expose, and dismantle these fraud operations. By analyzing patterns of user behavior, reverse searching images, tracking domain registration, and monitoring victim complaints, SOCMINT provides a comprehensive toolkit for uncovering scams and protecting the public. As online scams become more complex, the role of SOCMINT will continue to be vital in ensuring that fraudsters are brought to justice and that the digital space remains safe for everyone.

12.3 Identifying & Analyzing Disinformation Networks

In the digital age, disinformation has become a formidable tool used to manipulate public opinion, influence elections, and incite social unrest. With the rise of social media platforms, the spread of false or misleading information has become faster, more pervasive, and harder to detect. Disinformation campaigns often involve the deliberate spread of false narratives, manipulative content, and coordinated messaging aimed at deceiving audiences for political, financial, or social gain. The ability to identify and analyze these disinformation networks is critical for governments, researchers, journalists, and organizations working to safeguard the integrity of information online. In this chapter, we will explore the methods and tools used to detect, trace, and analyze disinformation networks across social media platforms, as well as examine the real-world impact of these efforts.

Understanding Disinformation Networks

Disinformation networks are organized groups of accounts or individuals that work together to spread false or misleading information across digital platforms. These networks often use multiple tactics to manipulate audiences, including:

- **Fake Profiles & Bots**: Disinformation campaigns commonly rely on fake accounts or automated bots to amplify the spread of false narratives. These profiles often mimic real users, making it difficult for regular users to distinguish them from authentic accounts.
- **Coordinated Hashtags & Content Sharing**: A key tactic in disinformation campaigns is the use of coordinated hashtags or viral content that encourages engagement and drives misinformation to a wider audience. Bots and fake accounts often engage with these posts to amplify their reach.
- **Influencers & Amplifiers**: Some disinformation campaigns recruit influencers, journalists, or celebrities, often with significant followings, to promote misleading or false narratives. These amplifiers provide an illusion of credibility to the disinformation being spread.
- **Echo Chambers & Filter Bubbles**: Disinformation thrives in echo chambers where individuals are only exposed to like-minded views. Social media algorithms contribute to this by showing users content similar to what they have previously engaged with, which can inadvertently increase the spread of disinformation.

By analyzing patterns of behavior and content spread across social media platforms, investigators can uncover the mechanisms behind disinformation campaigns and trace their origins.

Key Steps in Identifying & Analyzing Disinformation Networks

1. Identifying the Key Elements of a Disinformation Network

The first step in analyzing a disinformation network is identifying its key elements. This includes tracking the central figures involved, the types of content being spread, and the network of accounts engaged in amplifying the message. Key elements to consider include:

- **Originating Accounts**: Investigators can look for the source accounts that first publish or share the disinformation. These accounts may be influential personalities, fake profiles, or automated bots. The speed and pattern at which disinformation spreads from these accounts to others can provide crucial insights into the structure of the network.
- **Content Themes**: Disinformation networks often have specific themes or narratives that they promote. These could range from political misinformation, such as false election claims, to health disinformation, like misleading information about vaccines or COVID-19. Identifying the core message of the campaign helps in recognizing its scope and intent.
- **Amplifying Accounts & Engagement Patterns**: Disinformation networks rely on secondary accounts to amplify the message. These accounts may be highly active, with unusual posting behaviors, repetitive hashtags, or synchronized engagement patterns (e.g., the same group of accounts sharing content at the same time). Identifying these amplifiers is key to understanding how the network spreads its message.

2. Tracking and Analyzing Hashtag Campaigns

Hashtags are a powerful tool in amplifying content across social media platforms. In many disinformation campaigns, hashtags are deliberately crafted to trend, encouraging widespread visibility of misleading content. Investigators can track hashtag use and measure its spread by analyzing:

- **Hashtag Co-occurrence**: A simple yet effective way to detect disinformation campaigns is by tracking the co-occurrence of specific hashtags. Disinformation networks often employ a set of related hashtags to create a consistent narrative across posts. By identifying these hashtags, investigators can map the network's activity.
- **Engagement Metrics**: Social media engagement metrics such as likes, retweets, comments, and shares are vital for analyzing how widely a hashtag is being used and by whom. High levels of engagement from fake or suspicious accounts can indicate coordinated manipulation of content.
- **Hashtag Evolution**: Disinformation campaigns often evolve and adapt over time. Investigators can analyze how hashtags change or evolve as the narrative progresses, looking for patterns in how new hashtags are created to continue the spread of misinformation.

3. Network Analysis of Fake Accounts & Bots

Social media bots and fake accounts play a pivotal role in spreading disinformation. These accounts often share content at high volumes, post repetitive messages, or engage in coordinated actions across multiple platforms. Several techniques can be employed to analyze these accounts:

- **Bot Detection Tools**: Specialized tools such as Botometer, Bot Sentinel, and others can be used to identify automated or suspicious accounts. These tools analyze an account's activity patterns, looking for signs of automation, such as repetitive posting, rapid content dissemination, or lack of human engagement (e.g., no personal posts or comments).
- **Profile Analysis**: Many fake accounts are often created using stock photos, stolen images, or fake biographies. Investigators can use reverse image searches, profile analysis, and behavioral analysis to flag accounts that are likely to be fraudulent or part of a coordinated network.
- **Engagement Metrics on Suspicious Accounts**: By analyzing the engagement metrics of potential bots or fake accounts, investigators can identify patterns such as unusually high levels of likes, shares, and comments in a short amount of time. Suspicious accounts often show rapid engagement across multiple posts, suggesting they are part of a disinformation strategy.

4. Identifying Fake Content and Deepfakes

Disinformation campaigns increasingly use sophisticated methods to create misleading or completely fabricated content. This includes the use of deepfake videos, altered images, and fabricated news articles. Identifying these types of content requires:

- **Image and Video Verification**: Investigators can use tools like InVID and FotoForensics to analyze images and videos for signs of manipulation, such as inconsistencies in lighting, image compression, or pixel-level alterations.
- **Deepfake Detection Tools**: Deepfake technology has made it easier to create realistic videos that can deceive audiences. Investigators can use deepfake detection tools, such as Microsoft's Video Authenticator or other AI-driven solutions, to identify video manipulation. This can help uncover instances where disinformation is being spread through fake videos or doctored audio clips.
- **Cross-referencing Content Across Platforms**: Deepfakes and manipulated content can spread rapidly across social media platforms. By cross-referencing content across multiple platforms, investigators can identify the original source of the material and track its use in disinformation campaigns.

5. Mapping the Influence of Disinformation Campaigns

Once key accounts, hashtags, and pieces of content have been identified, investigators can use network analysis tools to map out the broader disinformation campaign. These tools analyze connections between accounts and how they interact with one another to amplify a false narrative. By doing so, investigators can uncover the architecture of the campaign, identifying key players and their roles within the network.

- **Social Network Analysis (SNA):** SNA tools, such as Gephi or NodeXL, allow investigators to visualize how accounts are connected and how information flows within the network. These tools can highlight clusters of fake accounts that interact with one another to spread disinformation and pinpoint the most influential accounts within the network.
- **Botnets and Fake Followers**: Disinformation campaigns often rely on botnets or fake followers to enhance the reach of their posts. Investigators can analyze the composition of followers and interactions on targeted accounts, revealing whether they are artificially inflated by fake profiles.

Real-World Case Study: Exposing a Disinformation Network in an Election

One of the most high-profile applications of disinformation network analysis came during a national election, where it was revealed that a coordinated disinformation campaign was used to sway voter opinions. The campaign involved a network of fake accounts spreading false information about candidates, misinformation about the voting process, and manipulated news articles that created confusion and doubt.

Through the use of SOCMINT, investigators traced the origins of the disinformation by analyzing hashtag trends, reverse image searching profiles, and identifying fake news articles being shared by a coordinated group of accounts. They used network analysis tools to map out how the disinformation spread, revealing a large bot network that was responsible for much of the amplification. Investigators identified several key individuals who were part of the operation, as well as the political affiliations behind the campaign.

The case led to widespread awareness of the threat posed by disinformation in democratic processes, resulting in stricter regulations and countermeasures to prevent the manipulation of public opinion during future elections.

The identification and analysis of disinformation networks represent a vital aspect of modern OSINT investigations. By recognizing the key characteristics of disinformation campaigns, utilizing tools for bot detection and content verification, and applying network analysis techniques, investigators can disrupt these campaigns and prevent further harm.

Disinformation is an evolving threat, but with advanced techniques and a vigilant approach, the integrity of information online can be protected, and those responsible for malicious campaigns can be held accountable.

12.4 Investigating a Cybercriminal Using Social Media Clues

The digital era has seen a rapid increase in cybercrime, with cybercriminals leveraging social media platforms to plan, execute, and cover their tracks. Social media can serve as both a tool for illicit activities and an unintentional source of critical information that investigators can use to expose the culprits behind these crimes. In this chapter, we will explore how social media can be a treasure trove of clues in cybercrime investigations, focusing on techniques for tracking and uncovering cybercriminals through their online presence. From hidden messages to careless posts, the digital footprints left on social media can reveal much more than intended, providing investigators with the necessary leads to solve these crimes.

Understanding the Role of Social Media in Cybercrime

Cybercriminals use social media platforms in various ways to further their criminal activities. They may:

- **Coordinate Attacks**: Cybercriminals often use social media to coordinate with co-conspirators, share resources, or plan attacks such as phishing schemes, malware distribution, or ransomware attacks.
- **Market Illicit Products**: Dark web markets and illicit services are often advertised or discussed on social media platforms. Cybercriminals may use forums or private groups to sell stolen data, malware, or hacking services.
- **Spread Misinformation or Deceptive Content**: Criminals may also use social media to spread misinformation as part of their scams, for example, spreading fake investment opportunities, fraudulent online stores, or fake tech support scams.
- **Cover Their Tracks**: Ironically, social media can also be a tool for cybercriminals to try and cover their tracks. By creating fake personas or misdirecting investigators, they may try to lead authorities away from their true identities. However, social media often betrays these efforts, offering subtle clues that reveal their location, activities, and intentions.

Understanding how cybercriminals use social media platforms is crucial for developing strategies to detect, track, and eventually identify those involved in criminal enterprises.

The key to successful investigation lies in using a combination of technical tools, investigative techniques, and a deep understanding of social media dynamics.

Steps in Investigating Cybercriminals Using Social Media

1. Profiling the Cybercriminal's Social Media Activity

A good starting point in investigating a cybercriminal is to build a comprehensive profile based on their social media activity. A profile can provide a wealth of information, such as:

- **Usernames & Aliases**: Cybercriminals often use multiple usernames or fake identities to conceal their true identity. By cross-referencing usernames across different social media platforms, investigators can begin to link these aliases together. For example, a hacker may use one name on Twitter and another on Telegram but may still share similar language patterns, interests, or clues that can connect the two accounts.
- **Content & Posts**: Investigators should examine the content the suspect posts, particularly focusing on anything that may relate to criminal activities. For instance, posts that describe hacking techniques, suspicious links, or even seemingly innocent interactions with other potential criminals could provide key clues. Cybercriminals often brag or share their activities online, even if it's indirectly.
- **Connections & Relationships**: A cybercriminal's connections on social media can tell investigators a lot. Friend lists, group memberships, and followers can reveal other individuals involved in criminal activities or even lead to the discovery of criminal networks. Social media platforms like Facebook, LinkedIn, and Twitter can provide insights into the suspect's social circles and associates.

Using social media intelligence tools such as OSINT framework, investigators can help map out connections, reveal hidden links between different profiles, and create a more accurate picture of the cybercriminal's identity.

2. Analyzing Digital Footprints and Patterns of Behavior

Cybercriminals may inadvertently leave behind a trail of digital footprints that can expose their actions. These footprints can often be traced back to their social media profiles, providing valuable intelligence for investigators.

- **Geolocation Data**: Many social media platforms automatically geotag posts, even if the user has disabled location sharing. Investigators can use this information to identify patterns in the criminal's movements. For instance, if the suspect has been frequenting particular locations, this could indicate their geographic area of operations or even lead to their physical location. By examining public posts with location data, investigators can narrow down the target's location and connect it to specific criminal activities.

- **Time Stamps & Activity Patterns**: By reviewing the time of posts, comments, and activity patterns, investigators can look for clues related to the cybercriminal's operational hours, possibly indicating when they are most active online. Time zone discrepancies or activity at odd hours could provide insights into where the cybercriminal is operating from or help rule out certain locations.
- **Language & Behavioral Cues**: Cybercriminals often slip up by revealing more than they intend to through their language. Investigators can analyze the tone, style, and context of posts to identify certain habits or personal details that might expose their real identity. In some cases, cybercriminals may use online lingo or jargon tied to a particular region or country, which can serve as a linguistic clue.

3. Tracking and Monitoring Dark Web & Private Forums Activity

While much of a cybercriminal's activity may occur in private spaces, such as dark web forums or encrypted messaging apps, clues can still be found on public social media platforms. Investigators should expand their search to include:

- **Cybercrime Marketplaces**: Platforms such as Reddit, Discord, Telegram, and even Facebook groups can host discussions related to illicit activities. Cybercriminals often communicate openly in private groups, discussing hacking tools, malware services, or stolen data for sale. Investigators can infiltrate these forums or use OSINT tools to track discussions, identify key players, and map out the broader cybercriminal network.
- **Cross-Referencing with Known Cybercriminals**: By checking the social media profiles of known cybercriminals or individuals with prior connections to cybercrime activities, investigators can trace connections and find new suspects. These connections may lead to criminal organizations or networks that specialize in cybercrime.

4. Tracing Cryptocurrency Payments & Financial Transactions

In many cases, cybercriminals rely on cryptocurrency for financial transactions, such as ransom payments, stolen funds, or black market exchanges. Investigators can use social media clues to help trace these payments and identify the criminal's financial movements.

- **Social Media Posts About Cryptocurrency Transactions**: Some cybercriminals brag about their illicit earnings, posting about cryptocurrency transactions on platforms like Twitter or Telegram. By analyzing these posts, investigators can trace the cybercriminal's crypto wallet addresses or connect them to specific ransomware campaigns or illegal activities.
- **Blockchain Analytics**: Although cryptocurrencies offer anonymity, blockchain analysis tools can still track the flow of funds across wallets. If the cybercriminal has shared any wallet addresses on social media, investigators can use this information to follow the money trail and link transactions to particular individuals or entities.

5. Building a Timeline of Events

Once a cybercriminal's social media profile has been established, investigators can begin building a timeline of events based on their online activity. This timeline can reveal critical moments in the cybercriminal's life and activities, such as when they first began engaging in cybercrime, major milestones in their operations, and when they attempted to hide or delete evidence.

The timeline can be constructed by combining multiple data points:

- **Posts & Messages**: Review the timestamps of posts and messages, particularly those linked to cybercrime activities, to build a chronological order of events.
- **Interactions with Other Criminals**: Social media provides an opportunity to uncover collaborations and partnerships with other cybercriminals. Investigators can track these interactions, identify key players, and gather additional evidence to support their investigation.
- **Data Leaks & Public Releases**: Cybercriminals often leak information about their criminal activities, whether it's through accidental posts, screenshots, or code snippets. These leaks provide invaluable clues for investigators to trace back to their source.

Case Study: Investigating a Cybercriminal Using Social Media

In one case, a notorious cybercriminal known for running phishing scams targeting financial institutions was identified using social media OSINT techniques. The suspect had a relatively low-profile presence on social media platforms, but after an in-depth investigation, several key clues were uncovered:

- The suspect used a pseudonym on Twitter to share tips on "hacking" email accounts, which were actually tutorials for phishing.
- They frequently posted about cryptocurrency, mentioning wallet addresses and encouraging others to engage in illicit transactions.
- Through image analysis, investigators uncovered metadata from a photo the suspect had posted, which included a timestamp and geolocation information.
- Investigators cross-referenced this data with known phishing campaigns and linked the suspect's posts to a series of scams targeting individuals across multiple countries.

Using these clues, investigators were able to track the suspect's activities across multiple platforms, leading to the eventual identification and arrest of the cybercriminal.

Social media has become an essential tool for cybercriminals to coordinate their activities, market illicit products, and disguise their operations. However, it is also a vital resource for investigators seeking to track and uncover the identities of cybercriminals. By analyzing social media profiles, tracing digital footprints, and using advanced OSINT techniques, investigators can identify key elements of a cybercriminal's operation and gather evidence to bring them to justice. Social media can often expose more than the criminal intends, making it an invaluable resource in the fight against cybercrime.

12.5 Using OSINT to Track Extremist & Radical Groups

In today's interconnected world, extremist and radical groups often use social media and online platforms to spread propaganda, recruit members, and organize activities. These groups thrive in the digital space, where they can disseminate their ideologies with little oversight. As a result, monitoring and tracking these groups using Open Source Intelligence (OSINT) has become an essential tool for law enforcement, intelligence agencies, and security researchers. By leveraging OSINT techniques, investigators can uncover hidden networks, detect early signs of radicalization, and identify key individuals within these groups. In this chapter, we will explore how OSINT can be employed to track extremist and radical groups, analyze their activities, and ultimately disrupt their operations.

Understanding the Role of Social Media in Radicalization and Recruitment

Social media platforms have become central to the radicalization process, especially for individuals who may be vulnerable or isolated. Extremist groups often use these platforms to:

- **Spread Propaganda and Ideology**: Radical groups utilize social media to share their ideologies, religious or political views, and to manipulate people into adopting extremist beliefs. Through videos, memes, articles, and posts, they create content that appeals to their target audience, pushing their narrative in a convincing manner.
- **Recruit New Members**: Social media allows extremist groups to reach a global audience, targeting individuals who may be receptive to their ideology. This process, often referred to as "cyber-recruitment," is particularly effective in reaching young people who are active on these platforms.
- **Coordinate and Mobilize Activities**: Many extremist groups use encrypted messaging apps, private forums, and closed groups on social media to organize and plan operations. These platforms provide a veil of anonymity, making it more difficult for authorities to track their activities.
- **Create a Sense of Community**: Radical groups often foster a sense of belonging and identity, which can be extremely attractive to those feeling alienated or marginalized. By creating a virtual "community," they make individuals feel supported in their beliefs, which can lead to further radicalization.

While these platforms provide an ideal space for extremist groups to grow and spread their messages, they also present a unique opportunity for investigators to uncover and monitor their activities.

Techniques for Tracking Extremist and Radical Groups Using OSINT

1. Identifying Key Platforms and Online Spaces

Extremist groups tend to operate across a range of online spaces. While major social media platforms like Facebook, Twitter, and Instagram are common, radical groups may also seek out more obscure, niche, or encrypted platforms to avoid detection. Investigators must use a combination of tools and strategies to identify where these groups are operating:

- **Mainstream Platforms**: Groups may have open or closed groups on Facebook, Twitter, or YouTube. While these may be more public-facing, they may still hold valuable information in the form of posts, comments, videos, or shared links.
- **Alternative Platforms & Messaging Apps**: Platforms like Telegram, Discord, or encrypted messaging services are frequently used by extremists for their anonymity and privacy features. Investigators need to monitor these platforms for specific keywords, group names, or hashtags tied to radicalization.

- **Dark Web Forums & Hidden Sites**: Extremists may use encrypted or hidden services within the deep or dark web to communicate without being detected. OSINT tools can help in discovering and accessing these hard-to-reach spaces, though a level of technical expertise is required.

Understanding the platforms used by extremist groups helps investigators set up monitoring strategies to detect their activities before they can do harm.

2. Keyword and Hashtag Monitoring

Once the platforms are identified, OSINT tools can be used to monitor conversations surrounding specific keywords, hashtags, or terms commonly associated with extremist ideologies. These terms may include political or religious phrases, hate speech, or references to groups known for their extremist beliefs.

- **Keyword Alerts**: Using OSINT tools like Social Search or specialized search engines, investigators can set alerts for terms associated with radical ideologies. These alerts can help track real-time developments in extremist conversations.
- **Hashtag Tracking**: On platforms like Twitter, Instagram, and TikTok, hashtags are a major tool used by extremists to organize, promote, and spread their content. By identifying and tracking hashtags linked to extremist ideologies (e.g., #WhiteSupremacy, #Jihad, #ExtremistGroupName), investigators can monitor discussions and actions tied to these movements.

By systematically tracking these terms, authorities can uncover emerging extremist groups or individuals who may otherwise fly under the radar.

3. Mapping Radical Networks

Radical groups are often organized into networks of individuals with shared goals, ideologies, and activities. OSINT can be instrumental in mapping out these networks by tracing interactions, connections, and affiliations across social media platforms. Investigators should focus on the following areas:

- **Follower and Friend Connections**: Examining an extremist group's social media followers or connections can reveal a network of people who are engaging with their content. By analyzing connections and followers of key influencers within the group, investigators can uncover additional members, sympathizers, or even facilitators.

- **Content Sharing & Cross-Platform Activity**: Many extremists operate across multiple platforms, using different spaces to disseminate their messages. Investigators can trace the sharing of videos, articles, or memes across various platforms and connect the dots to uncover coordinated activity between seemingly independent groups.
- **Inter-Group Messaging**: By monitoring conversations between members of different groups or individuals with cross-group involvement, investigators can uncover alliances, collaborations, and common objectives among seemingly disparate radical factions.

Mapping out these networks can provide critical insight into how extremist groups collaborate, recruit, and spread their messages.

4. Geolocation Analysis

Extremist groups often have a geographical focus, and certain events or activities are tied to specific regions or locations. By analyzing the geolocation data associated with posts, photos, and videos, investigators can gather intelligence about where these groups are active or where potential threats may arise.

- **Geotagging in Posts**: Social media platforms like Twitter, Instagram, and Facebook often allow users to share their location when posting content. Investigators can extract this geolocation information from public posts to track extremist activities in specific regions or identify areas where the group is likely to have physical presence or influence.
- **Event Location Tracking**: Extremist groups frequently organize physical events, protests, or rallies, which are often promoted or discussed on social media. By monitoring event-related posts and using geotagging data, investigators can predict or track where these events are taking place, providing advance warning for law enforcement agencies.

Geolocation analysis helps in identifying key locations where radical groups operate and can provide actionable intelligence.

5. Behavioral Analysis and Radicalization Signs

OSINT can also be used to track the behavior of individuals who may be in the process of being radicalized. Social media platforms often reveal shifts in an individual's tone, interests, and associations, which can signal their growing involvement in extremist ideologies.

- **Changes in Social Media Activity**: A sudden increase in engagement with extremist content, such as liking, sharing, or commenting on posts with radical or hateful messages, can be a strong indicator that someone is becoming radicalized.
- **Disruptive Content**: The content that individuals share or engage with can be analyzed for signs of ideological shifts. For example, an individual may initially share harmless political opinions, but over time, their posts may evolve to include violent rhetoric, extremist views, or glorification of terrorism.

By identifying these behavioral patterns early, investigators can intervene to prevent individuals from progressing further into extremist activities.

6. Reporting & Collaboration with Authorities

Once extremist activity is identified using OSINT techniques, it is essential to report the findings to relevant authorities, such as law enforcement or intelligence agencies. Investigators can provide valuable insights into the activities, networks, and individuals involved in extremist groups, which can then be used for further investigation or intervention.

Collaboration with international organizations, non-governmental organizations, or cybersecurity experts can enhance efforts to track and dismantle these radical networks. These groups may have additional resources, access to specialized tools, or intelligence networks that can help disrupt extremist activities.

Case Study: Tracking an Online Radicalization Network

In one case, an OSINT investigation uncovered a covert network of individuals promoting violent extremism across multiple social media platforms. Through keyword monitoring and hashtag tracking, investigators identified a group using coded language to communicate their intentions while avoiding detection. By mapping out the connections between group members and analyzing their posts, investigators were able to identify key influencers within the network.

Further analysis revealed that the group was planning to organize a series of public protests aimed at radicalizing local communities. Geolocation data from posts helped pinpoint their physical locations, enabling law enforcement to intervene and disrupt the group's operations before any violence occurred.

The use of OSINT to track extremist and radical groups is a critical tool in the fight against terrorism and hate-based violence. By leveraging social media monitoring, keyword tracking, network analysis, and behavioral cues, investigators can uncover hidden extremist cells, predict radicalization patterns, and intervene before these groups can act. While the process can be challenging due to the anonymity of many platforms and the encrypted nature of some communications, the opportunities OSINT offers to expose and disrupt radicalization make it an invaluable tool in modern counterterrorism and law enforcement efforts.

12.6 Final Challenge: Conducting a Full Social Media OSINT Investigation

As we wrap up the book, it is time to put the various tools, techniques, and knowledge learned into practice by conducting a full Social Media OSINT (SOCMINT) investigation. This challenge will guide you through the steps of a complete investigation, from initial data gathering to analysis, and ultimately, drawing actionable conclusions. It will require a deep understanding of the methodologies covered throughout the book, as well as the ability to synthesize multiple data points to form a coherent picture of the target's digital footprint.

In this final challenge, we will simulate an OSINT investigation of a hypothetical case where you are tasked with investigating a person or event of interest. This scenario will test your ability to apply various OSINT techniques, such as tracking digital footprints, uncovering hidden connections, identifying suspicious activity, and using ethical practices to gather data without violating privacy laws.

Step 1: Define the Scope of the Investigation

Before diving into the investigation, it is crucial to clearly define the scope of your OSINT effort. Understanding what you need to find will help narrow the search and avoid unnecessary tangents.

Ask yourself the following questions to establish the scope:

- **Who is the target?** This could be an individual, a group, or an event. In this example, let's say the target is an individual suspected of being involved in a recent cybercrime.

- **What information do you need?** Are you looking for social media profiles, digital connections, past activities, geolocation clues, or other specific data points?
- **What platforms will you focus on?** Based on the target's age, profession, or background, decide which social platforms are most likely to hold valuable information. Common platforms include Facebook, Instagram, Twitter, LinkedIn, Reddit, and niche social networks.
- **What tools will you use?** Based on your investigative objectives, select the OSINT tools that are most suited for your investigation. These could range from social media search engines like Social Search or Pipl to more specialized tools like Maltego, Hunchly, or FOCA for metadata extraction.

Once you have answered these questions, you'll be ready to begin gathering information.

Step 2: Data Collection

With the scope in mind, the next step is to start collecting data from available open sources. During this phase, you'll gather both public and semi-public information that could shed light on your target's digital footprint.

- **Social Media Profiles**: Start by searching for any known profiles associated with the target on major platforms such as Facebook, Instagram, Twitter, and LinkedIn. This can be done by searching for their name, email addresses, usernames, or other personal details that may be available. If the target uses pseudonyms or nicknames online, be sure to account for these when searching.
- **Public Posts & Content**: Examine their posts, photos, comments, and activity on different platforms. For example, you might explore Facebook groups, public forums, Twitter posts, or Instagram feeds that the target has interacted with. Look for patterns in their behavior, possible connections to other people or organizations, or changes in their activity over time.
- **Hashtags & Keywords**: Use advanced search operators and keyword alerts to track hashtags or topics relevant to the target. For example, if the suspect is associated with an extremist group, you might monitor specific terms and hashtags to find references to the group's ideology, events, or discussions.
- **Metadata Extraction**: Whenever possible, extract metadata from images or videos associated with your target. This could reveal valuable information such as locations (GPS coordinates), timestamps, and device types that were used in creating the content.

digital footprints, uncover hidden connections, and analyze social media activity to draw actionable conclusions.

However, it's essential to always adhere to ethical guidelines and legal boundaries when conducting OSINT investigations. Your work may have real-world implications, and the accuracy, integrity, and legality of your findings should never be compromised. With proper training, diligence, and a strong understanding of OSINT tools, you'll be well-equipped to tackle even the most complex digital investigations.

Social media has transformed the way people interact, communicate, and share their lives. But beyond its social functions, these platforms are goldmines of intelligence for investigators, analysts, and researchers. Whether you are conducting background checks, tracking digital footprints, or investigating cyber threats, social media offers a wealth of publicly available data—if you know where and how to look.

Social Media OSINT: Tracking Digital Footprints is a comprehensive guide to gathering, analyzing, and verifying intelligence from social networks. From Facebook and Twitter to LinkedIn, Instagram, and emerging platforms, this book provides a step-by-step approach to navigating the digital trails people leave behind.

What You'll Learn in This Book

- **Understanding Digital Footprints**: Learn how social media activity creates lasting online records.
- **Facebook Investigations**: Master techniques for uncovering hidden profiles, tracking interactions, and analyzing public posts.
- **Twitter & X Intelligence**: Extract valuable insights from tweets, hashtags, followers, and metadata.
- **Instagram & TikTok OSINT**: Discover techniques for analyzing visual content, tracking trends, and mapping relationships.
- **LinkedIn & Professional Networks**: Learn how to leverage LinkedIn for corporate intelligence and background checks.
- **Social Media Graph Analysis**: Use mapping tools to visualize relationships between accounts.
- **Username & Handle Investigations**: Uncover connections by tracking usernames across multiple platforms.
- **Social Media Metadata Analysis**: Extract hidden data from images, posts, and videos.
- **Fake Accounts & Disinformation**: Learn how to detect bots, troll farms, and manipulated narratives.
- **Privacy & Ethical Considerations**: Understand the legal and ethical boundaries of social media investigations.

With real-world case studies, hands-on exercises, and expert tips, Social Media OSINT transforms you into a skilled investigator, capable of extracting intelligence from the vast and ever-changing landscape of social platforms. Whether you're tracking a subject, verifying information, or conducting corporate due diligence, this book equips you with the essential techniques to navigate social media OSINT effectively.

Thank you for choosing Social Media OSINT: Tracking Digital Footprints as part of your OSINT journey. Social media is one of the most dynamic and complex sources of intelligence in the digital age, and by exploring this book, you've taken an important step in mastering its investigative potential.

The ability to gather and analyze social media intelligence is a powerful skill, but with power comes responsibility. We encourage you to use the techniques in this book ethically and legally, ensuring that your investigations respect privacy laws and ethical standards.

Your curiosity and dedication to learning fuel the OSINT community, and we deeply appreciate your time and effort in studying this field. If you found value in this book, we'd love to hear from you! Your feedback helps us refine future editions and continue delivering practical, high-quality OSINT resources.

Stay curious, stay ethical, and keep uncovering the truth.

Continue Your OSINT Journey

Expand your skills with the rest of **The OSINT Analyst Series**:

- **OSINT Foundations**: The Beginner's Guide to Open-Source Intelligence
- **The OSINT Search Mastery**: Hacking Search Engines for Intelligence
- **OSINT People Finder**: Advanced Techniques for Online Investigations
- **Image & Geolocation Intelligence**: Reverse Searching and Mapping
- **Domain, Website & Cyber Investigations with OSINT**
- **Email & Dark Web Investigations**: Tracking Leaks & Breaches
- **OSINT Threat Intel**: Investigating Hackers, Breaches, and Cyber Risks
- **Corporate OSINT**: Business Intelligence & Competitive Analysis
- **Investigating Disinformation & Fake News with OSINT**
- **OSINT for Deep & Dark Web**: Techniques for Cybercrime Investigations
- **OSINT Automation**: Python & APIs for Intelligence Gathering
- **OSINT Detective**: Digital Tools & Techniques for Criminal Investigations
- **Advanced OSINT Case Studies**: Real-World Investigations
- **The Ethical OSINT Investigator**: Privacy, Legal Risks & Best Practices

We look forward to seeing you in the next book!

Happy investigating!

www.ingramcontent.com/pod-product-compliance
Lightning Source LLC
LaVergne TN
LVHW060120070326
832902LV00019B/3054